Collaborative Media

Collaborative Media

Production, Consumption, and Design Interventions

Jonas Löwgren and Bo Reimer

The MIT Press
Cambridge, Massachusetts
London, England

MIT Press books may be purchased at special quantity discounts for business or sales promotional use. For information, please email special_sales@mitpress.mit.edu.

This book was set in Stone by the MIT Press. Printed and bound in the United States of America.

Library of Congress Cataloging-in-Publication Data

Löwgren, Jonas.
Collaborative media : production, consumption, and design interventions / by Jonas Löwgren and Bo Reimer.
  pages   cm
Includes bibliographical references and index.
ISBN 978-0-262-01976-7 (hardcover : alk. paper)
1. Social media. 2. User-generated content. 3. Mass media—Technological innovations. I. Reimer, Bo. II. Title.
HM851.L69 2013
302.23'1—dc23
2013009443

10   9   8   7   6   5   4   3   2   1

Contents

I   Starting Points

1 ⦚⦚⦚ Introduction

—What's on your mind?

As of October 2012, Facebook had over 1 billion users who were active at least once a month, and more than half of them were active on at least six days out of seven. If being an active user would constitute citizenship, the country of Facebook would be the third largest in the world—after China and India. The "friend" network consisted of over 125 billion connections in the summer of 2012, averaging 139 connections per monthly active user. Over 300 million photos were uploaded per day; over 3 billion likes and comments were produced per day (Facebook 2012).

It is safe to say that Facebook is the biggest thing that has happened to the world of mediated communication for quite some time. People use it to stay in touch and get in touch; to brag and to share; to seek comfort and sympathy; to experience belonging and otherness; to hate and blow off steam; to advocate and campaign; to market and trade. More than anything else, people use it habitually. Facebook truly forms a communicative infrastructure in the sense that its reach and penetration in certain demographics is large enough to make it a primary channel. It has become mainstream to the extent that early adopters and cool hunters started abandoning it years ago in the search for the next avant-garde venue. What is left is in some ways like a global phone directory where you can find anybody from your high school days, and in some ways like a local pub with some 140 regulars, where you can't help listening in on the ramblings of less-than-interesting people talking a little too loud at the next table.

We might speculate that Facebook is a significant part of why most people today mostly think of their computers as a communication portal. It wasn't always like that; only a few years ago, the computer was primarily a personal tool with a great library and some communication channels attached. But as a mainstream communication medium, Facebook has a very unusual feature: all the content is created by users. In other words, there are no designated producers planning and executing the transmission of messages using dedicated means of production. Facebook as such is an empty shell, keeping track of people and their connections but at the same time leaving it entirely up to the same people to craft the messages going out via the connections.

The way we see it, Facebook is a *collaborative medium*: a form of mediated communication whereby people collaborate on messages, content, meaning. This book is about collaborative media, and our aim is to identify their qualities and characteristics in terms of what they enable people to do. As the book proceeds, we will illustrate and analyze the forms of practice related to collaborative media, showing among other things how collaboration entails not only production and consumption of what media scholars call texts (including all manner of media content), but also design of infrastructures. We will also argue that knowledge about collaborative media is best produced by combining analysis and criticism with design-oriented interventions.

Contemporary Communicative Practices

In everyday Internet parlance, Facebook is the leading member of the "social media" denomination, which according to Wikipedia

includes web-based and mobile-based technologies which are used to turn communication into interactive dialogue among organizations, communities, and individuals. Andreas Kaplan and Michael Haenlein define social media as "a group of Internet-based applications that build on the ideological and technological foundations of Web 2.0, and that allow the creation and exchange of user-generated content." Social media is ubiquitously accessible, and enabled by scalable communication techniques.[1]

There is something confusing with this jargon-laden definition: What does it mean to turn communication into interactive dialogue? How is communication not interactive? From a media studies standpoint, you would be hard pressed to find a medium that could not be characterized as social—and thus the label of "social media" is hardly a meaningful one.

Nitpicking aside, there is a relatively clear public perception that "social media" entails communicative practices where the people formerly known as the audience step into various production capacities. The atomic unit of content production is arguably the Like action in Facebook, and from there a wide span extends to include Twitter microblog entries, Flickr photo uploads, Spotify playlist sharing, YouTube videoblogging, and a myriad of other ways to create and distribute messages without being a formal producer with access to a privileged production and distribution structure.

However, even though the mainstream penetration of "social media" is a relatively recent phenomenon, collaborative media as such predate Facebook and Twitter and the rest by several decades, as illustrated by examples such as ham radio, local TV, mix tapes, and fanzines. Yet it would be fair to say that the emergence of digital technologies and the Internet has offered significantly greater potential to disrupt traditional production-consumption media structures. An Internet-connected computer from twenty years ago already represented the necessary means for creating and distributing messages in a variety of media forms, including text and image as well as video and audio. Production technology was less approachable, to be sure, and the reach and coverage of the distribution infrastructure was much more limited, meaning that many-to-many communicative practices (the possibility for a large group of producers, not only professional ones, to reach many consumers) belonged largely in the realm of early adopters. For us, though, this is where the story starts, and as a vignette we would like to briefly introduce some early and emerging subcultures of collaborative media.

The history of art and professional culture production is full of examples of reappropriation, from Marcel Duchamp's *Fountain*—the ready-made piece in the form of a signed urinal that was voted the most influential piece of art of all time in 2004 (BBC 2004)—to intra-literary references in novels, pop culture cameos in blockbuster movies, and samplings in hip-hop and DJ performances. Public reception has shown over the years that reappropriation is highly appreciated by consumers; what the digital media are increasingly showing us is the pleasure of not only consuming, but also *producing* reappropriations.

You only have to say, "Hitler reacts to . . ." for many people in Western culture to smile knowingly and start telling you about their personal favorite spoof based on the German film *Der Untergang* (2004), titled *Downfall* in English. An Internet phenomenon that took off in late 2008, the *Downfall* parody involves taking a scene from the controversial, Academy Award–nominated film and subverting it by subtitling the German dialogue with a different storyline in English (or other language). At the time of writing, we estimate that well over five thousand such parodies have been published on video sites such as YouTube. Broadly speaking, the first wave of parodies all were based on the famous scene that takes place in the command bunker when Hitler realizes Germany's defeat is inevitable and throws a massive tantrum. Most of the parodies shift the subject of Hitler's rage in time or context in order to create a humorous contrast; according to knowyourmeme.com, the first known *Downfall* parody showed Hitler fuming over the lack of new features included in the demo trial of Microsoft's game *Flight Simulator X*. The collective creativity of the online crowds led to variations such as using different scenes from the movie and creating meta-jokes, a particularly popular one being "Hitler reacts to the amount of *Downfall* parodies on the Internet."

As *Downfall* parodies turned into a viral phenomenon, their huge popularity and mainstream media coverage also meant that debate ensued on recurrent issues having to do with originality, artistic intention, and intellectual property in digital media. In 2010, the production company owning the rights to *Der Untergang* took legal action on several occasions against YouTube and other video sites publishing the parodies, claiming that they violated copyright law (Clay 2011). Advocates of more contemporary rules for intellectual property, such as the Electronic Frontier Foundation, claimed that *Downfall* parodies were clear-cut examples of fair use under U.S. law, which provides an exception to normal copyright rules. Interestingly, the director of the movie—Oliver

Hirschbiegel—felt that the parodies were very much in line with the intentions of the movie: to "kick these terrible people off the throne that made them demons, making them real and their actions into reality" (Rosenblum 2010).

The idea of making and publishing a *Downfall* parody would be inconceivable if it hadn't been for the availability of scenes from the movie in digital formats that lend themselves to modification and re-publication, as well as tools that make subtitling a digital video clip a feasible task for anyone with a computer and an Internet connection (Templeton 2009). In fact, as often happens online, interest begot automation and someone even created a dedicated tool (downfall.jfedor.org) for *Downfall* parody production, whereby the dialogue is entered line by line on a web page of keyframes and the click of a Create button puts the video clip together and uploads it to YouTube. More generally, what this shows is how the low material and communicative thresholds of contemporary online media make it possible for people outside professional media production and distribution to engage in creative expression and to participate in public discourse using a variety of expressive forms.

The best illustration of accessibility thresholds and their relations to widespread use in this context is arguably the expressive form known as *machinima*, a form based on using 3D animation engines in order to make films. It stepped onto the public scene in 2005, when a thirteen-minute animation called *The French Democracy* was circulated widely on the Internet and covered thoroughly in most European mainstream news media. The animation, made by French industrial designer Alex Chan (aka Koulamata), comments on the outbreaks of civil unrest in suburban Paris and connects them to the cultural and racial discrimination of immigrants in France. However, machinima has a history that dates back to the early 1990s and the first 3D first-person shooter games that introduced the feature of recording game play for later playback. In games such as *Doom* and *Quake*, players could record playing sessions and stage death matches in game demo files that were small and easily distributed. However, what distinguishes machinima from shooter games is the use of the 3D animation engine to tell stories that are not directly drawn from the actual playing of the game. In effect, to make machinima is to use the game software as a virtual recording studio.

First-generation machinima had a relatively high accessibility threshold. The first machinima subcultures were comprised almost exclusively of gamers, partly because some technical inside knowledge of the games was required to be able to fulfill the expressive intentions of a machinima movie; but, perhaps even more obviously, because the movies were distributed as demo files that could only be played back in the game itself. The subsequent initiative by Hugh Hancock to create the machinima.com community (and thereby coin the name of the art form) in 2000 and to allow contributions based on video frames rather than on demo files meant that machinima became amenable to editing tools familiar to people outside the gamer culture, and, equally important, to people who did not play *Quake*.

Machinima, as well as other subcultural gamer practices such as creating and distributing independent game content ("modding"), was well known to the game industry and new tools were continuously incorporated in the games to offer creative value for the players beyond the anticipated play action and prepackaged game contents. Many of the tools in effect served to lower the threshold of engaging creatively with the games as opposed to "merely" playing them. This development culminated with the 2005 release of the game *The Movies* by Lionhead Studios. *The Movies* is labeled a business simulation game. The main plot is that the player runs a movie studio, including tasks such as overseeing the finances and keeping the actors happy. What the game also contains, however, is an easy-to-use studio for making 3D-animated movies—in other words, a machinima production facility.

The studio functions of *The Movies* proved easy enough to use for Alex Chan to complete *The French Democracy* in three or four days, despite his lack of previous filmmaking experience. He uploaded his movie to the dedicated site where *The Movies* users could share their work, the site editors selected *The French Democracy* as a Hot Pick, and it quickly gained attention.

One striking aspect of Chan's *The French Democracy*, which was also commented on by several critics, is the dissonance between the sinister subject matter and the cartoon-like qualities of some of the visuals. For instance, the teenagers running for their life from armed policemen in the opening scene do, in fact, move a lot like the cartoon character Bugs Bunny. The overt reason for this is that *The Movies* provides large libraries of characters, props, and movements for making 3D-animated movies mostly of a lighter kind. However, there is also another reason, which has to do with the aesthetic codes of the machinima genre.

As stated earlier, machinima was initially dominated by hardcore gamers and carried certain elements of a hacker culture in terms of high requirements for technical production expertise and in terms of frequent references to subcultural jargon. And—going back to the visual dissonance of *The French Democracy*—the contrast between in-game assets and out-of-game storylines was generally appreciated and even sought, as in the case of the famous *Apartment Huntin'* piece from The ILL Clan, in which lumberjacks Larry and Lenny go through the customary process of renting a new apartment, but in a visual environment with sliding spaceship doors, futuristic computer centers, and metal corridors that come straight out of *Quake* (which was used to make the movie).

It has been argued that *The French Democracy* was an anomaly in the development of machinima (Jones 2011). However, there is no doubt that it still is a lively genre of creative audiovisual expression, moving slightly out of the avant-garde and into the mainstream not only with the introduction of production tools like *The Movies* but also with the growing audiovisual literacy across the Internet. There are popular websites for distributing and socializing around machinima movies, for teaching production techniques and sharing production resources, as well as sites upholding and nurturing the mythology of the genre by, for example, carefully tracing and crediting the pioneering works. In short, machinima can be described as a commune of digital media expression. It should be clear from the historical sketch here that it was never "designed" in the conventional sense of master plans or premeditated outcomes; instead, we consider it to be a useful example of an emergent phenomenon, a creative grassroots subculture gradually growing into more widespread recognition and acceptance.[2]

It may be interesting to note that machinima originated in subcultural subversion, where highly skilled consumers reverse engineered game engines to perform tasks never anticipated or endorsed by the developers of the games. And it turns out that there are quite a few other examples of collaborative media cultures sharing similar origins. *Fan fiction*, the works produced by fans when rewriting the stories of their favorite TV shows, films or books, for instance, can be understood as a subversion of mainstream producer-consumer assumptions on who does what in the entertainment industry (Jenkins 2006).

What we mean is that it is generally assumed that it is the producers, and the producers only, who decide what will happen to, for instance, the bold crew of the USS *Enterprise*. The role of the Star Trek fans is just to consume and enjoy the creative efforts of the producers. However, it turns out that the fans do not stop at that, but rather create vast amounts of unauthorized fiction in various media forms to elaborate on the stories and characters provided by the producers. A particularly engaging branch of Star Trek fan fiction is K/S fiction or "slash fiction," where the letters stand for Captain Kirk and Mr. Spock and the stories explore the possibilities of a homoerotic relationship between the two shipmates. The production of fan fiction generally takes place in a community-like structure of digital media production, and it is subversive in the sense that it is often critical of the original producers' intentions and the scope of their work. The potential for far-reaching conflict between "producer" and "consumer" over fan fiction is perhaps best illustrated in the case of Star Wars, where Lucasfilms Ltd. sent a letter to several fanzine publishers to assert the copyright to all Star Wars characters and specifically to ban any material, such as pornography, that would corrupt the family friendly character of the brand (Jenkins 2006).

At the time of writing, the novel *Fifty Shades of Grey*, the first in the so-called *Fifty Shades* trilogy, is sweeping the world and its author E. L. James has replaced J. K. Rowling as the best-selling author on Amazon.com. What is interesting about this phenomenon is that it marks the point where fan fiction stepped into the cultural and economical mainstream. Why? Simply because the *Fifty Shades* novels started as fan fiction based on characters from *Twilight*, the extremely popular series of vampire-themed fantasy novels, later to be rewritten and published as an original work.

Another illustrative example of online DIY (do it yourself) culture concerns the emergent collaborative response to the smash hit music video for Eric Prydz's song "Call on Me," directed by Huse Monfaradi and released in 2004. The video features an all-but-one female aerobics group, wearing more makeup and hair spray than clothes, performing a workout routine that borders on the pornographic. The video was very successful in terms of broadcasting airtime and download statistics, for instance becoming the most downloaded music video in Australia in 2005. However, it also stirred up a fair bit of controversy due to its sexually exploitative nature. The interesting aspect of the controversy, for our purposes, is that some of it took place in online media and used the same expressive form as the original—music videos.

More specifically, people started publishing satirical video parodies and mashups in order to communicate how they felt about the "Call on Me" music video and what it signified. The most popular technique by far was to simply reverse the gender order of the video and show an all-but-one male aerobics group emulating the moves from the original as closely as possible. The effect is quite striking, to say the least.

Nearly all of the gender-reverse examples are produced by recording new video to the same soundtrack. There are also examples of more conventional mashups, with already published video and audio material combined in new ways (Gunkel 2008). Perhaps the most elegant satire to be found is the *Brokeback Mountain 2* trailer directed by "Dan Colon." Here, the creator picks up on the wafer-thin storyline in "Call on Me," suggesting a romance between the aerobics instructor and the sole male group member. The mashup subverts this into a lesbian relationship between the instructor and one of the female members, using footage from the original video combined with text screens and music from the *Brokeback Mountain* movie trailer.

There are also more indirect traces of cultural influence to be found. For instance, the pelvic-thrust motion that was so droolingly depicted in the original video has intertwined with the popular-culture meme of humping in subcommunities such as ihumpedyourhummer.com, a video site built entirely around user-contributed video clips where people hump Hummer SUVs as a way to protest against the environmental implications and military connotations of driving said vehicles in civil society. On the site, there are contributions in the Music Videos category that use "Call on Me" as their soundtrack.

In most of the cases of machinima, mashups, and parodies produced and distributed by nonprofessionals online today, there is an unmistakably amateur quality to the production and execution. Whether we focus on the humorous or the political, the sincere or the satirical, the whole scene belongs in the aesthetic realm of do-it-yourself. Similar to the DIY movements in design and social innovation in the 1960s and 1970s, what we find in collaborative media is, above all, authentic and genuine. For instance, a recurring point critics made in their responses to *The French Democracy* is how moving and heartfelt the contrast is between the message and the form. The production tool that Chan used to create the movie was obviously designed for other kinds of animation, such as light comedy: the power station where the two teenagers hide from the police and die from electric shock is modeled as a quirky shack in the woods; the Empire State Building appears in the skyline of Paris; and, as mentioned earlier, the characters run like Bugs Bunny. The critics' point is that this discrepancy in fact enhances, rather than detracts from, the communicative quality and perceived authenticity of the film.

Perhaps this is where some of the attraction lies, harking back to early 1990s Internet evangelism, which raised hopes for a truly egalitarian medium. When widely distributed and widely noticed creations (such as novels, music videos, and films) appear to be made by your next-door neighbor in his or her bedroom, they might speak to you like your neighbor might speak to you: on your level, inviting you to engage in dialogue and, potentially, action. This is something very different from the awe-inspiring but passivizing spectacle of mass media and perfect production value.[3]

More generally, the stories of parody, machinima, mashup, and DIY illustrate well what we find to be the most salient trait of digital media: the grassroots and emergent nature of communicative practices, cutting across established media structures of society and its institutions. These practices, and the media infrastructures enabling them, define what we choose to call *collaborative media*. The book is devoted to studying the properties and practices of this new cultural form.

At the Intersection of Academic Disciplines

The form of this book is a scholarly monograph, and it is based on nearly fifteen years of collaboration between an interaction designer (Löwgren) and a media scholar (Reimer). The first project we did together started in 1998 and addressed the future of the established news media in the face of the then-exploding Internet penetration in the Western world. We worked together with members of the newspaper and news magazine industries, exploring trends in Internet use and online news and experimenting with new possibilities for news services and modes of production. (One of the ideas at the time concerned extremely local news curation through a then-imaginary service most similar to today's microblogging platforms, such as Tumblr.)

Since then, we have devoted much of our work to the field we now call collaborative media. And most of that work has followed the original pattern, in the sense that we have aimed to combine studies, analysis, and criticism with experiments, interventions, and change facilitation. In other words, we have been keen to study existing communication practices as well as to propose and explore new communication practices that could exist. This balancing act characterizes a *transdisciplinary* mode of research whereby the descriptive and analytical is combined with the design oriented.

From the point of view of our respective disciplines, the work we have done is somewhat difficult to pin down. In media and communication studies, on the one hand, the dominant mode of inquiry is descriptive, analytical, and critical, focusing on existing communication practices and their properties. Experimenting with communication practices that might exist is not considered standard practice. In interaction design, on the other hand, most research is design oriented and involves experimenting with the not-yet-existing. Here, though, there is a strong heritage of viewing computers as tools, and the idea of computers as communication media of a sociocultural fabric still represents a minority view.[4]

What we hope to accomplish in this book is to pull together and reflect systematically on a considerable body of experience from working in this borderland of collaborative media. We envision our readers as a relatively advanced academic audience, including researchers and PhD students with an interest in collaborative media and their trajectories. In terms of academic affiliation, we expect a mixed readership representing interaction design and media and communication studies as well as other subjects pertinent to collaborative media, such as computer science, social and behavioral science, and perhaps also some of the fine arts. Our transdisciplinary approach in combination with this kind of audience will certainly lead to situations where the individual reader finds some of our points elementary, others quite obscure and perhaps irrelevant. This follows inevitably from the disciplinary structures of academia, and our best advice is simply to look at the whole and to think about how well-known subject matter may take on different meanings when juxtaposed with material from other fields.

Bearing the diversity of the readership in mind, then, our aim is to achieve two purposes. First, we want to outline the qualities and characteristics of collaborative media as a new cultural form. In conventional terms, it can be stated that our main knowledge contribution is a characterization of the forms of practice that collaborative media make possible, and the abstraction of our insights into a communication model that seems to accommodate or capture collaborative media. Second, as a call to action, we want to facilitate a transition toward transdisciplinary ways of doing research in collaborative media where analytical and design-oriented modes of working are combined, and where interventions are carried out in everyday settings. The following section presents our approach to achieving the dual purposes.

Overview of the Book

Part I, Starting Points, defines collaborative media in more detail and positions our work in the emerging landscape of new media scholarship and design (chapter 2). Moreover, it looks at the roles of research more generally. We explore contemporary notions of knowledge production, and we outline a transdisciplinary research approach to collaborative media, where analysis and design are combined (chapter 3).

Part II, Interventions, consists of ten case studies. These are all examples of research projects in collaborative media that we have done ourselves or have had privileged access to through our close colleagues. The cases are chosen to form a broad repertoire of exemplars, spanning different use situations, different intervention purposes, different user population sizes, and different technologies.

We find that there are three meaningful levels at which to discuss collaborative media, and these levels are also represented in the three chapters of part II. Chapter 4 addresses the level of society and particularly the roles of collaborative media in societal change and transformation. The level of institutions (chapter 5) is mainly concerned with existing and established media structures, and their relations to—potentially disruptive—collaborative media. Finally, the level of tribes (chapter 6) is chosen to underscore the potential of collaborative media to nurture communality within a myriad of relatively small social structures coexisting on top of the same technical infrastructure.

Part III, Insights and Conclusions, allows us to reflect on our experience and situate it in the contemporary scholarly landscape. The structure mirrors part I, with a chapter reflecting on the specificities of collaborative media practices (chapter 7) followed by a closing chapter addressing the practice of transdisciplinary collaborative media research (chapter 8).

2 〰〰 The Cultural Form of Collaborative Media

As we describe in chapter 1, something is happening with people's media practices in everyday life. Increasingly, people not only consume media, they also produce media: blogs, music videos, and so on. And they organize their media practices in new, innovative ways.

As we see it, the situation can best be understood by considering the changes intimately related to the emergence of a new *cultural form*. The concept of cultural form comes from the British cultural studies theorist Raymond Williams, who introduced it in *Television: Technology and Cultural Form* (1974). In the book, he used it in order to outline the specificity of television: its form. This form is dependent on many factors, but in the end, the form is primarily cultural, by that meaning that the form always is historically and contextually specific—and contested. Television is shaped both by technological properties and historical, social, and cultural circumstances. Even though technological properties make some uses possible and other uses impossible, television has no necessary, predetermined form or function; that is, it is continually changing. In discussing the cultural form of a medium such as television it is thus necessary to be historically specific.

We will regard the phenomenon under study here in a similar way, as a cultural form. We will outline its specific properties without forgetting the contextual character of these properties. It is a way of treating the technological properties of the cultural form seriously, but neither treating these properties as essential or "natural," nor believing it possible to deduce simple "effects" out of their properties.

As our suggestion for how best to capture this cultural form, we will introduce the concept of *collaborative media*. We will also critically discuss—and reconceptualize— what is meant by digital media practices and we will outline our approach to collaborative media.

Delineating Collaborative Media

In looking back at the examples of people's everyday media practices presented in chapter 1—practices dealing with parody, machinima, mashup, and DIY—we find that they share some characteristics.

1) The practices are based on media services and tools that
   a) are easy to use;
   b) can be used creatively and pleasurably in many different ways.
2) The practices are to a great extent collaborative. People work together to create things that are not possible for the lone user to create. And this occurs not only face to face; to a great extent, the collaborations take place online on a potentially global scale.

In other words, the precondition for the appearance of these new everyday-life practices is the development of new media technologies that make new practices possible, and it is tied to the design work that is required to make these technologies fun and interesting to work with. The technologies furthermore "reward" people who work collaboratively with them. However, collaboration does not follow "naturally" from the technologies. It is rather the outcome of an intricate interplay among technological, cultural, and social factors at historically specific points in time.

How may one best conceptualize this cultural form? Different concepts have been used to capture contemporary media. The three most common ones are arguably *digital media*, *social media*, and *new media*. However, we do not find any of them adequate for capturing the salient properties we identify earlier.

Why not digital media? The media in question are unquestionably digital; that is, in a sense, a precondition. But not all digital media have the properties we have outlined. The concept of "digital media" made sense at a point in time when there was a clear distinction between analog and digital media. Today all major media run on digital infrastructures and, consequently, the concept has lost its meaning as a marker of contemporary media and contemporary media practice.

"Social media" is a term used frequently in everyday life and the media themselves seem to find it appropriate. But it is a term whose scope is too narrow in relation to the properties we have described. In practice, it mainly refers to social networking services such as Facebook and Twitter. At the same time, it is too wide: in principle, all media are social in the elementary sense that they mediate social (communication) processes.

The main contender to collaborative media is "new media." It is by far the most commonly used term within academia for capturing contemporary media and contemporary media practices. Influential books include Bolter and Grusin's *Remediation: Understanding New Media* (1999) and Manovich's *The Language of New Media* (2001). Academic journals within the field have names such as *New Media & Society, Television & New Media*, and *Convergence: The International Journal of Research Into New Media Technologies*, and a large number of textbooks covering the area use the term "new media" in the titles.[1]

However, due to its widespread use, new media is also a very broad and imprecise concept. As Fuery writes: "'New media' is, after all, a catch-all phrase that takes in the internet, television, and sound; transgenic art; digital photography; body modification; installations, and so on" (2008, 1). There are of course occasions when broad concepts are useful; it depends on what one wants to do with a concept. But if the focus is on contemporary, digital media practices, using the concept of new media is not ideal. As Benjamin Peters argues: "the concept of 'new media' cannot refer to any particular set of technologies: the term must sustain fascination across time and space divisions, history and social groups" (2009, 17).

Those media that we today consider to be old have also been new (cf. Marvin 1988). Similarly, the media that we today consider to be new will one day be considered to be old. And for young people growing up today it certainly makes no sense to speak of, for instance, the Internet as a new medium; for them it has always been there. Thus, the concept of new media is useful as a concept dealing with media in particular stages of their existence, when they are new. It is not useful for describing a group of media that happened to be developed at one particular point in time only. And thus, it is not useful in describing what is happening today.

We propose the concept of "collaborative media" as the most fruitful one in describing those media properties outlined earlier and in chapter 1. Collaboration is the one feature that in the clearest way indicates the particular kind of communication that is typical within this context. Rather than focusing on technology, collaborative media focuses on the action-oriented component of media; it focuses on the kinds of practices the cultural form makes possible. We do not define collaborative media as some specific media forms rather than others. "Collaborative" is a relative, rather than an absolute, concept. Some media forms have properties that make them more suitable for collaboration, but it is only at those occasions when they are put to use collaboratively they become collaborative media. Similarly, some media forms are less likely to be used collaboratively, but on those occasions when that happens they "are" collaborative media. It is also crucial to point out that we conceive of the concept of "media" very broadly to include any channel that facilitates communication. This in turn means that in line with technological development, more and more things may function as media, as portrayed with the help of terms such as "The Internet of Things" (Atzori, Iera, and Morabito 2010). Thus, what we focus on, and want to delineate, is the specificities of certain media as *forms for practice*; the specificities of what they can make possible. *Collaborative media is a particular cultural form for collaborative, mediated practice.*[2]

Collaborative Media Practices: Design, Production, and Consumption

Having defined "collaborative media" from the perspective of what such media potentially can make possible, the next logical step is to outline what these potentialities are.
In so doing, it makes sense to start with the large body of work that has been amassed
during the last decade on the possibly new relationship between media production and
consumption.

Previously, in times of traditional mass media, this relationship was rather straight-
forward. A small number of media producers produced *media texts* (a term used in
media studies to refer to all manner of media content) that were subsequently distributed to a large number of media consumers. The consumers discussed the texts
in everyday settings, and they made different kinds of use of them, but they did not
produce media texts themselves.

The emergence of new media technologies led to new relationships between production and consumption, where the two processes became less distinct. What happened
was that, as we hinted in chapter 1, people who used to only consume media—the
people "formerly known as the audience" (Rosen 2006)—increasingly also started to
produce their own media texts; they became media producers themselves.

Academically, the debate concerning this development has been rather lively. First,
it has been questioned whether the change actually is that significant. Even though it
may be the case that people to a certain extent do produce their own media texts today,
one should not forget that people always have used the media available to them in quite
different ways, often in ways not imagined by the media producers. Using the media
has always been a productive and creative practice (Livingstone 2003; van Dijck 2009).

Second, it has been argued that even though some people do produce their own
media texts, on the whole it is a marginal practice. Most people are content with consuming the things media professionals produce (Bird 2011).

Third, a debate has raged concerning the consequences of this development. On one
side researchers have argued that the change is highly positive. People have become
increasingly productive in their spare time. Instead of reading or watching what professionals have produced for them, they make their own blogs or videos. The work
they produce—often collaboratively—functions as an exciting alternative to the work
produced by the traditional media companies and institutions, and it raises a kind of
criticism toward power structures that has never been heard before (Benkler 2006; Jenkins 2006; Gauntlett 2011). However, the arguments against these lines of reasoning
have been fierce. It is true, it is argued, that amateurs produce media texts of their own
today. But these texts are of extremely low quality and do not add anything substantial
to material produced by media professionals. It could rather be argued that important,
high-quality work will drown in the flood of amateur production (Keen 2007). There is
also the question of exploitation. In enjoying the possibilities of being able to express

themselves, and being able to make their expressions available to a wide audience, people are very happy to work for free, and to give away their work for free to media corporations that subsequently make a profit off the work. This, furthermore, makes it increasingly difficult for professionals to make a living on their work. If some people work for free, why should others get paid? (Terranova 2004; Andrejevic 2011).

The question of whether these changes are positive or not is of course a crucial question (albeit a very difficult one, and not one lending itself to a simple yes or no answer). We will return to it in the final part of this book. Right now, however, the two initial discussion topics are of more importance for our argument.

We agree that media use always has had a constructive aspect. Studies within the academic field of audience studies have shown this convincingly (Brooker and Jermyn 2003). But there is still a substantial difference between consuming other people's media texts and producing one's own. And even though it can always be discussed when a practice has grown to such a magnitude that it should be seen as substantial, for us figures such as 1 billion Facebook users and over 150 million bloggers worldwide (Pingdom 2011) indicate that these are practices of some significance.

There is, thus, a need for taking the changing relationship between production and consumption seriously. And this is also something that has been done for quite some time. On a more general everyday-life level, not restricted to media practices, the concept of "Pro-Am" (Professional-Amateur) has been coined to indicate how people in their leisure time conduct activities with such conviction, endurance, and quality that the work produced meets professional standards (Leadbeater and Miller 2004; Leadbeater 2008).

More specifically connected to media practices are concepts proposed to capture the new position taken by people who both produce and consume media, expressed in terms such as "prosumption" (production and consumption) (Tapscott and Williams 2006) and "produsage" (production and usage) (Bruns 2008).[3]

There are often good reasons for coining new terms. They make us rethink things we used to take for granted. Prosumption and produsage, for example, cause us to think anew on what production and consumption entail. However, in our view these two concepts are problematic in that they confuse the increasing interlinking and simultaneity of two separate practices—production and consumption—with the conflation of these two practices. In an article concerning everyday life practices more generally, Beer and Burrows write that "participation in acts that genuinely blur the line between production and consumption are now an established part of the everyday lives of millions of people" (2010, 10). It is this blurring of distinctions we would like to question. It is certainly true that people spend more free time than ever before consuming and producing media. It is also true that consumption and production can be carried out more or less simultaneously. But that does not mean that the practices as such are blurred. To the contrary, we find it more analytically useful to uphold the distinction and speak of production and consumption as two distinct practices.

More important, though, we would like to point out that it is not only production that has been added to people's repertoires of everyday media practices. There is another practice that needs to be taken into account.

When thinking in terms of production and consumption, the point of departure is a mass communication model based on the idea of a small number of media with relatively well-determined production possibilities, historically changing since they are culturally shaped, but fairly static on a momentary timescale. According to this model, media production entails, for example, making a film, or a newspaper, or a radio program. Carrying out these productions requires media infrastructure, including facilities and production equipment. Media producers do not really have to think about the infrastructure beyond having to learn how to use it to the best advantage; it recedes into the background and becomes part of the given preconditions for media production.

Such a model is not valid in relation to collaborative media. In this context, a new possibility has opened up. Not only can people produce media texts, they also can take part in *the design of the infrastructure*—the programs, software components, and web services that can be used for media production. People working within the media industries (broadly defined) as well as interested citizens can now participate in creating the tools that enable different kinds of media productions. In this sense, designing Facebook or Flickr is not the same as producing a TV show. A TV show is produced by a group of professionals at a particular point in time; only that group has access to the production facilities needed. In the case of Facebook and Flickr, as we shall see in the following discussion, aspects of their functions and appearance are actually open for modification by users. This means that Facebook and Flickr, like many other collaborative media services, are being continuously redesigned by both professionals and amateurs. Designing the infrastructure is now an option, in principle, for everyone—and an increasing number of people are seizing the opportunity. This can happen on both the private and public levels.

On the private level, it is possible for people to modify the infrastructure simply for it to function in ways that better suit them. For instance, it is quite common for people to customize web pages. Accordingly, designers of the infrastructure purposely make products so they can be customized. However, it is also possible for people to make adjustments and modifications that software designers never could have imagined. In traditional media, such reappropriation was a rare exception requiring high levels of specialized skill—the classic example is how hip-hop culture transformed record players into musical instruments with scratching and other performance techniques (White 1996). In contrast, collaborative media is, generally speaking, much more open to infrastructural modification due to the prevalence of open source software, open APIs (application programming interfaces), and components that can be combined at will into different constellations known as mashups.

The openness of the collaborative media infrastructures also extends to sharing, since most of what is made by nonprofessionals is executed in digital form and lends itself to effortless duplication and distribution. This is the link between the private and the public level of infrastructure modification. The proverbial example of collaborative open source development (i.e., public infrastructure modification) is the Apache web server, which was launched in 1996 and is now estimated to run over half of all the web servers on the Internet. Three more recent and widely used examples of collaborative-media infrastructure components that are developed as collaborative open source products are the publishing platform Wordpress, the content management system Drupal, and the Linux-based operating system Android.

For private as well as public infrastructure modifications, it holds true that some of the work follows rather closely the intentions of the original designers, whereas other modifications go way beyond initial ambitions. A venerable example, but still worthy of consideration, is the mundane 160-character text message service of mobile phones. SMS, or short message service, was conceived as part of the specifications for the first generation of digital mobile phone communication systems in the mid-1980s, and at the time it was described in purely functional terms. The first commercial implementations of SMS in mobile networks for customers, introduced around 1992, used the service to send automated notifications from network stations to mobile-phone users of, for example, pending voicemails. The idea that people would use text messages for communicating with each other initially was not considered very promising: the service was not marketed very strongly, and there were severe technical restrictions and billing inconsistencies. Predictably, consumer adoption was quite slow during the 1990s. What happened, however, was that despite the technology's limitations, teenagers saw its social potential and jump-started the SMS industry by choosing text messaging as their medium for interpersonal communication. Today, this industry clearly is significant in commercial terms: global earnings for 2010 were estimated at over $100 billion USD (Potts et al. 2008).

A similar but more recent example is Twitter, where the retweet function—as well as the whole family of services growing from the hashtag—is now considered part of Twitter DNA. Yet, both the hashtag and retweet function were designed by users rather than by the original producers of Twitter (Löwgren and Reimer 2012).

As we see it, the possibility for people to take part in designing media infrastructures is at least as significant for our understanding of collaborative media as the possibility of producing media texts. To summarize, we suggest that the key everyday practices collaborative media make possible are *design, production*, and *consumption*. These are different kinds of practices, and each has its own specific logic. However, within the framework of collaborative media, they are not isolated from each other. Quite to the contrary, they are intimately related, and it is this intimate relationship which has led to the confusion concerning production and consumption. In order to make sense of the practices, it is thus necessary both to identify the specific logic of each practice and to view the practices as parts of a system, within which they structure each other.

Our point of departure for so doing is the work carried out by British Cultural Studies scholar Stuart Hall on mass communication processes, and primarily his book chapter "Coding and Encoding in the Television Discourse" (1980). The chapter deals with television, primarily news programs, and with the question of how meaning is produced, transmitted, and received. In the chapter, he presents his influential encoding/decoding model.

For Hall, a mass communication process consists of a number of distinctive moments: production, circulation, distribution/consumption, and reproduction. By "moment," Hall means a particular section of a process that at least analytically can be delimited from other sections. Each moment has its specific logic, but it is important to note that the logical framework of each is only relatively independent. The moments belong in a structure within which they are linked to each other. These linkages depend on the specific historical situation, which implies that their nature can vary but that they are never random.

Although all moments are needed in order for the communication circuit to "work," some are more determinate than others. These are the discursive moments, in which the event to be covered—"reality"—is translated into language (which for television means an audiovisual form). The first discursive moment is the production moment. This is the moment in which reality is translated into a message encoded with certain meanings that the encoder/producer wishes to deliver to its receivers. But there is also a second discursive moment, when the receivers make sense of—decode—the message. And this they can do in different ways.

Hall suggests three possible ways of decoding the same message, depending on the position from which the decoding is done. One can take a dominant-hegemonic position, in which case the decoding follows the encoding quite closely. It is also possible to take a position Hall calls negotiated, which means largely accepting the viewpoint from which the encoding has been made but making some adjustments or modifications. The third position he calls an oppositional one. From this position, the decoder rejects the message the encoder tries to convey.

Stuart Hall was not the first person to note that a message encoded by a producer may be decoded in ways not intended by that producer. This was recognized already by Claude Shannon and Warren Weaver in the 1940s (Shannon and Weaver 1949). For Shannon and Weaver, this constituted a communication problem they sought to overcome. For Hall, this lack of fit led instead to two more general observations:

1. People within the same society have different worldviews. It is not reasonable to expect that messages transmitted to a large segment of the population will be encoded uniformly.

2. Consumption—or decoding—is a discursive moment in its own right. The encoding moment may be "predominant" (Hall 1980, 130) and it may structure the decoding, but it is impossible to predict the meanings people will make from the message itself, or from the intentions of the producers.

In making sense of collaborative media practices, Hall's model for understanding communication processes constitutes a good point of departure. Building on that, we will present our model for how to understand collaborative media practices. However, since the cultural form of collaborative media is different from the cultural form of television, the model will have to be modified.[4]

First, Hall's model focused on how one particular message—one television program—was encoded and decoded. We are interested in how collaborative media practices in general can be understood.

Second, when dealing with television in the 1970s and 1980s, there was a very clear distinction between producers and consumers. Producers were professionals working for big corporations, private or public. Consumers were the general audience. The producers obviously did not only produce television programs; they also watched programs. But the general public only consumed. There was no way they could move into a producer position. As already discussed, when it comes to collaborative media, the situation is completely different. People in general not only consume media, they also produce.

Third, for Hall, two moments were determinate: production and consumption. This was based on the idea that these were the two discursive moments in the process. As we have already discussed, one major characteristic of collaborative media is that people are able to also take part in the design of their infrastructure. That infrastructure has come into play, so to speak; it is not preordained, once and for all. It is furthermore the case that when it comes to collaborative media, the distinction between infrastructure and media texts is less clear than for other media forms. Thus, design of the infrastructure contains discursive elements, and just as production and consumption, it should be considered a determinate moment.

Finally, in dealing with one particular television program, which is produced at one particular time and then broadcast to the general public at a later stage, but also at a particular point in time, the model is sequential by necessity: first production, then consumption. Generally speaking, the situation is quite different when it comes to collaborative media processes. It is certainly true that for a new collaborative media process to take place, there has to be some kind of media service, platform, or tool— some element of infrastructure. In other words, in most cases there has to be a moment of design in order for the other moments to occur. But this initial design moment can be very brief and sketchy. For instance, it could be limited to the introduction of a rudimentary private beta version of a new service. There are also examples of how new collaborative media processes take off through reappropriation of existing infrastructural components, thus requiring no upfront design at all. Either way, once a process is initiated, the moments of design, production, and consumption take place simultaneously. Thus, our model for collaborative media practices is essentially nonsequential.

Figure 2.1 presents our model for collaborative media practices. It is based on the interrelationship of the three moments of design, production, and consumption, and it

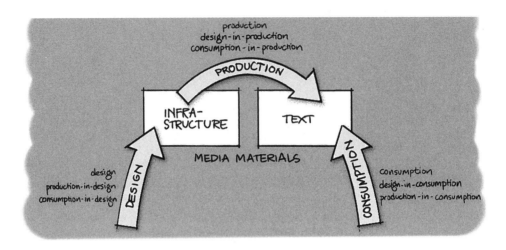

Figure 2.1
The moments and practices of collaborative media.

links the roles of designing, producing, and consuming to one another without making them exclusive (the same person can both design, produce, and consume). It furthermore makes clear the close relationship between the collaborative media infrastructure and the collaborative media texts produced with the help of the infrastructure. Together, the infrastructure and the texts produced may be conceived of as *collaborative media materials*.

Each moment contains three kinds of practices. Within the moment of design, design practices, production-in-design practices, and consumption-in-design practices take place. Design practices are of course the most common ones within this moment, but production and consumption also occur. For instance, when creating and designing a collaborative media infrastructure, before launching it, it is often deemed necessary to test its functionality. This is typically done through the creation of initial products or texts (production-in-design) and by conducting user tests (consumption-in-design). Take as an example the video-sharing website YouTube. It was launched in November 2005, but the moment of design started long before that with design processes at work creating an initial version of the site. Six months before the launch, beta tests were carried out (involving production-in-design as well as consumption-in-design).

The production moment primarily consists of production practices, but it also includes the practices of design-in-production and consumption-in-production. By design-in-production we mean the practices carried out when existing infrastructures in use are modified, either by professionals or by amateurs. Similarly, consumption-in-production refers to practices when people consume media texts in order to produce. To continue with the same example: YouTube is based on the idea of people sharing video clips. Some of these are taken from movies or TV shows, for example, but a substantial number consist of material specially produced for YouTube by its users. All of this making of video clips is production. Moreover, the functions and features of the website (the infrastructure) are continuously refined and many YouTube users take part in this design-in-production work, actively endorsed by the company. An even more clear-cut example of design-in-production is when a YouTube user styles her channel page to her liking. Finally, a YouTube example of consumption-in-production is when a user watches a batch of existing *Downfall* parodies in preparation for creating a new one (see chapter 1).

The practice of consumption dominates the consumption moment, but design-in-consumption and production-in-consumption practices also take place within that moment. Consuming video clips is the most common practice on YouTube. But by watching clips, people (albeit unintentionally) take part in the ongoing redesign of the website, since the selection of "most watched" clips—prominently displayed on the website—is based on viewers' consumption practices. Finally, an example of production-in-consumption is when someone posts a comment about the video clip she has just watched. This comment is a form of production, but it takes place within the context of consumption.

Understanding Action—and Interaction

Thus far in this chapter, we have identified collaborative media practices and we have related them to the cultural form that they depend on. However, we have not yet discussed what it is that make these practices occur. In everyday life, some people use collaborative media frequently, others do not. Why is that? It is easy to find examples of overwhelming energy and effort being poured into collaborative media design, production, and consumption: people upload their music and their photos for worldwide audiences. They digitize vintage TV sitcoms from video tapes and share online. They donate hours and hours of their spare time to answer questions in their particular field of technical expertise. They contribute news reports. They create dozens of elaborate machinima episodes. They reflect in public writing on big and small things in life. And they talk for hours with people they have never met. Why?

More generally, this concerns the notion of *action*. What is it that makes people decide to do what they do? Obviously, this is a huge question that we cannot deal with exhaustively, but it is still a question we need to touch upon in relation to media practices.

Turning to the academic field of media and communication studies—a reasonable starting point given the topic—one could initially state that in order to understand why people use the media the way they do, it is necessary to take into account both the medium in question (the cultural form of the medium as well as its output) and the interests and competencies of the people involved. Action furthermore occurs within a sociocultural context. These statements are not exactly controversial. However, within the field, there are differences to be found when it comes to the weight one assigns to the different factors. Do people choose to do what they do owing to personal interests, to socioeconomic background, to social circumstances, or something else entirely? How important are the media themselves?

In general, social science traditions have prioritized studies of media users, placing less attention on the actual study of the media output. On the humanities side, some traditions have put their focus exclusively on media texts, and their properties, whereas others have tried to deal more concretely with the roles played by the individual (within a social context) and by the media and their texts.[5]

Obviously, many important insights can be drawn from studies carried out on mass media practices when studying collaborative media. But the ways that media and communication studies have treated mass media practices cannot simply be transferred to the study of collaborative media practices. And this is not surprising. Collaborative media represent a new cultural form and it is not reasonable to expect existing studies of the cultural forms of mass media to provide insights of immediate relevance for our purposes. The cultural form of collaborative media demands its own explorations and studies in order to build a relevant body of knowledge and insights.[6]

The primary problem with the work carried out within the major traditions within media and communication studies is their exclusive focus on media texts and media users; they have not treated the media infrastructure necessary for the production and consumption of media texts in a serious manner. And as discussed earlier in this chapter, collaborative media practices cannot be understood without taking those infrastructures into the discussion.

Why is it that media infrastructures have not been treated seriously? Their importance would seem to be self-evident. But it has to do with the curious role that technology has played within the media and communications studies paradigm. Even though different mass media obviously in some ways are dependent on technology, it has not been deemed a priority for study.

To simplify only a little, one could regard the role played by technology in relation to human action as either crucial or marginal. The first position is associated with what has been called medium theory, with Marshall McLuhan (1964) its best-known proponent (Meyrowitz 1994). The second position traditionally is referred to as the social shaping of technology (SST) (MacKenzie and Wajcman 1999). Even though the first position originated in the field of media and communication studies, and concerns media specifically, it has been subject to repeated accusations of technological determinism and hence been forced to function more or less in isolation from other traditions within media and communication studies. Lately there have been signs of an opening between the two positions, as the title of John Potts's 2008 article in *The Fibreculture Journal* makes clear: "Who's Afraid of Technological Determinism?" A similar discussion is taken up by Kristoffer Gansing (2013). However, for the time being, studies of media properties—including infrastructure—are not a crucial part of mainstream media and communication studies.[7]

It may be understandable why infrastructure has been left outside the analytical framework for studying traditional forms of mass media. But as we have pointed out, in dealing with collaborative media this is not a viable option. What interests us is not just how and why people consume media but also how they take part in the design of media infrastructure and in media production. We are interested not in action generally but in *interaction*—the interaction of people mediated by different types of collaborative media. And since we cannot get that much help from the academic field of media and communication, in order to gain a better understanding of how this media form actually "works," we have to look elsewhere, to academic fields dealing more explicitly with the relationship between people and things.

One field that is fundamentally driven by an interest in the relations between people and things (and specifically man-made things, or artifacts), as well as how those relations can be improved, is obviously design research. The field can be characterized as an umbrella construction in the sense that it comprises several design disciplines, such as architecture, industrial design, and interaction design (which entails the design-oriented branch of human–computer interaction), and the underlying assumption is that design processes and knowledge share common traits across those disciplines. For the purposes of exploring collaborative media, it turns out that design research within interaction design—focused on digital materials—is the most appropriate venue. A representative example of how the relation between people and things has been conceptualized in that subfield is the concept of *affordance*. Originally proposed by ecological psychologist James Gibson (1977), it was introduced to (interaction) design by Donald Norman (1988) as a way to understand what it is in a thing that makes it interesting or relevant for a potential user. In Gibson's original work, the affordance was purely a property of the thing itself; Norman modified the perspective to consider *perceived* affordances, referring to how the properties of a thing that a user perceives makes the user act upon it in certain ways.

The notion of (perceived) affordances became hugely popular in interaction design, and to this day it is common to find design guidelines for optimal usability and functionality along the lines of "Design clear and unambiguous affordances." It is also a fitting illustration of mainstream approaches to the relations between people and things within interaction design: It concentrates on the interaction between one user and one thing in a social vacuum, and it aims at making that interaction as efficient, error-free, and pleasurable as possible. For our purposes, such approaches are of limited value since our atomic grain of analysis is rather the social level of people in mediated communication with each other.

Fortunately, design research also offers other conceptual approaches to the relations between people and things where sociality is a fundamental starting point. One such approach, which has gained widespread recognition in design research, is actor-network theory (ANT), originating with sociologist Bruno Latour and colleagues (Law and Hassard 1999; Latour 2005). Of particular interest to us is the ANT notion of *inscription*, referring to the way in which designers inscribe artifacts with meaning. For each artifact, there is a script. As argued by Akrich: "Thus, like a film script, technical objects define a framework of action together with the actors and the space in which they are supposed to act" (1992, 208).

The concept of inscription is similar to the concept of encoding, discussed earlier, but inscription is connected to an artifact as such, not to a media text. There is furthermore one distinctive trait in the way action is viewed in ANT, which makes it a particularly interesting construct for our purposes.

Within social science in general, focus traditionally is put on understanding or explaining human behavior. Things, or physical objects, have been left to the natural sciences. But can one understand human behavior without treating the objects people use seriously? On one level, as Latour argues, it is difficult to see why objects are not in focus for the social sciences since they obviously are involved in action: "At first, action should appear innocuous enough. After all, there is hardly any doubt that kettles 'boil' water, knives 'cut' meat, baskets 'hold' provisions, hammers 'hit' nails on the head. . . . Are those verbs not designating actions? How could the introduction of those humble, mundane and ubiquitous activities bring any news to any social scientist?" (2005, 71).

The reason these activities are left outside social analysis, as Latour reminds us, is because of how action is regarded within social analysis. It is tied to the notion of intentionality, and obviously in the examples Latour offers, there is no such thing. There was no intention on the part of the kettle to boil the water, no intention on the part of the knife to cut the meat, and so on.

However, even though there is no intention, is it not the case that these activities *change conditions and states of affairs*? Shouldn't they therefore be included in social analyses, even if the changes are partly due to the things—to the nonhumans—involved? Is there not a big difference between boiling water with or without a kettle, or cutting meat with or without a knife?

Latour's point is that analyses of social action should include all actors that make a difference. Actors *"make others do things"* (2005, 71).[8] They transform situations. And, as shown in this example, actors can be things, physical objects, artifacts. This does not mean, of course, that there is no difference between humans and nonhumans. As already spelled out, nonhumans do not have intentions. But that is not a reason for excluding them from analyses.

Including nonhumans is relevant for any study of social action—and "device-centred" approaches to public affairs show the importance of such studies (Marres 2012). But the inclusion of nonhumans is especially relevant in relation to a study of collaborative media practices, since collaborative media can play such crucial roles as actors (as we begun to show in chapter 1 and will return to in Part II of this book). This is one reason for moving toward an ANT perspective. However, it is not the only one. It is not only about extending the number of actors—even if that is crucial in itself. It is also a question of getting a different understanding of action, and the forces behind action.

Within the media and communication studies traditions, as well as within other traditional social science practices dealing with human action, a major concern is dealing with, and preferably overcoming, the system/actor distinction. Which is most important? The system or the actor? Traditionally, this is dealt with by conceptualizing human action taking place within a "context." This context can be described more or less concretely, but it stays outside the analysis of human action. It is a context within which things happen.

The perspective put forward in ANT is not to overcome this distinction, but—put somewhat provocatively—to ignore it (Latour 2005, 216). Instead of situating systems and actors on different conceptual levels they are joined through analyses in which all things—all actors—that make a difference are taken into account simultaneously. They need not be active simultaneously, though: to the contrary, many relevant actors are historical.[9] But the point is that by treating every actor in a similar way—by keeping the social "flat"—analyses can take all powers into account. It also means not hiding or disregarding difficult problems by simply making them part of the context, thereby placing them outside analysis.[10]

An Approach to Collaborative Media

Thus, we end up in a situation where we establish that (1) the new cultural form of collaborative media appears to have properties that set it apart from traditional mass media forms, and (2) mainstream approaches to media studies are of somewhat limited value to us. Specifically, as we argue for the significance of collaborative media infra-structures and their ongoing design (as opposed to the taken-for-granted infrastructures of traditional mass media), we need 3) a perspective on media practices that treats people and artifacts together.

This is not to say that we need to reinvent the wheel, though; our concerns resonate quite well with cultural studies approaches to media as outlined in the previous section. Latour speaks of the necessity of tracing the different associations among the different actors involved in a setting. Such phrasing is similar to the way Stuart Hall (1986) speaks of identifying articulations among different actors or elements. By "articulations," Hall means those linkages that can exist between actors, linkages that are more or less probable but never "necessary" or essential. Our concerns also fit well with the current materialist turn in social analysis and social theory (Coole and Frost 2010). It is a turn in which *Communication Matters*—as the title of the book by Packer and Crofts Wiley (2011) makes clear. Or as Jussi Parikka writes: "Instead of philosophical traditions, let us read modern physics, engineering and communications technology as mapping the terrain of new materialism" (2012, 96).

Our interest in the three moments of design, production, and consumption as well as in the infrastructures of collaborative media has consequences for how we approach the phenomena under investigation. As will become apparent in this book, our case studies and our reasoning include technical details of collaborative media services and platforms as well as the social and communicative actions that people take around them. We find this necessary in order to provide a rich understanding of the full socio-technical complex that is collaborative media practices.

Moreover, as Hall (1980) reminds us, the articulations of linkages in sociotechnical webs of media practices depend on what the articulator brings to the analysis. In our case, this corresponds to the stance and perspective of the collaborative media researcher—which is the topic for the next chapter.

3 〰〰 Researching Collaborative Media

Academic work traditionally is highly disciplined. Research areas are divided among different groups of researchers who organize themselves into disciplines or fields, within which they speak the same language. They may disagree upon research matters and on specific analyses but they share a common understanding concerning what research within the field entails, what one should study, and how. This does not mean that each research area necessarily is exclusive to one discipline, but it means that each discipline deals with the area in its particular way.

Thus far we have discussed how to theoretically, conceptually, and empirically grasp our area of focus, collaborative media. The researchers involved in these discussions come primarily from the humanities and the social sciences. Many of them come from media and communication studies (including television studies and journalism) or cultural studies, but definitely not all. Also involved are researchers coming from political science; sociology; ethnology; human geography; and science, technology and society studies (STS). These researchers differ in many ways, but they make up an academic community in the sense that they all work theoretically/empirically and they agree to a great extent on which questions are relevant to address, and which researchers are crucial to discuss.

The reason for initially focusing on this academic community is that it is the one that has most explicitly dealt theoretically and conceptually with collaborative media (thus far). And even though, as stated, researchers within a particular field agree upon what research within that field entails, it is still the case that academic fields change and develop. Or at least, the dominating positions in the field can be challenged. A case in point is the study of media within the field of media and communication studies. In order to set the stage for the research approach we propose later on in this chapter, we will next summarize the recent debate within media and communication studies on how to approach media, and then touch upon practice-based approaches to collaborative media and the issue of nonacademic knowledge production.

Media Studies 2.0 and Onward

In 2006, media scholar Will Merrin created a blog dedicated to Media Studies 2.0, in which he argued that technological developments have created the need for a revision of media studies.[1] His point was that the field of media studies traditionally only has focused on a small number of media, and almost exclusively on content and reception, leaving technology and production outside the scope of the field. Mass communication gave the field its reason to exist. Today, however, it limits the field, Merrin argued. His blog launching Media Studies 2.0 led to the journal *Interactions* devoting a special issue to the topic, in which Merrin further outlined his position: "MS2.0 is a call for every part of media studies to recognize and open itself up to the changes caused by digital media. It is a call for media studies to broaden and update its knowledge and references and to test its ideas, assumptions and arguments against the contemporary world. Above all it is a call for media studies to remain relevant" (2009, 27–28).

In the special issue, most voices were critical to Merrin's call for Media Studies 2.0. The main criticism concerned what was regarded as a highly uncritical view of what is happening in the current media landscape. Critics argued that Merrin had failed to see that power relations have stayed the same even though people use the media in new ways, and that interactivity is not by definition empowering (cf. Andrejevic 2009; Taylor 2009). However, he did receive support from David Gauntlett, who argued that Merrin's position was not about celebrating the new situation; rather, it was about acknowledging that things are changing, which arguably should have consequences for how media scholars work (2009).

In a similar vein, Toby Miller subsequently argued that today's media landscape needs a new version of media studies, a version he denotes Media Studies 3.0; a form of media studies which goes beyond simple dichotomizing, where either the media are regarded as having simple, unidirectional effects on unsuspecting audiences (Media Studies 1.0) or the audience is considered all-powerful, doing whatever it wants with the media output (Media Studies 2.0). To make sense of today's situation, it is necessary to broaden one's outlook and bring in ethnographic, political-economic, and aesthetic competencies in a global as well as a local way (Miller 2009, 6). Miller's call for a new version of Media Studies led to a special issue of the journal *Television and New Media* (2009) in which more than fifty media researchers got the opportunity to outline their own "Media Studies."

What Merrin and Miller argue is that the new media situation has created the need for new ways of thinking. And it is primarily the role played by consumers—or citizens—that lead to this rethinking. In the new media environment, people who traditionally only consumed media now also produce media themselves. And that has created both new communication patterns and new power relations between traditional media producers and citizens.

There is obviously "ferment in the field."[2] Things are happening in the "real world," things which demand new approaches. And it seems as if the researchers who have dealt with these phenomena need help. Miller explicitly voices the need for bringing in new perspectives from other academic disciplines. We agree with that call. However, Miller's call is a soft one; it does not seem to be intended to be heard very far away. It is only addressed to the closest friends of the discipline of media studies, friends doing academic research in the same way media studies researchers do.

But this is not the only academic community with an interest in collaborative media. There are others, with other objectives and other ways of conducting research. In the user manual to what is arguably the most comprehensive anthology of the field, Wardrip-Fruin and Montfort's *The New Media Reader* (2003a), the editors write that the texts they selected come from computer scientists, architects, artists, writers, and cultural critics (2003b, xi). Thus, for them the field also includes people working with what broadly could be called a *practice-based approach* to collaborative media.[3]

The New Media Reader is one of the few examples of attempting to create a space for the meeting between analytical and practice-based approaches to collaborative media. Otherwise, it is more reasonable to speak of two cultures (see Snow 1959/1998). For instance, the key journal *New Media & Society* is characterized as engaging in "critical discussions of the key issues arising from the scale and speed of new media development, drawing on a wide range of disciplinary perspectives and on both theoretical and empirical research."[4] In other words, the journal is open for engagement for researchers from different disciplines and it spells out that it accepts both theoretical and empirical contributions. But it does not state anything about the possibility of submitting practice-based work to the journal. Similar descriptions and similar content can be found in other social science/humanities journals devoted to the field, journals such as the aforementioned *Television & New Media* and *Convergence: The International Journal of Research into New Media Technologies*. It would be highly unusual to find an article in these journals based on practical work. Similarly, in the introductory article to the first edition of *The Handbook of New Media* (Lievrouw and Livingstone 2002/2006), the editors address the question of whether new media demand new research methods. According to them, there are two research positions. Either one believes that new media can be treated like any other area under investigation by the social sciences, with surveys, case studies, interviews, and so on—or one believes that traditional methods must be changed. But "change" here only refers to reformulating criteria within one's traditional way of working, rethinking, for instance, criteria for survey sampling and reasonable response rates when studying virtual environments. It does not mean working in any new ways. Researchers within this community theorize and conduct empirical studies, but they do not create things. For practice-based work—whether through design, art, or engineering—you have to look in other directions.[5]

Interaction Design and Practice-Based Approaches to Collaborative Media

A practice-based approach to collaborative media cannot be found in a homogeneous discipline in academic terms. It may rather be seen as a mosaic of fragments that can be found in different academic communities. Hence, the big picture of practice-oriented work on collaborative media is a multidisciplinary one, where the constitutive disciplines are not always acting in coordination.

One of the more notable academic fields in this context is *media technology*. Here we find scholars from information and communication technology and other engineering fields, together with social scientists, behavioral scientists, and the occasional media scholar, working on topics such as the Internet, the World Wide Web, hypermedia and multimedia, and ubiquitous computing. To generalize, the work is somewhat dominated by engineering perspectives where the central aims are to understand what is possible in technical terms, and to improve technology in order to offer new communicative possibilities.[6]

The field of media technology is related to the relatively new field of *digital humanities* (Berry 2012; Svensson 2012). Placing the digital humanities in this context rather than the social sciences/humanities context is by no means self-evident; the whole point of digital humanities is to transgress the borderline between technology and the humanities. However, under the original name *humanities computing*, digital humanities were more of a computing support service than a multidisciplinary research field (Hayles 2012, 43). It still deals primarily with the systematization and analysis of large-scale data materials, but lately has moved more and more toward treating other kinds of materials than traditional print.[7]

The independent fields of *digital arts* and *media arts* have a long history of practical, creation-oriented approaches to the new media. Even though they originally had very little to do with academia, there is a distinct and worldwide trend in the last ten years or so to pull art practice and art schools into closer cohort with conventional academic practice. This has led to the emergence of the brand new academic field of *artistic research* (Hannula, Suoranta, and Vadén 2005; Biggs and Karlsson 2010). For collaborative media more specifically, this has manifested in the emergence of a whole new range of art+academy educational offerings, a lively debate on practice-based research methodology, and the appearance of academic publication venues.[8]

However, the most important field to bring up in this context is *interaction design*. It originated from human–computer interaction, where there has always been a strong tradition to focus on individual use of digital technology. But as digital artifacts have evolved from workplace tools to everyday media in recent years, interaction design has increasingly also started to take note of social and communicative aspects. Indicative examples here include the "reader-to-leader" framework by Preece and Shneiderman (2009), and the recent work by Chan (2012) on concepts for "social interaction design."

Academic work in interaction design is generally characterized by the aim to contribute to better interaction—where "better" used to mean more efficient and error free, but nowadays includes hedonistic and aesthetic qualities to an increasing degree. In interaction design research, the practical element is prominent. Most research results consist of proposals for new digital artifacts and interaction practices, together with assessments of their predicted qualities.[9]

What these disciplines have in common is some degree of topical proximity to collaborative media and collaborative media practices, and a research orientation toward design, intervention, and change where creative work is part of the knowledge production process. There is also a focus on how something could be, rather than how something is. But as already mentioned, interaction design is not a homogeneous field.

In the introductory chapter to *The New Media Reader* anthology, Janet Murray describes the field of new media as a meeting point between humanists and engineers: "The humanists see the contradictions and limitations of the great systems of thought and it causes them to question the very project of systemized thinking. . . . The engineers are grounded in a tradition that emphasizes solution and defines the needs it cannot satisfy" (2003, 4). For her, the practice-based approach means adding a problem-solving ability to humanists' critical thinking facilities.

In "The Lab," David Edwards distinguishes between the aesthetic and the analytical as two ways of thinking in relation to creative processes:

Through aesthetic thinking, we embrace uncertainty and complexity, we induce, follow intuition, and draw inspiration from images and sound. This process especially thrives in aesthetic environments, like theater companies or design studios. Through analytical thinking, we simplify a complex world, reduce its challenges to resolvable problems, and pursue the logic of equation. This process thrives in scientific environments, like a pharmaceutical company or a bank. (2010, 4)

Problem solving or embracing complexity? These are two completely different views on what a practice-based approach may mean. And those are not the only possible ones. However, this is not surprising; there is no reason to assume that the actors within this heterogeneous field, including computer scientists, interaction designers, and artists, would agree on what such an approach should entail, or what its objectives should be. The main point, however, is that they all are based on the idea of doing things, of not "merely" observing or analyzing. In this way they stand apart from researchers coming from the social sciences/humanities.

Thus, social science/humanities approaches are strong when it comes to empirical analysis, conceptualization, and critical perspectives. But a practice-based approach can also add substantially to the process of theoretical development of the field. "Learning by doing" is of course a research tradition with a long history, from John Dewey (1916/1944) onward. That tradition is highly relevant for this field, and there are a number of researchers steeped in it who have worked concretely within the areas of design and media. Not least important here is the work of Donald Schön and his notion of the "reflective practitioner" (1983, 1987).

Generally speaking, we find reasonable support for our position that researchers with practical knowledge and experience from collaborative media design interventions are in a position to say other things about such practices than researchers having "only" analytical, critical, or theoretical knowledge of collaborative media. Moreover, such practical experience forms a useful part of the foundation for theorizing about collaborative media practices. And finally, the products of practice-based research constitute forms of knowledge in themselves, either in Murray's (2003) sense of solutions to concrete problems or as artistic work that helps challenge traditional ways of representing knowledge.

Non-academic Knowledge on Collaborative Media

The preceding sections are in a sense written as if academia is the only place to go to if we are to understand what is happening with collaborative media today. But that is of course not the case. Generally, it could be argued, as done by Ziman in his book *Real Science*, that science today is *post-academic*. A radical transformation is under way, changing dramatically how science is organized, managed, and performed (Ziman 2000, 67). This concerns, among other things, an increasing focus on collaborative research and a strengthening of the relationship between academia and industry.

The picture Ziman paints bears strong relationships to the idea of a so-called Mode 2 type of knowledge, as put forward by Gibbons et al. in their book *The New Production of Knowledge* (Gibbons et al. 1994; see also Nowotny, Scott, and Gibbons 2001, 2003). According to this view, Mode 2 knowledge is generated within a context of application, it is transdisciplinary, it is heterogeneous (as compared to Mode 1 knowledge), it is reflexive, and it is based on novel forms of quality control (Nowotny, Scott, and Gibbons 2003, 186–187).

The debate around the notion of Mode 2 knowledge has been lively. In a review, Hessels and van Lente note that "*The New Production of Knowledge* has been cited in more than 1,000 scientific articles. Criticism has been raised primarily towards its empirical validity, its conceptual strength and its political value" (2008, 741).

The book is without a doubt open to criticism. But for us, the main point is that Gibbons et al. (2008) have identified certain features concerning knowledge production that seem hard to question—at least on a general level. These include the notions that today knowledge increasingly is produced collaboratively, with actors coming both from within and outside academia (and with academic actors coming from different disciplines) and that it has become increasingly difficult to arrive at a consensus concerning what knowledge actually "is" (with more and more researchers arguing for the notion that knowledge is context specific).

Similar points are raised also by researchers coming from other traditions than Gibbons and his colleagues, such as the science, technology, and society tradition. Callon (1999) argues for the need to include laypeople, or nonspecialists, in crucial debates concerning science and technology, and he shows how interaction between, for instance, patients and doctors may lead to the production of crucial knowledge. Similarly, Latour (2001) argues for the need for new "collective experiments." Such experiments involve both scientific knowledge and everyday-life performance. The experiments are both social and technical and they are conducted on a large scale and in real time.

Thus, collaborations between academics and non-academics are crucial in general when it comes to the production of new knowledge. But—important to note in this context—it is especially crucial for the field of collaborative media. When it comes to collaborative work, in many occasions digital media, and the technologies guiding them, serve as necessary preconditions for collaborations to take place at all: it is with the help of digital media that it becomes possible to coordinate work, and to distribute its results. Collaborations are made based on the idea of open innovation, and user-driven innovation—letting lay people become central actors—is a key notion (Chesbrough 2003; von Hippel 2006). The traditional producer-centered innovation model is increasingly challenged generally, but particularly so within the field of digital media. As Potts et al. write: "This new model is increasingly important in the creative industries, and especially within the domain of new digital media, where both the technology effects, and the impact of socially networked creative consumers-as-producers are strongest" (2008, 463).

It is also interesting to note that collaborative work has not only led to knowledge with relevance for what is happening in everyday life in many different ways, but also to knowledge about collaborative work as such. And to a significant extent this knowledge has been produced by actors on the borderline between academia and journalism rather than by traditional academics, including writers such as Chris Anderson, Charles Leadbeater, and Clay Shirky. Furthermore, their books—*The Long Tail* (Anderson 2006), *We-Think* (Leadbeater 2008), and *Here Comes Everybody* (Shirky 2008)—have influenced not only public discourse, but also academic work.

A Transdisciplinary Approach to Collaborative Media: Theorizing and Experimenting "in the Wild"

We have discussed the academic field of collaborative media in relation to two loosely coupled groups of researchers: one group coming from the social sciences/humanities and one from a practice-based tradition. They are loosely coupled in the sense that there are similarities within the groups when it comes to views on what academic work is and how it should be carried out, but, as we have shown, there are also differences within the groups that occasionally may be greater than the differences between them (these are not closely knit communities). In other words, working together across the borderline is by no means impossible.

We have also discussed the knowledge production carried out outside of the academy. It is impossible to argue that academics have a monopoly on knowledge anymore—if they ever had (Adkins and Lury 2009). This situation could be interpreted as problematic. Savage and Burrows write about the "coming crisis of empirical sociology" (2007), but the problem may be extended to academic science as a whole.

How should one deal with this? One way is, of course, to paint a bleak picture of the future of academia. Another way, which we find more promising, is to acknowledge the new situation not out of necessity but for its inherent possibilities. This means taking part in new collective experiments, and even more, stepping up and taking a lead in organizing such experiments. In other words, for academics it means getting out into the "real world" and addressing real-life problems, at the same time invigorating academic life.[10]

In short, we propose a research approach to collaborative media whereby social sciences and humanities join forces with practice-based research to conduct real-life experiments "in the wild" together with non-academic actors.[11]

The approach we propose entails that we not only talk critically about what collaborative media are and how they are used, but also that we do things. It is an experimental approach, involving design of preferred communication practices and, more generally, preferred partial states of the world; it is also an analytical/theoretical approach involving systematic reflection on those communication practices. Moreover, it is a collaborative approach, with researchers taking on roles in co-production structures that are sometimes quite intricate and involve a wide range of actors outside academia.

This new researcher role carries a new set of responsibilities: the disinterested stance of Mode-1 research is not an option for researchers who set out to explore and assess the potential of collaborative media in creating a space in the mediascape for underprivileged groups to influence public opinion, for example. Initiating such transformation processes corresponds to taking societal action, and the researchers are responsible to the extent that their actions have real consequences for the lives of real people. The primary goal for the researchers is still knowledge production, to be sure. Yet the means of producing that knowledge entail acting with engagement, commitment, and a clear picture of the researchers' responsibility—and, perhaps most important, a clear picture of the demarcations of that responsibility.

We have called our approach a transdisciplinary one. This choice of a term is not self-evident, since the inclusion of non-academic actors in the collaborative networks also implies involving people for whom the notion of academic disciplines makes no sense. However, what we are looking for is the connotation of actors coming from different communities of practice, bringing their competencies with them and working together.

To be a little more specific, our notion of transdisciplinarity is specifically geared toward collaborative media. Elaborating on the previous description of the approach being the meeting place between theorizing and designing in real-life environments, a more precise denomination of our approach would be *collaborative media design interventions*. In this approach, researchers with different competencies work collaboratively with professionals and laypeople "in the wild" in processes of change and transformation. As we outline what this entails, we will discuss what we mean by "design interventions" by first discussing the interventionist part of the approach and then the design part. With the help of the Living Lab concept, we then outline how one may construct or produce physical spaces in real-life settings within which the design interventions, and subsequently the collaborative media practices, can take place. The approach we propose is based on detailed readings of work, theoretical and practice based, carried out within a number of disciplines, but it is of course also based on the experiences we ourselves have gathered during the last decade working both theoretically and practically with the matters at hand.

Everyday-Life Interventions

One of our key convictions concerns the importance of leaving the academic environment and conducting work in everyday-life settings, without limiting ourselves to objective observer roles. Our approach concerns taking part in what is happening, and even starting processes. That is, the role of the researcher is an active one, devoted to making things happen that may not have happened otherwise.

The origins of this approach can be found in the social science tradition of *action research*, a tradition building on the work of John Dewey and other pragmatists, but primarily associated with the works of Kurt Lewin, who coined the term. In his words, "action research" consists of "comparative research on the conditions and effects of various forms of social action, and research leading to social action. Research that produces nothing but books will not suffice" (1946, 35).

The key notion is the interest in change—or even *Massive Change* (Mau 2004). There is a will not only to observe and analyze, but also to take part, to intervene and to start processes. As argued by Brydon-Miller, Greenwood, and Maguire:

Action research challenges the claims of a positivistic view of knowledge which holds that in order to be credible, research must remain objective and value-free. Instead, we embrace the notion of knowledge as socially constructed and, recognizing that all research is embedded within a system of values and promotes some model of human interaction, we commit ourselves to a form of research which challenges unjust and undemocratic economic, social and political systems and practices. (2003, 11)

Historically, media research has had few ties to action research. Recently, attempts have been made to rectify this situation, but the connection is still weak (Hearn et al.

2008; Napoli and Aslama 2010).[12] This is surprising, given the possibilities of such a connection. As we see it, these possibilities should be obvious both from the perspective of the media researcher and from the perspective of the action researcher.

In any case, our approach will build on such possibilities, and on the knowledge gathered from the action research perspective. We will not use the phrase "action research," however. Instead we will speak in terms of *interventions*. The difference is not great, but the term "intervention" implies a clearer focus on what concerns us in this book. One "intervenes" in a particular situation. "Action" is a broader and less precise term.

Designing Interventions

In order to carry out collaborative media interventions in everyday life, these have to be set up and organized. Or to put it another way, they have to be designed. By design, here we do not mean the design of an artifact or an infrastructure, but the design of a situation making practices and collaborations possible, a situation in which many different groups of stakeholders are involved, and in which their respective agendas, competencies, and mandates are put into play in collaborative transformation processes.

This approach to design can historically be traced to participatory design, a philosophy and approach to information systems development for work settings that grew out of Scandinavia in the 1970s.

Participatory design emerged in part as a reaction to rationalistic approaches to systems development missing out on important issues in regard to the human, social, and political contexts where information systems were developed and used. Researchers conceived participatory design as a way to facilitate work-life democracy in a time when systems development for work contexts mainly aimed at creating instruments for management and control. In a participatory design process, the eventual users of a new information system are empowered to shape and influence the decisions on what the new system should be like, what it should do, and how the work involving the new system should be done.

More specifically, participatory design is a process of mutual learning in which designers and users learn from each other and about each other's professional practices. Users participate in design activities, but the designers equally participate in the users' professional work activities. Planning and facilitating the design process entails creating new design practices related to the daily practices of both users and designers, and participation is based on skill rather than on articulation, formalization, and abstraction. In other words, a premium is put on practical understanding. Participatory design processes involve engaging design artifacts such as games and low-fidelity mockups to provide the means to experiment with interventions into the social construction of an organizational setting, to explore the users' professional competence, and to introduce the possibilities of new technology (see Ehn 1989; Sanders and Stappers 2008).

The participatory design approach concerns the whole process surrounding different forms of collaborative practices—or design interventions. Here, we concentrate on how such interventions are set up from the point of view of the researcher, or rather, the research team.

Setting up entails identifying the problem area one intends to work with, and making clear how it is to be dealt with, which stakeholders to bring in, and so on. Here there is an obvious need for a design competence, but this is a competence concerning how to design for things to happen rather than the competence of how to design things. In design research, this level is denoted as meta-design (Fischer and Giaccardi 2006).

Two points are crucial to discuss in this context. The first concerns the relationship between research and design—or between the two roles of researcher and designer. There is a fundamental difference between the roles in terms of intentions. To simplify slightly, we can say that research aims at producing knowledge, whereas design aims at producing things (in a broad sense, including products as well as practices and more). In other words, and still on the level of suitable simplification, when researchers with design competence engage in design work during an intervention, they can do so for two different reasons. One is to produce knowledge, and the other is to produce things. The challenge lies in the fact that the two reasons imply different expectations and success criteria, since they emanate from different constituencies. For example, academia conventionally requires knowledge contributions to be novel in the sense that they should not already be known to the academic community. Producing a thing through design in a particular real-life situation, on the other hand, might entail creating something responding to a market need. It is quite uncommon that the "best" solution from a commercial point of view also represents a viable academic knowledge contribution. In our experience, this tension needs to be taken into account when planning and performing an intervention, such that multiple agendas are accommodated and appropriate resources are allocated for addressing both research and design intentions.

To complicate matters further, the notion of design in this context entails meta-design (designing conditions for intervention) as much as conventional design (designing things—products, practices, etc.). The same reasoning applies here: meta-design for purposes of knowledge production is not the same as meta-design for purposes of thing production. We end up with a plethora of possible practices at the intersection of research and design, including meta-design for knowledge production, meta-design for thing production, thing design for knowledge production, and thing design for thing production. This may seem overly complicated, but it is in fact an inherent consequence when researchers engage in participatory intervention and there is no way to deal with it other than to recognize its complexity and make it part of the preconditions for the work.

The second point concerns the composition of—and relationship within—the academic research group. In dealing with collaborative media theoretically, critically, empirically, and practically, there is obviously a need for researchers with different competencies. That is an easy, self-evident statement to make; no one would argue against it. But what does it mean in practice to work in groups like that? Given the novelty of such an approach, there is a lack of academic writing on the subject. Our own experiences tell us that it is easy to underestimate the problems inherent in multidisciplinary research on this kind of scale.

Most readers of this book will have experienced research seminars where peers representing different disciplines end up having difficulty communicating. Such barriers are, of course, even more accentuated when it comes to not only debating for an hour in a meeting room but actually engaging in joint, long-term, real-life experimentation together. Working across the theoretical-practical borderline introduces particular gaps in terms of not only language and methodology, but also the fundamental purpose of research and academic activity.

However, in our experience, such difficulties become easier to overcome with time and practice. Working in multidisciplinary research teams in a shared environment for over a decade, as we have done, and doing so within a number of large-scale projects, we find that communication gradually becomes easier. Increasingly, we also create a common ground of words, concepts, practices, and values. This does not mean that everybody agrees on everything, but the conversations do become increasingly meaningful. It does not mean, either, that everybody becomes an expert on everything. Rather, the main point is to increase the understanding of what other people's competencies are, and how these different kinds of competencies can be used together. The media researcher should not take on the role as the designer; the programmer should not get the primary responsibility for writing a chapter on hegemony.[13] But it does mean that when it comes to setting up a design intervention, for example, research team members other than the formally trained meta-designer/researcher will be able to provide valuable input and contribute to a better intervention setup.

Setting the Stage for Design Interventions: The Living Lab

With our approach to collaborative media, we insist on the importance of not only theorizing but also doing things. For this you need space, and traditionally it is within the confines of the university that such spaces are made available. In the context of design research, Binder and Brandt (2008) distinguish between the workshop, the studio, the atelier, and the lab (or, in their way of writing, the Design:Lab) as alternative kinds of spaces for such work.

For Binder and Brandt, the research lab contains the potential for meaningful design research that the other alternatives do not, where standardized, controlled experiments can be carried out. For them, the *controlled environment* is a crucial notion:

If we think of the laboratory as a shared "facility" for the partners, whether these are potential future users or other stakeholders, then the *controlled environment* can be seen as the setting where we let this "as-if world" live and be explored under the explicit condition that we have not yet decided if this world should be translated into a more permanent reality. In this respect, the Design:Lab is a hypothetical space where we can negotiate among the participants how much of the world outside we want to take in and how far we will allow the exploration to go. (Binder and Brandt 2008, 119)

The idea is that the design lab enables controlled experiments that to a certain extent can take real-life circumstances into consideration. That is of course true. However, being set within a university setting, it still ultimately represents a constructed situation.

The Living Lab attempts to move such laboratories out "in the wild." Developed by William Mitchell and colleagues at MIT, the Living Lab concept engages users in research and innovation processes and experiments in real-life settings. In Europe, research based on the Living Lab concept has been carried out since the 1980s, and in 2006, the European Network of Living Labs was created with the support of the European Union (Katzy and Klein 2008).

Today Living Labs can take many different forms, and it could be argued that the differences among them are as big as the similarities, thereby making the concept relatively meaningless. But if one regards the Living Lab as a general concept for research and collaborative practices involving different stakeholders taking place in real-life settings, then it still makes sense—as long as that characterization is tied to a closer description of the specific use one intends to make of the concept.

In relation to our approach on collaborative media design interventions, the Living Lab concept makes sense as the space for interventions to take place. With this term, one may make clear that even though the practices in question take place in real-life settings, some kind of space has to be constructed in order for the interventions to take shape. However, this does not mean that the Living Labs have to be physical. They could equally well be digital.

It is also important to point out that in moving outside of academic spaces, and moving into collaborations with different stakeholders—laypersons, companies, municipalities, and so on—one should not assume that the different actors involved share the same interests. Quite the contrary: the normal situation would be that actors who take part in Living Labs do so for completely different reasons. A way of conceptualizing the potential in such collaborations is to use political theorist Chantal Mouffe's distinction between antagonism and agonism (2000). According to Mouffe, the point of democratic politics is not to eradicate an us/them distinction. That is not possible. Rather, the point is to envisage a way forward that makes conversation and deliberation possible, whereby one does not see one's enemy as someone to destroy. Antagonism concerns differences that cannot be overcome, while agonism concerns differences between enemies who share some common ground. They may not agree on many things, but they can communicate. And when that is the case, it may be more reasonable to speak of adversaries instead of enemies.

In other words, it is possible to envision a space where adversaries can meet. Living Labs may be conceived of as such spaces, characterized in recent design-theoretical work as spaces for "agonistic participatory design" (Björgvinsson, Ehn, and Hillgren 2012) or "adversarial design" (DiSalvo 2012).

A Call to Action

To close this chapter and part I on starting points, we summarize in five imperatives our stance as design interventionist researchers in collaborative media. We offer these imperatives not to impose dictates or to instruct, but to distill a transdisciplinary interventionist research approach (not a small thing!) into essential desiderata that underpin the case studies of part II and reemerge in our synthesis and conclusions in part III.

Be collaborative. We find the combination of media and communication studies with interaction design to be essential for the kind of research we advocate. What is more, we find that the mainstream notion of knowledge transfer from academia to society needs to be questioned; sustained co-production for collaborative knowledge production is a more promising perspective, in our view.

Be interventionist. There is no place for conventional academic distance and ceteris paribus in the kind of collaborative media research we represent. Development of theory and concepts happens in parallel with interventions and with design of possible new collaborative media practices, and the two strands presuppose and inform each other.

Be public. Collaborative media research needs to happen in public spaces, physical as well as mediated ones. This is more than a simple matter of knowledge dissemination from the academic ivory tower to the general-interest audience; collaborative media researchers are but one group of actors in a field where action takes place in constant consideration of and in plain view of other constituencies.

Be agonistic. The field where collaborative media researchers play their parts in intervention and knowledge production is a real and public one, which among other things means that we have to move beyond naïve notions of consensus. Different constituencies have their own agendas, normally conflicting ones; issues of power and influence are at the forefront of the ongoing infrastructuring taking place.

Be accountable. Playing a part in the agonistic field of collaborative media also means assuming responsibility for your standpoints and actions. Neutrality regarding consequences is a luxury that spectators in the stands may indulge in, but it is not an option for actors taking part in the unfolding events in the field.

II Interventions

In chapter 3, we elaborated on our approach to what we called collaborative media design interventions. The practices evolving out of these interventions involve different actors, as well as these actors' different objectives in participating in the processes. Our particular interest lies in the roles that researchers can play in the processes. As we have argued, there is a possibility—even a need—for researchers to take on new roles and responsibilities. These new roles and responsibilities may seem appealing, perhaps even energizing, but talking about them in the abstract does not offer much guidance on how to heed the call to action. Hence, part II is devoted to case studies: examples of knowledge production where analysis and intervention on the part of researchers are integrated in the field of collaborative media. We focus on examples where we have been actively involved in the work or have enjoyed privileged access to the context and the details of the work in question. The perspective of our presentation is generally the one of academics acting as change agents, catalysts, or facilitators in a collaborative process of change and transformation. This choice of perspective reflects our intention to characterize a *design-oriented mode of knowledge production, integrating analysis and intervention in collaborative media research.*

However, we recognize that the academic position per se is by no means unique or required in order to initiate change and produce knowledge. The cases reported in part II span a decade, and at the time when the first cases were executed there was much less public recognition of the Internet and digital technologies for mediated communication in general, and of collaborative media in particular. Essentially, for experimental interventions into everyday collaborative media to happen, researchers had to initiate them. In recent years, the preconditions have changed significantly and whole economies are forming around collaborative media and related fields. Some of the more recent cases we report are entrepreneurial efforts without any academic intentions, but which are amenable to analysis yielding new knowledge on the qualities and possibilities of the cultural form that is collaborative media. And that is, of course, of equal interest.

When addressing processes of transformation, such as the collaborative media cases introduced here, it is always essential to consider the particular situation at hand. What

characterizes the stakeholders involved in the process? What do the different agendas look like and how do they relate to each other? What competencies and other resources are available to fuel and facilitate the transformation process? For this reason, we have chosen to concentrate on cases where we have privileged inside knowledge.

More specifically, the cases we present are all connected to the research environment that we have helped establish and develop for fifteen years (the School of Arts and Communication and the Medea Collaborative Media Initiative at Malmö University, Sweden), thus growing out of a set of shared ideas and values that can be summarized roughly as follows:

• Digital technologies are primarily media for human communication.
• To understand and shape the practices around digital media, several academic disciplines must be brought together, most prominently interaction design with media and communication studies.
• Research (and teaching) must be performed in experimental and explorative ways as well as analytical and critical ways.
• Artistic modes of working represent promises of new knowledge and new modes of knowledge.
• Academic research (and teaching) is part of the world and plays a role in the development of society.

Within this environment, a large number of collaborative media design interventions have been instigated and executed over the years—some that we have had the privilege to participate in directly, others that have been operated by our colleagues but based in an environment that we share on a daily basis. For the purposes of this book, we feel that choosing cases from this institutional portfolio enables us to provide a level of depth and richness in the case studies that would otherwise be impossible to attain. Moreover, since all the cases to some degree are guided by the same set of values, we expect the internal consistency of the case selection to be strong—thus allowing us to synthesize them comfortably for the conclusions in part III of this book.

The cases are divided into three categories: society, institutions, and tribes. These categories represent a rather intuitive attempt to capture essential levels of operation for collaborative media practices, rather than a systematic taxonomy or an analytical necessity.[1]

First, the *society* category in our presentation leans toward a perspective of grassroots change and emancipation that follows closely from the collaborative potential inherent in collaborative media practices. This is not to be taken as romantic 1990s Internet evangelism, though; we are fully aware that the potential of collaborative media is equally available to totalitarian regimes as it is to local activist movements (as evidenced, for example, in how the Sudanese regime used fake social media personas in 2011 to round up and imprison regime critics and activists by posting invitations to protest meetings). However, we find that the emerging collaborative media practices do hold the potential for partially new ways to approach societal development and governance. In our work, we have strived to explore such potentials by creating agonistic collaboration processes rather than antagonistic processes.

Three examples of such cases are presented in chapter 4. The first case, *Avatopia*, reports the design and deployment of a collaborative cross-media platform for young teenagers concerned with societal issues and societal action. In the second case, we examine the societal implications of *Bambuser* live-video streaming via consumer-grade mobile phones and networks. The final case is *Parapolis*, exploring the potential of collaborative media for citizen involvement in urban planning and development.

Second, the whole process of collaborative media practices emerging and growing takes place against the backdrop of an existing, and already quite densely populated media landscape. The "traditional" mass media structures represent *institutions* of everyday life in many ways, and developments in collaborative media have often been construed as threats or challenges to these institutions. What we focus on here is how transformation and change can be initiated and explored by researchers and institutions in collaboration, in order to examine possible futures of collaborative media practices in which the established media institutions play rewarding and meaningful roles.

The institution-level cases are presented in chapter 5. The first case, *MyNewsMyWay*, illustrates how an established public service television company concentrates on innovating its offerings toward adaptive personalization, while still struggling to uphold an essential production/consumption asymmetry. The other three cases show the analytical and transformative leverage of collaborative media in established institutions that are conventionally not thought of as media industries, namely technical information (the *Substrate* case), medical care (the *Kliv* case), and the fashion industry (the *Hacktivism* case). Specifically, the Hacktivism case is not a "media" case in the conventional sense, but rather elucidates the issues of interventionist research in a setting that is structurally analogous to a collaborative media setting.

Third, we find the level of *tribes* to be characteristic of many collaborative media practices in that the emerging social structures we can observe very often are distinguished by a significant degree of cohesion, altruism, and a sense of belonging. Before the massive penetration of online communication forums, the word "community" would have been apt—but it was quickly subverted into referring to the platforms and infrastructures for online communication, before it more or less disappeared from general parlance a few years ago. For instance, Facebook and its precursor/competitor Friendster were both at times described as online communities, which is obviously ridiculous. More accurate would have been to talk about them as containers for thousands or millions of communities, each consisting of a relatively small network of people who perceived some degree of communality. In talking about tribes rather than communities, we connote an even stronger emphasis on cohesion, communality, and altruism—which are, as we said, traits that we find to be rather characteristic of collaborative media practices.

Cases on the tribe level are presented in chapter 6. The first, *OurNewsOurWays*, addresses the question of how to cope with the task of finding something to watch on TV in a near future when overwhelming volumes of user-generated video and broadcast company archives are accessible in one's own living room. The suggested approach of *OurNewsOurWays* illustrates a tribal approach to social navigation. The second case details the growth and dynamics of the *Arduino* community, a rapidly growing group of open-source hardware tinkerers and advocates with strong activist and tribal characteristics. In addition to insights into tribal process dynamics, the Arduino case illustrates the emergence of a technological direction often referred to as the Internet of Things—which is arguably growing rapidly in importance as a collaborative media infrastructure. The final case, *Malmö City Symphony*, deals with place-specific and cross-media collaborative media productions.

The reason for presenting the cases in part II is threefold. First, they can be seen as reporting in some depth the "data" we need for our synthesis and conclusions on collaborative media practices and research in the final part of the book. Second, they provide richer and more concrete images that should help readers elaborate their understanding of collaborative media practices beyond the general concepts we provide. Finally, and following standard practice in design-oriented research disciplines, the cases serve as exemplars that in a sense carry actionable knowledge in themselves for readers who wish to engage in collaborative media design interventions of their own. Proficient design always requires a repertoire; in our view, part II provides raw material for other collaborative media designers to extend their repertoires.

Part II consists of three sets of case studies, illustrating collaborative media design interventions in various settings. The first collection, presented in this chapter, is devoted to collaborative media on the level of society; our particular interest lies in the design and use of collaborative media as part of societal change and transformation. We introduce three cases that share this orientation; they demonstrate the breadth of design approaches and communicative practices that collaborative media entail on the societal level.

Targeting young teenagers with ambitions toward social activism, Avatopia was an early exploration of the potential of collaborative media working in conjunction with established mass media to facilitate social change. The project functioned as a participatory design process involving geographically dispersed groups of teenagers as well as a national public service television company. The work led to the design and deployment of a cross-media platform and an activist community where collaborative media played crucial roles.

The next case examines Bambuser, a mobile service for live video streaming that was launched more recently and occupies an interesting spot at the intersection of media democratization and new media capitalism. What is particularly interesting about Bambuser is that it has been designed from the start against the backdrop of emerging collaborative media societal practices, and that it illustrates how new services can be grown into organic parts of the new collaborative media fabrics.

Finally, we look at the Parapolis project, which involves the design and deployment of collaborative media in the context of urban planning and development. Key insights in Parapolis concern how notions of participation and influence move beyond simple majority consensus and representative democracy when collaborative media are treated as integral parts of societal transformation processes.

Avatopia: Participatory Design of Societal Media for a Narrow Stakeholder Group

Avatopia was an early experiment in combining mass media with collaborative media, and specifically broadcast TV with a collaborative, creative online environment, in order to create a cross-media platform for young teenagers who feel strongly about changing society (Gislén, Löwgren, and Myrestam 2008). The cross-media approach nowadays is standard practice, of course, but the case still offers a few valuable insights into collaborative media practices that we find relevant also for contemporary discourse.

In Sweden, as presumably in most Western countries, there is a relatively small proportion of thirteen- to seventeen-year-olds who are deeply engaged in societal issues such as environmental protection, gender equality, racial segregation, globalization and consumerism, social injustice, and societal influence of young citizens. Young activists fortunate to live in urban areas generally find companionship and social support in one-issue organizations, organized actions, and ad hoc meeting places. Those in rural areas, however, often find themselves more lonely and disempowered. Further, a subcultural perception common to most young activists in the country, urban as well as rural, is that they are denied the access to mass media and other channels of public influence that the heartfelt issues deserve.

In 2001, one author (Löwgren) noted a possible congruence between the young activist subculture and the intentions of Swedish Television (SVT), the ad-free public TV broadcasting company funded by the government and viewer fees. One of the very few television networks available to every household in Sweden, SVT is considered a cultural institution in many ways. Its viewer numbers and credibility are extremely strong; it is also considered among teenagers to be distinctly adult and authoritarian. At the time, SVT was struggling with low ratings among the younger audiences as well as the formidable task of redefining its position and public-service mission in an emerging landscape of new media and increasing competition from commercial TV broadcasters.

We set up a joint project, involving SVT and a number of academic sites, to explore the intersection of young teenagers wanting to change society and SVT wanting to experiment with new cross-media formats and new interpretations of its public-service mission.

The Avatopia project started with a preparatory phase during which the institutional partners reviewed their joint knowledge regarding cross-media services, the Swedish TV audience, and sociological theories of subcultural activism. The Avatopia team also performed exploratory fieldwork among young activists in Southern Sweden. Based on this preparation, the team formulated a project vision that essentially amounted to a cross-media platform providing the social substrate for planning societal action and influencing public opinion on key issues. This was to be realized in the form of a small, collaborative web forum in conjunction with a daily or weekly TV show; the material to be broadcast would be produced by forum members and SVT staff. The idea was for the web forum and the TV program to form *a positive spiral of participation*: the material the forum produced would be seen by a large TV audience, motivating some viewers to join the community by committing to action. In order for this to work, the Avatopia team assumed that the collaborative forum would use audiovisual representations suitable for TV broadcasting. Moreover, the Avatopia community was envisioned as a small and highly involved group, comprising some 2,500 members, of which a few hundred at most would be online at any given time. The access to a major national broadcast channel would ensure appropriate potential for influencing public opinion.

The next step in the Avatopia project involved *concept development and community building*. To this end, the project team set out to create a participatory design process involving twenty to thirty young teenagers in the dual tasks of contributing to the cross-media platform's design, and adopting the roles of mentors and norm carriers in the community once it opened to the public.

The teenagers were recruited in December 2001 and January 2002 by means of a Christmas gift and an initial workshop. The gift was a gym bag containing a loaf of bread stuffed with various creative exercises, along with an invitation to bring the results to the workshop. The exercises were inspired by work on cultural probes carried out at the Royal College of Art in London (Gaver et al. 1999) and comprised a disposable camera for a photo diary, a set of prestamped postcards with questions concerning views on societal change and social values, a small device for creating a personal avatar, and a cassette tape with instructions and some mood music.

The team sent some forty Christmas gifts to teenagers selected from the initial fieldwork and from other contacts with activist groups and organizations. Twenty-seven recipients signed up for the workshop. This surprisingly good result can be attributed to some degree to the unusual and inspirational qualities of the invitation and gift. The workshop participants spent a weekend understanding the initial project vision, sketching initial ideas for the collaborative forum and for the social mechanisms of the community, and generally getting to know and trust one another. The participants' individual preparation work on the creative exercises was used as the raw material for joint creative work (see figure 4.1) and for discussions in small groups and in plenum.

The workshop ended with the formation of four *task forces*, committing to working together during the spring of 2002. The tasks comprised determining (1) the look and feel of the collaborative forum; (2) the functions and features of the collaborative forum; (3) the norms and values of the community—and ways of upholding them; and (4) formats for the TV show. It was understood that the work of the task forces would be deeply intertwined, despite the realities that the participants lived across most of Southern Sweden and attended high school, thus having to work on the project in their spare time. The four task forces included researchers and artists from the institutional project partners (including Malmö University, SVT, the Interactive Institute, and the department of Animation and Animated Film at Konstfack), who would coordinate the work.

Toward the summer of 2002, all four task forces had achieved substantial results. For instance, the task force in charge of determining look and feel had produced a music

Figure 4.1
The initial Avatopia workshop.

video for the song "Star" by the Swedish rock band Silverbullit (aka Citizen Bird) in order to develop ideas for a visually eclectic style that would invite participation and collaborative creation.

The Avatopia project team synthesized the results into a coherent *concept design* focusing on the visual and functional aspects of the collaborative forum, and on strategies for building and sustaining a desirable set of values in the community. The collaborative forum was to become a 3D avatar world with a highly eclectic, collage-style visual quality (see figure 4.2). In order to intensify interaction and energy, the world would be small enough to hold only about a hundred avatars at any given time. There would be buildings with dedicated purposes (such as the Knowledge Bank, where mythological matter including collaborative stories and useful activism material would be stored). To stimulate collaboration and communication aimed at the society outside Avatopia (rather than individual projects), there would be no tools for constructing or modifying buildings in the world.

The primary form of communication in the collaborative forum would be chat-style typed text, with the spatial metaphor upheld in the sense that users would only be able to talk to avatars nearby. In addition, there would be communicative tools for

Figure 4.2
Scenes from the collaborative online forum, showing the limited size of the "world," the subtitle-style chat, and the use of posters to organize action.

arranging hearings and other forms of public debate, for initiating and participating in forum-style asynchronous text conversations, for creating propaganda bots, for placing posters and flyers in the avatar world, and for joint creation of machinima-style avatar animations.

Concerning the *social aspects of community building*, it was clear that the young teenagers placed much faith in open and critical dialogue. Virtually all ideas on technical enforcement of community rules, such as blocking and automatic monitoring, were ruled out by the task force in favor of an open democracy where every voice should be heard, even though some could then be thoroughly refuted in debate. The overall social character of the community would be a collaborative environment marked by tolerance, with proposals and positions judged based on their merits rather than on who stated them. It was clear that the key to successful growth of the Avatopia community would be the creation of a shared set of core values and a means to carry those values forward into a growing membership upon launch.

As part of the community building strategy, the project team planned a series of half-hour TV programs to be broadcast immediately prior to the public launch of the Avatopia platform. The programs would feature a number of young teenagers from the design team, traveling around Sweden and initiating actions together with local people in large and small cities (see figure 4.3). The actions would address issues of interest to the Avatopia community and the final episode would contain strong lead-ins to the launch of the collaborative forum, where the teenagers featured in the TV series would carry on their work by acting as mentors for the newcomers.

A rather extensive *implementation* phase followed, in which the design team mainly engaged in validating aspects of the collaborative forum as it grew into a usable online platform. Another task for the design team during this phase concerned the format for the TV show complementing the collaborative forum.[1]

Avatopia launched in September 2003 with four half-hour TV episodes of the traveling activist series, leading into the public opening of the collaborative forum and the

Figure 4.3
Scenes from the traveling activist series. In this episode, the Avatopia activists help organize a ceremony where high-school students get to grade their teachers.

launch of a weekly half-hour Avatopia show in SVT's youth programming block. The collaborative forum implemented the concept design described earlier, with two exceptions due to resource prioritization: there were no propaganda bots and no tools for collaborative animation. The three core community members from the traveling activist series and a number of other members from the participatory design team assumed the roles of mentors in the collaborative forum, taking care to address newcomers and share the Avatopia values and "methods" with them as they joined.

The *launch plan* predicted a small but steady growth in numbers of active members in the collaborative forum, and similarly a small but steady growth in the proportion of relevant topics addressed by the community. Only the first two months would be dominated by questions concerning how the collaborative forum worked and should be used, before the community would gradually move into using the Avatopia platform for societal-change purposes. A critical mass of 1,000 active members was expected by the end of six months, when a longitudinal evaluation of social community practices and societal outcomes would start.

The development of the community during the fall of 2003 adhered to the launch plan. However, the operation of Avatopia entailed a small running cost to be paid by SVT for part-time editorial staff and server hosting. When SVT suffered an unexpected budget cut toward the end of 2003, the company decided Avatopia was not part of its core business and therefore was terminated in early 2004. Hence, no systematic evaluation was performed of the project, and no perceivable societal impact was achieved.

The Avatopia project clearly "worked" in the sense that it engaged a group of highly committed and talented young teenagers over a sustained period of time. The joint efforts of the young participants and the institutional partners led to the successful deployment of an innovative media platform, which seemed to have some potential for achieving its aim of empowering societal change. Due to the project's premature termination, however, the team was never able to observe how that potential was realized in actuality.

Still, there are a few insights to be gleaned from the Avatopia case in terms of collaborative media's potential for societal change and transformation. First, we propose that a combined cross-media platform can be a fruitful way to leverage specific properties of different media channels. Specifically, the essential idea in Avatopia was to create a *positive participation spiral* that would grow organically from a core tribe. To this end, much effort was spent in the project to create an audiovisual collaborative forum where suitable material could be produced for TV broadcasting, thus minimizing the barriers between the two main media channels of online forum and broadcast TV. Moreover, the main channels were chosen to combine high engagement and low reach (online forum) with high reach and low engagement (broadcast TV). These two strategies together served to support a small tribe of dedicated activists in efforts to reach a much larger audience with messages creating awareness, stimulating curiosity, and providing clear paths of action for the few who would be motivated to engage with the activist cause. The preliminary results from the fall 2003 launch phase did seem to support the notion of a positive participation spiral, in that new members joined and at least some of them did so with a fairly clear image of what to expect of Avatopia. Similar results on positive spiral phenomena are reported by Hartmann (2009) in a cross-media experiment at radio eins, Berlin.

Second, the Avatopia case illustrates a *community-building strategy* with potential for societal change for a narrow stakeholder group characterized by strong, shared commitment and geographical dispersion. Specifically, the strategy consists of setting up a participatory design process: participants develop the community core values and practices, then transition into roles as mentors or model members as the community opens to a wider audience. In the years following Avatopia, as the field of collaborative media gains more widespread recognition, media scholars have addressed the issue of how to facilitate participation in collaborative media. Using concepts such as sociable media theory (Jackson 2009), the tentative conclusion seems to support the strategic choices made in the Avatopia case. However, it must also be noted that the participatory design strategy for community building is an extremely costly one in terms of project resources. When it comes to participation in settings addressing wider audiences and requiring lower degrees of commitment, recent examples of massive-penetration "social networks" such as Facebook show that more cost-effective strategies are sufficient.

Bambuser: Global Broadcasting for Anyone

On February 17, 2012, the following was published as the introduction to an article in the web edition of the *Guardian*:

Syrian government has blocked a premiere live stream website a day after one of its users broadcast images of a bombing believed to have been carried out by President Bashar al-Assad's forces.

Bambuser—a mobile live stream service based in Sweden—has been in close contact with activists on the ground in Syria for over eight months. The dissidents use the service to broadcast
streaming video of conditions in their country in real time. With foreign media blocked, online
citizen journalism has become a crucial medium for telling stories from within Syria's borders.
(Devereaux 2012)

The "mobile live stream service" Bambuser was conceived in 2007[2] and, briefly, the
intention was to make live video broadcasting generally available. In the same way
that text publishing was put within reach of everybody on the Internet through the
development of blog and microblog engines, and rich media such as images and video
clips found outlets on sharing sites such as Flickr and YouTube, the Bambuser founders
concentrated on live video. Technically speaking, their starting point was the increasing penetration of mobile phones with capabilities to capture video and communicate
with the mobile Internet over broadband-speed connections.

Initial development of Bambuser was motivated largely by an ideology of democratization, which acknowledged the social power of broadcast media and contended that
public debate should benefit from empowering citizens with expressive media tools for
accessing the influential channel of broadcast live video. In 2007, there were only a
limited selection of mobile phones with adequate video camera quality and connectivity; the concept of smartphones had not yet made it into general parlance; the iPhone
3G and the first generation of Android phones were still a year away; the concepts of
apps and app stores were unheard of. The Bambuser founders staked their efforts on
three key trends, which in retrospect seem rather accurate: the increasing bandwidth
of mobile Internet communication, the decreasing cost of the same, and the increasing
processing power of mobile phones. These forecasts formed the basis for designing a
service for a technical infrastructure that was clearly not ubiquitous at the time the first
Bambuser prototype was launched.

While on the topic of forecasting as a design parameter, it is worth noting that
the explosive growth of apps and app stores for disseminating mobile phone services
was not something the founders of Bambuser had counted upon. Since then, it has of
course proven to be a key factor contributing to the uptake and popularity of the Bambuser service—mainly because Bambuser, unlike many other mobile services, is built
on an architecture that actually requires distributing and running a dedicated program
(an "app") on the mobile phone.

More specifically, the core Bambuser concept was to run a client program on a
mobile phone that would allow the user to capture video and send it in real time to a
server, where it would be available via web access for live viewing as well as archival
viewing after the broadcast. Following the proof-of-concept work of this core technology, development work was strongly oriented toward creating a service that would find
a meaningful place in the emerging ecology of collaborative media. There were two
main indications of this orientation, and they were strongly related. First, much effort
was spent on making Bambuser broadcasts part of the collaborative-media content

fabric—by providing convenient hooks for sharing broadcasts via Twitter, Facebook, and Jaiku, as well as mechanisms for embedding broadcasts in, for example, blog posts through a dedicated player. Second, it was quickly found in the actual use of early versions that broadcasting live also encouraged responding live. In other words, communicative practices were quickly forming, including viewers using Twitter to communicate with the Bambuser broadcaster during the live transmission, providing input and asking questions as well as requesting camera pans and the like. To cater for this back-channeling and to provide a more dynamic, interactive live environment, a chat room was quickly added to the core Bambuser service.

Since then, the Bambuser service has grown steadily in terms of popularity as well as public recognition. As indicated in the *Guardian* excerpt cited earlier in this section, there are strong connotations of activism and societal change; the use of concepts such as democratization might have seemed like stale 1990s Internet evangelism for a casual observer in 2007, but the development of Bambuser has in fact been guided by a fairly strong ideological stance throughout. The connections to grassroots activism and perhaps particularly the events surrounding the Arab Spring in 2011 are not coincidental.

When the uprising in Egypt picked up speed with the January 2011 events centering on Tahrir Square in Cairo, it was found that Bambuser broadcasts occupied a somewhat special position in terms of bringing news of the unfolding events to the attention of international news media. Adler (2012) tells the story of how the SVT news desk was struggling with a flood of tweets indicating the scale and force of the Tahrir demonstrations, sensing the importance of the events but failing to verify the information in reliable ways. Flickr photos and YouTube clips could be located, but they raised questions concerning authenticity and currency. However, when the Swedish journalists found multiple live broadcasts by Bambuser-using mobile phone owners in the square, showing large crowds of protesters from different angles, verification was asserted and massive reporting efforts began.

The claim that live video broadcasting represents particular potential in terms of unsanctioned and radical citizen journalism is also somewhat substantiated by the fact that Bambuser was the second online channel to be blocked by the Egyptian regime, shortly after Twitter but several days before the bulk of Internet-based services (Raoof 2011).

As the passage from the *Guardian* indicates, Bambuser appears in similar roles in the Syrian events that are unfolding at the time of writing, as well as in other areas of unrest throughout the world.

The relation between Bambuser and global mainstream media concerning political events is reinforced by the recent collaboration agreement between Bambuser and AP, the international news agency. Bambuser users can now choose settings on their profile pages that give AP general rights to distribute their video streams. AP undertakes to credit the originators appropriately, with their Bambuser user names appearing in all media, and in return the agency asks for contact information for follow up on particularly interesting material (Bambuser 2012b).

At the time of writing, a Bambuser clip has recently appeared on CNN, Sky, BBC, Al Jazeera, and some eighty other TV news networks on five continents, with over six hundred airings in total (Adler 2012). The clip originated from Bambuser user Homslive in Homs, Syria, and it shows the intense bombing of the city (see figure 4.4). This dissemination is made possible through the AP agreement; news editors can access a source of live footage from the events in Syria as they unfold.

These are all examples of the political activist stance of Bambuser in relation to news media, but any service offering the innovative and pleasing experience of being able to broadcast live video from an ordinary mobile phone is, of course, going to be used in many disparate ways, from the playful to the earnest to the artistic and the purely silly. Bambuser is currently available on all major mobile platforms, and the standalone viewing and archival platform at bambuser.com is quite comprehensive. The archived broadcasts show the diversity you might expect, including sports and general media content with links to established media production as well as scores of local TV hobbyist projects, marketing events, and general leisurely use.

The strategy of connecting Bambuser with emerging online media practices has been maintained, and the current service offers seamless integration with all mainstream collaborative media platforms including Facebook, Twitter, MySpace, WordPress, and Blogger.

The broadcasting app has been downloaded nearly 3 million times, and the number of active users is estimated at 10 percent of that, or 300,000 broadcasters. The number

Figure 4.4
Bambuser video syndicated through AP reaches the world's major news networks.

of broadcasts per day is between 5,000 and 10,000; the viewing platform at bambuser. com serves between 20 and 30 million views of broadcasts per month (Adler 2012).

A slightly more in-depth look in the broadcast archives of the official Bambuser site reveals a somewhat interesting pattern: much of the leisure, nonactivist use seems to represent spur-of-the-moment material that is captured on the move. There are clips captured and broadcast while attending a concert, watching a boat race, going on a school trip, sightseeing in a city, having a good time in a club, celebrating a young nephew's birthday, documenting a graffiti piece being made, cooking a special dish, spotting a pet doing something unusual, waiting for the graduation ceremony to end, and so on. This sets Bambuser leisure practices apart from the standard fare of video blogging captured in the bedroom using the laptop webcam, and reflects the mobile-oriented origins of the service.

Another notable trait of Bambuser is its close affiliations with mainstream media, presumably due in part to the close links among activist use, citizen journalism, and established media houses. The influential trade blog *The Next Web*, for example, called Bambuser No. 1 on its list of the top ten media apps of 2011 (Heim 2011). Quite a few journalists and news desks are experimenting with Bambuser as a complementary channel for their own production, in order to provide live coverage that engages viewers in conversations as events are happening. Another oft-cited benefit among journalists is being able to cover unexpected events that could not be captured in any other way. Yet another idea, which has seen some exposure, is to offer a Bambuser feed in the format of an anchor spy cam, showing the behind-the-scenes activities of news shows and the like in an allegedly covert and honest way. And of course, as illustrated in the AP agreement, when moving beyond the professional journalists' own production, Bambuser is sometimes perceived in the mainstream media as a step toward curated citizen journalism.

In the consumer-oriented discourse outside professional media contexts, Bambuser is sometimes classified as a live streaming service provider. As such, it occupies the same space as better-known services such as Ustream, Livestream, and Justin.tv, all of which are regarded as having the edge on Bambuser in terms of commercial structures and audience reach. However, those competitors are all based on webcam broadcasting, which means that the mobile DNA of Bambuser still provides a differentiating factor. In a recent and authoritative consumer-report-style review of the main options, Ozer (2012) closes with the following recommendation: "Consider Bambuser for your live broadcasts if you need extensive mobile support. . . . It's also a good choice for those looking for overall ease of use, since the relative lack of features does translate into a cleaner interface with fewer options. Avoid Bambuser if you're seeking eyeballs or established programs for video monetization."

To summarize this characterization of contemporary Bambuser, it might be fair to call it a mobile-first live video streaming service with an activist flavor and a positive trend in terms of synergy with established news media structures. Thus, it comes as no surprise that the most viewed clip in the Bambuser archives at the time of writing was an interview in 2009 with Peter Sunde, co-founder of the controversial file-sharing facilitator website The Pirate Bay, in relation to the trial against the website's founders. The clip also draws rather heavily on back-channeling where viewers of the live broadcast would send questions for Sunde to the interviewer who would pick them up and address them during the broadcast. For comparison, the No. 1 clip on YouTube at the same time was an official music video featuring Justin Bieber (and in fact, nine out of the top ten clips on YouTube were corporate-produced music videos, whereas the only user-generated clip on the list was finger-biting baby Charlie at spot no. 6). Moreover, Bambuser's grassroots activism toward free speech and democratization is clearly discernible on the official website—in the dedicated archival collection pages on the Middle East events and on the Occupy movement, as well as in the strong positioning of the service in the open source culture.

More generally, we consider Bambuser an example of a collaborative medium that was designed from the start to be part of societal communication practices, even to play a role in reshaping them through ideals of democratization. It is interesting to note how the sense of democratization has deepened, though, throughout the first years of Bambuser's life cycle: From a general approach toward equalizing access to live-video production and distribution, to democratizing in the sense of taking active part in societal change. The original designers of Bambuser were not merely providing a neutral tool for society to pick up and use as it may. Recently, for example, they have engaged directly with Egyptian and Syrian activists through contacts in person and via online media to provide training and other kinds of moral and practical support for the activist causes (Messieh 2011). The explicit promotion of Middle East and Occupy archives on the official Bambuser website is another case in point.

At the same time, there is an apparent trade-off to be negotiated between grassroots activism and mainstream capitalist perspectives on collaborative media. Ideals are important vectors in the ongoing design work, but they do not lend themselves as easily to funding development and marketing for a startup incorporated company. The general sense of looking into the ongoing societal and economical process that is the development of the Bambuser service is that the trade-off is handled rather comfortably by adopting an inclusive position. There are no "either-ors," but rather a "both-and" that seems to keep many options open for positioning Bambuser and its continued development as part of the mediated fabric of contemporary society. Or, in the words of the official Bambuser blog in a post addressing the first anniversary of the Egypt uprising:

Although we know and understand that the Egypt uprising and revolution actually has little to do with social media and online tools, we're honored to be a service appreciated and used by so many to show the world from their perspective, somewhat democratizing news reporting.

We continue to follow and observe the events and we do our best to create a service that can be used for broadcasting everything from children's birthdays to revolutions. (Bambuser 2012a)

Parapolis: Designing the Future Cityscape

The general interest in innovation has boomed in recent years, and a significant subset of that interest concerns alternative innovation models that engage broader constituencies. There are many reasons for this move, ranging from stimulating creativity and diversity by including alternate perspectives to increasing customer acceptance and buy-in. When it comes to societal processes of development and change, it is clear that interest is growing for new models for citizen participation and codetermination—which is closely connected to recent developments in collaborative media as enabling platforms as well as drivers of new approaches. The city of Malmö, Sweden, is no exception in this regard.

In 2007, the traffic environment unit of Malmö city administration decided to put an open question to the citizens: Which way should we go to reduce car traffic in our city? The response exceeded expectations: Over one thousand suggestions were posted on the dedicated web page, ranging from innovative sky train designs to more down-to-earth approaches such as free public transportation and raised parking fees.

In order to continue and develop the dialogue, Malmö's administration enlisted the local design and innovation studio Unsworn Industries to propose ideas for a follow-up based on the collected suggestions. Erik Sandelin and Magnus Torstensson[3] of Unsworn, in collaboration with the traffic environment unit, created a campaign called See the Future for which the operative idea was to make the citizens' own ideas and suggested changes more tangible. A device called the Parascope was designed as a "future periscope" of sorts, using augmented reality technology to display a future panorama with visualized changes to the cityscape superimposed on the present (see figure 4.5). The goal of the See the Future campaign was to invite Malmö citizens to imagine possible future developments and engage in ongoing discussions about what their city should, or could, be like in the future.

Professional architects, artists, graphic designers and cultural geographers were recruited to work on future panoramas for three significant places in Malmö. Their work was to be based on the citizens' suggestions, but they were also given specific themes to explore, penetrate and express. The See the Future campaign ran in early 2009, and Parascopes were placed in the city to show possible futures like a car-free zone covering what is currently a traffic-plagued square in the heart of the city (see figure 4.6), and a boat-taxi service using the channels cutting through Malmö.

The form of the Parascope is reminiscent of traditional sightseeing binoculars that you might find as coin-operated and quaint attractions on mountain tops or in sky bars, but its function is less concerned with magnifying the existing. Instead, it provides a

Figure 4.5
The Parascope.

visual overlay showing indications of how a place might look in the future through pan-and-tiltable augmented reality technology. There are buttons for zooming and for accessing text annotations. More important, though, it is also possible using another button to switch between different visualizations—some of which are even mutually contradictory.

Specifically, a Parascope is built around a complete laptop computer with the screen used as the display and the processor receiving input from sensors in the joints of the construction to be able to respond to pan and tilt. Some custom electronics are used to filter and convert sensor signals (and button presses) to the regular serial input port of the laptop. When the Parascope is deployed at a new location, it is calibrated using a specific piece of calibration software running on the laptop with the existing buttons as input devices. Importantly, the laptop inside the Parascope runs Wi-Fi that continually searches for a peer with a specified name. This means that when you come close to the Parascope with another laptop that runs Wi-Fi with the specified name, a

Figure 4.6
Through the Parascope, visualized urban planning ideas are superimposed on the actual cityscape.

password-protected peer-to-peer connection is established between the Parascope and the outside laptop. Using VNC (virtual network computing) client and server software, it is now possible to control and communicate with the laptop inside the Parascope without stopping it or dismantling the Parascope itself. This feature was, strictly speaking, not necessary for the initial Parascope commission in the See the Future campaign, but Unsworn Industries, which designed the Parascopes, was already looking ahead toward other uses (as shall be detailed further).

The Parascope is powered by six car batteries hidden in its base, which means it can run for a week before recharging. The whole piece is constructed in industrial-strength stainless steel to withstand harsh Nordic climates as well as possible vandalism. Moreover, it turns out to be heavy enough to discourage its frequent relocation—which ameliorates the possible inconvenience of manual calibration. Still, the somewhat flexible and interventionist nature of the work is underlined by the fact that it is quite feasible for two people to move a Parascope using a typical van.

The whole purpose of a Parascope is to empower citizens to visualize, compare, and discuss several possible urban futures, rather than visualizing a projected change that has already been decided. The reasoning behind the design is that augmented reality overlays are more direct and accessible than maps and models, which are the typical representations through which dialogue is sought on issues concerning urban planning. Overlay visualizations require less specialist training for their interpretation, and flicking through different scenarios by pressing a button makes it easier to develop the sense that a place can appear in many forms and serve various urban functions. Moreover, taking the Parascope to the streets implies that the focus of the discussion is kept close to the actual site (and at the height of the human eye!), the essential and immediate qualities of the place being discussed, with all the localized and non-abstracted dimensions of knowing and feeling that the particular place implies.

The Parascopes and the See the Future campaign largely worked as intended, but did not leave any sense of closure or completion. Rather, it was felt that they represented a mere first step into a much larger field of participatory urban planning. Specifically, the intermediate step between citizen suggestions and professional future panorama renderings was seen as a distancing move. Further co-production work was initiated in the form of the Parapolis project, involving the research environment of this book's authors as well as public actors and professionals in the fields of architecture and collaborative innovation.

Unsworn Industries, being a key member also of the Parapolis project, from the start had foreseen the use of the Parascopes in participatory planning processes—hence the extra work to make a Parascope controllable and modifiable from the outside while in operation. A key idea Unsworn designers brought to the Parapolis project was the panorama studio, essentially corresponding to a mobile meeting place where citizens can discuss and sketch their own visions for the possible future of a particular place. The studio has the tools and capability to take the sketches directly into a Parascope, such that they can be experienced in place and form the basis for further dialogue and development.

In 2010, a series of experiments on participatory workshop methodology ran in a part of Malmö called Nydala. This is a rather average subcentral residential area, and the aim of the experiments was to find ways to stimulate engagement and participation in local urban planning.

The first phase of experimentation focused on a drop-in approach to participatory planning in the central square of Nydala. In a publicly available office space on the ground floor at Nydala Square, a panorama studio was set up with large sheets of line drawings of the square, lots of material for sketching and making collages, and a photo rig with proper lighting for capturing images of the sketches. A Parascope was placed in the square together with appropriate signage guiding curious passersby to the office space, and some active soliciting yielded a number of participants who would come into the office space and take part in sketching ideas for what Nydala Square could, or should, be like (see figure 4.7). The workshop organizers photographed the produced sketches twice a day, used stitching software to create panoramas with the right measures, and then uploaded the panoramas to the Parascope. During the night, the Parascope was left running and the intention was for people walking across the square to explore the new ideas and perhaps be inspired to come back the following day to join the workshop in the public office and take part in the ongoing discussion of what their square should be like.

Figure 4.7
The Nydala panorama studio in action.

The first workshop phase ran for three days in Nydala Square, leading to a fair number of panoramas showing different citizens' ideas on how the square could be developed (see figure 4.8). Overall, the panoramas have a sketchy and tentative feel to them, which is quite appropriate considering the aim of the workshop is to stimulate discussion and direct participation by those most immediately concerned, rather than visualizing a completed development proposal. It is easy to see how the whole setup of the workshop and the choice of tools were made with this kind of ongoing, tentative expression in mind.

After the first workshop phase, Parapolis project members summarized the results in two ways: first, what seemed to be the major issues concerning Nydala Square, and second, what was learned regarding the use of Parascopes and panorama studios to facilitate participatory planning.

The example panorama in figure 4.8 has a stickie in the middle saying "FYLL IGEN TUNNELN," which means to block or fill the underpass. This refers to what was identified as a recurring issue on Nydala Square, namely the driveway through the square and how it interferes with other needs that a subcentral square has to fill. In a public web page produced after the first phase, Parapolis researchers point out that the stickie

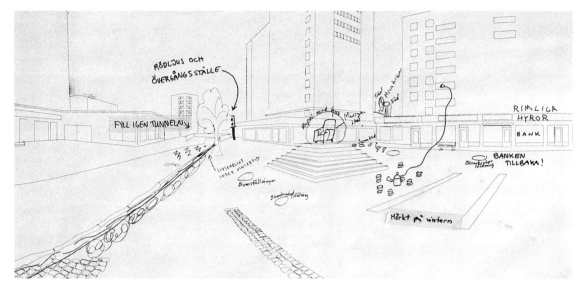

Figure 4.8
A panorama from the first Nydala workshop phase (detail).

indicates an important concern—the existing underpass is an unpleasant passage, and the driveway splits the square rather harshly—but that the proposed solution is not necessarily the only one. Instead, they pose the open question of what the existing underpass could be used for if the traffic in the driveway was controlled instead by pedestrian crossings with traffic lights and perhaps more strict speed limitations: An outdoor theater stage? A subterranean tropical park? An ice-skating arena in the winter? This and other actions taken by the researchers demonstrate quite clearly how they aim to work with the panorama studio workshop as part of a larger process, being inherently participatory and discursive.

The second phase of the Nydala experiments was slightly more complicated, in that it entailed several different interventions. One direction was to set up and operate a panorama studio in the middle of the square, next to the Parascope, in order to reduce the distance between the eye-catching Parascope itself and the practical setting for engaging hands-on with the issues symbolized by the Parascope. It had been found in the first phase that only rarely did people come into the panorama studio after having looked into the Parascope and reacted to one of the ideas presented there. On the one hand, having the studio in plain view in the middle of square was found to work well in terms of attracting more people, but on the other hand those who participated in the discussion-through-sketching were generally more shy and self-conscious as the whole process took place in public. Here, it was found that a professional illustrator could facilitate the process and liberate ideas to a great extent by taking part in the discussion and "holding the pen" when it came to sketching panoramas for the Parascope.

In another second-phase experiment, a panorama studio with a professional illustrator was used as the venue for a meeting of stakeholders in the development of Nydala Square, including representatives from the urban planning offices of Malmö as well as the major housing companies owning the buildings around the square. The idea was to create panoramas as meeting notes, thus forcing decision makers away from abstract discussion of, for example, densification, and toward concrete experimentation with physical future possibilities. The experiment was not very successful, mainly due to the illustrator's lack of expressive initiative (but the researchers still see some potential in the approach).

A final experiment in the second phase, representing rather interesting insights into the properties of different representation forms, was a photorealistic rendering of a particular panorama that had been sketched in a very light and tentative way with stickies and rough marker strokes on a white line drawing. The rendering, which was made overnight by one of the workshop facilitators, was found to draw much more detailed reactions on the level of physical realization. For example, Nydala residents pointed out that the square shown in the realistic rendering lacked adequate greenery. The rendering even stimulated attempts at expressing similarly detailed proposals in panoramas made from collages of photographic images from magazines. This experiment initiated further thought among the researchers on possible roles of designers in participatory planning processes, where particular skills in visual expression could be used to stimulate dialogue in a systematic way.

The Parapolis project as such is concluded, but work continues toward a more comprehensive approach labeled Prototyping the City, based on the insights gained in the project. At the time of writing, Unsworn Industries has used the Parascope over twenty times in different participatory planning settings, in Sweden and abroad. The city of Malmö has commissioned Unsworn to help make the participatory planning methods and tools a larger part of common practice in urban development. Moreover, there is an emerging conceptualization of Parascopes and panoramas as one part of a much larger, mediated whole forming the venue for ongoing discussions of urban development. This venue spans multiple media channels and incorporates processes on different timescales, from momentary interventions to several-year political initiatives. And most important, this venue already exists to a major extent, and designing a new forum requires a clear view of connections to already ongoing communicative practices. One clear example of this can be found in the initial See the Future campaign. The original intention was to provide an online forum for citizen discussion that the Parascopes in the city were intended to stimulate. However, the amount of energy and participation in that forum was generally unsatisfactory. At the same time, the regional newspaper

Sydsvenskan saw lively debates in its online forum on issues pertaining to urban change and development—in fact it was the second most debated group of topics at the time, surpassed only by Zlatan Ibrahimovic (a world-class professional soccer player who grew up in Malmö). One of the Parascope designers summarizes this insight as follows: "There is clearly engagement in these issues, but we need to find the formats and channels to put it to work" (Sandelin 2012).

To conclude this case, we offer a few remarks on Parapolis as seen through the lens of collaborative media and society. The basic approach is arguably to reify citizen participation in urban development into mediated forms that are accessible to most citizens, rather than requiring specialized planning competence. This ambition of "translating" the dialogue into more widely "spoken languages," as it were, echoes the whole 1970s participatory movement in architecture and urban planning. The idea of digitally mediating the arenas for participation has been thoroughly explored ever since—for example, in the work of Arias (1996), Underkoffler and Ishii (1999), and Eden, Hornecker, and Scharff (2002); it is also what makes Parapolis an interesting case from our point of view.

It can be noted that the Parascopes themselves are unique in that they offer an experience that is new to most people: the ability to actually see alternative futures through a richly embodied and situated way of seeing. The physical form of a Parascope also makes it stand out in a city square or a street corner, and Parascopes are designed for more or less temporary interventions rather than long-term, mundane everyday use. On balance, the Parascope when seen as a media channel is perhaps best understood as a process tool for catalyzing energy and engagement, rather than as a stable and permanent part of the media infrastructure in itself. Already when the Parascopes were designed for the See the Future campaign (which was commissioned from a more traditional, hierarchical standpoint), their use was anticipated as one of the vehicles for participatory planning processes, in concert with panorama studios and other techniques.

As we also observed, the digital mediation foundational to the Parascopes and the panoramas also implies connections to a vast and largely established set of communicative practices in collaborative media as well as digitized broadcast media. Work is underway at Unsworn to develop an online venue called FuTube, corresponding to a YouTube of alternative urban futures in the form of panoramas. One might speculate that collaboration with an established media provider addressing local and regional citizen concerns would be a valuable approach here, in order to connect more closely to established communicative practices dealing with urban change and development.

More generally, though, the Parapolis case illustrates the highly dispersed and distributed processes of design, production, and consumption that we find to characterize collaborative media. What is more, it moves in the territory of agonism and ongoing dialogue as a meaningful alternative to traditional notions of majority consensus and representational democracy where expert planners are appointed through political mechanisms and are trusted to make decisions under some form of more or less informed consent. The close-to-the-ground facilitation processes explored in Parapolis also shed light on the nature of small-scale, local communicative structures with tribal characteristics. We find that none of these characteristics are limited to participatory urban planning, but rather appear as quite ubiquitous traits of collaborative media.

5 〜〜〜 Collaborative Media and Institutions

In this chapter, we examine four cases of collaborative media design interventions in contexts dominated by institutionalized views of media production and consumption. The selection of cases aims to elucidate how the design work evolves from different ways to approach the media institutions. More specifically, the cases can be characterized as follows.

In MyNewsMyWay, the work grows out of a larger project frame that more or less takes existing modes of production within the institutions of mass-media broadcasting for granted. The case deals with new production technology for audiovisual broadcasting enabled by digital production and distribution, and the possible improvements that could follow from such technology for consumers of news and sports. It should be read as complementary to OurNewsOurWays in chapter 6, which was spawned as a way to explore some of the more long-term implications of collaborative media starting from the same project frame.

The Substrate case starts from a similar institutionalized position but within another media field, and one which is perhaps not always recognized as such: the field of technical information, including user guides and product manuals. In technical information, the notion of specialists producing and users consuming is very strongly entrenched; the Substrate case reports ongoing work with an explicitly change-oriented perspective whereby researchers and professionals work together to explore the implications of collaborative media for technical information.

The venerable Kliv case addresses knowledge management within healthcare, another area that normally is not affiliated with the media sector but turns out to be usefully approached from a collaborative media perspective. Kliv employs a grassroots empowerment approach within an existing set of institutional practices for mediating knowledge (i.e., formalized training, instruction manuals for intensive-care equipment, centralized dissemination through intranets, etc.), more or less aiming to operate under the radar and develop results that can later be institutionalized by demonstrating their appropriateness in practice. The results, in this case, comprise concrete collaborative media products as well as insights on the practices of interventionist collaborative media research.

The final case called Hacktivism concerns the fashion industry, read as a media institution. It is similar to Kliv in terms of grassroots empowerment, but uses more openly confrontational and critical methods and rhetorics. The overt topic is alternative design practices within fashion, but the results turn out to be highly relevant to our notions of collaborative media and collaborative media research.

Thus, the overall arc of this chapter spans different ways for collaborative media researchers to approach the institutions of mass media, ranging from working incrementally within a mass-media mindset, to collaborative planning and execution of change toward collaborative media, to interventions through grassroots empowerment and critical practices.

MyNewsMyWay: From Time Shifting to Shape Shifting

In 2004, a three-year grant was awarded from the European Commission to a collaborative research proposal called "NM2: New Media for a New Millennium." The project, which was later renamed "NM2: New Millennium, New Media," involved thirteen partners from research organizations and the media industry. According to the project proposal, the main emphasis was on the two general areas of technology and media production (NM2 n.d.).

The project as a whole took its point of departure from the tradition of broadcast audiovisual media with specialist organizations producing and distributing media content for subsequent consumption by large audiences. The challenge posed by the project was to create "prototype production tools for the media industry that will allow the easy production of non-linear media genres based on moving audiovisual images suitable for transmission over broadband networks" (Williams et al. 2004). The project envisioned a new kind of audience experience in the realm of *interactive narratives*, in other words, storytelling for which the readers or viewers themselves can influence the story arc and outcome. The general interest presentation of the project speaks of "the easy production of non-linear broadband media that can be personalized to suit the preferences of the individual user," where "[v]iewers will be able to interact directly with the medium and influence what they see and hear according to their personal tastes and wishes" (NM2 n.d.).

It is clear that this is a significant challenge from a mass-media production and consumption point of view, and one certainly warranting a coordinated research effort, mainly due to the fact that viewer interactivity combines rather poorly with traditional notions of producer narration. This topic has been explored for over twenty years in computer games and digital narrativity research, starting with simple ideas of branching narratives and moving on to sophisticated applications of artificial intelligence to create story engines and other mechanisms for enabling interactive narrative (see, e.g., Murray 1997; Mateas 2001). The approach of the NM2 project was to reify the challenge to a question of devising production tools that would enable media producers to create some sort of interactive narratives across a range of genres, including fiction as well as documentary and news. Success criteria for those tools would be that they enable media producers to create compelling and profitable offerings in a cost-efficient way. Essentially, the media production partners in the project would represent the knowledge of what tools would be needed, the technical partners would create the tools, and the media production partners would test them in experimental interactive-narrative productions, thus forming a loop of refining and testing the tools that would become the main result of the project.

Stepping back, it is equally clear that the NM2 project took for granted certain core values of the established institutions of audiovisual mass media, such as the distinction between production and consumption, the individual interaction between the viewer and the media provided by the producer, and the ability of production tools to cut across established media genres (and in fact, the nonlinear audience experiences anticipated by the project are described as a new genre in itself, which is somewhat unorthodox).

Within the NM2 frame, one of this book's authors (Reimer) together with research colleagues and with subcontracting partner Swedish Television (SVT) (Sweden's national public-service television network) took on the role of media producers for the genres of news and sports. In other words, their task was to design an experimental news and sports TV format that would demonstrate the principles of interactive narrative and the capabilities of the NM2 tool suite for future production of compelling and profitable interactive news and sports.

The project was called MyNewsMyWay, and it was immediately clear that it had a few characteristics that set it apart from designing interactive narratives in other genres such as fiction or documentary. Most important, news and sports is never a one-off production to be distributed and consumed in a standalone fashion, but rather a question of selecting, interpreting, and communicating material from a continuous stream of real-world events. A "story" in the context of news is not preconceived and the way the story ends is not known to the producers at the time they choose to bring it to public attention. Instead, it unfolds over the course of days and weeks, sometimes reaching a dramaturgically satisfying conclusion but equally as often losing traction and eventually being swapped for the next major story. What this also means is the producers possess ever-growing temporal archives of news and sports material, where the significance of a particular item is similarly impossible to judge once and for all. All archival material is potentially relevant at a future time, depending on the direction of the real-world event stream.

The notion of *shape-shifting media* was coined within the larger NM2 project as a variation on the well-known concept of time shifting, which gained currency in the early 2000s as a way to refer to on-demand services for media consumption, various

technologies for recording broadcasts, and other ways for viewers to liberate themselves from the broadcasting schedules of the ether media. Within MyNewsMyWay,
shape shifting became an important guideline for initial design of the new audience
news and sports experience. The concept was taken to entail superficial manipulation
of the media content, such as the viewer's ability to set the duration of a news summary and have the contents changed accordingly, as well as deeper issues concerning
the news and sports contents, including the specification of personal-interest profiles
to guide the selection of news and sports material to display. The academic motivations for these and other design ideas included the degradation of broadcast media in
relation to concerns such as the democratic needs for well-informed citizens, relevant
grounds for societal action, and the general desirability of more dignified and meaningful media experiences. For instance, Ignatieff's (1997) analysis of TV news was used to
characterize the present problems:

Television has unfortunate strengths as a medium of moral disgust. As a moral mediator between
violent men and the audiences they crave, television images are more effective at presenting consequences than in exploring intentions; more adept at pointing to the corpses than in explaining
why violence may, in certain places, pay so well. As a result, television news bears some responsibility for that generalized misanthropy, that irritable resignation toward the criminal folly of
fanatics and assassins, which legitimizes one of the dangerous cultural moods of our time—the
feeling that the world has become too crazy to deserve serious reflection.

Based on this kind of analysis, the goal of MyNewsMyWay for producers was to
provide tools that would enable them to produce more in-depth and varied news and
sports output without unreasonable amounts of extra work for the journalists and editors concerned. The goal for the audience was to provide material for more meaningful
news and sports experiences.

The final results of the MyNewsMyWay project are a demonstrator illustrating a
shape-shifting news and sports experience built using the NM2 tools, as well as a number of reflections on further improvements (Lindstedt et al. 2009). Further insights
from media studies were used to guide the design on a more detailed level. For instance,
the news genre is comparatively rigid in terms of its formats, meaning that the expectations of what constitutes TV news are stable and deeply rooted. Moreover, it is known
that news consumption for many people form part of their daily routine, and is ritual-
istic in nature. These insights directed the design work toward creating a TV experience
(rather than a computer experience), working with the notion of a program (a news
show) rather than isolated news stories, using a conventional remote control plus a TV
screen as interactive devices, and finally, creating a format that would encourage but
not demand viewer action.

More specifically, MyNewsMyWay starts with the entry screen, showing visual head-
lines for the six different departments of the service: MyNews, General News, Sports,
Culture and Entertainment, Economy, and Home and Leisure (see figure 5.1). MyNews

Figure 5.1
The entry screen of MyNewsMyWay.

is a personalized news show, which will be detailed further. The other five departments are based on editorial selection of contents. Moreover, a general search function is available as well as functions for maintaining settings and profiles.

Selecting MyNews with the remote control takes the viewer to a news show (see figure 5.2) that is dynamically assembled by selecting twenty minutes' worth of material whose metadata fit the viewer's personal interest profile.

While watching a clip in MyNews, three main functions are available to the viewer. The More function retrieves further material on the topic of the clip that is playing, thus providing an in-depth view of that news item and a better understanding of its context. For example, while watching a clip on Middle East diplomacy, the More function might yield a new clip summarizing the background of the U.S.-Iraq conflict. The

Figure 5.2
Watching MyNews.

Related function presents a list of clips that are more laterally related to the clip in play, thus encouraging serendipitous consumption based on a notion of content relevance. Finally, the Increase Time and Decrease Time functions change the overall playing time of the news show by increments of five minutes by adding or subtracting material.

A number of young participants tested the demonstrator, and the results were generally favorable. Participants appreciated the idea of personalized news and the capacity to explore different perspectives and viewpoints on a particular news event. They considered the experience appropriate both for individual watching and for watching with family and friends, and perceived the user interface as easy to learn and use.

The demonstrator was built on a relatively small database, consisting of material from Swedish Television's archives that had been manually augmented to contain all the metadata required by the NM2 tools. Specifically, news and sports clips in MyNews-MyWay are tagged using an extended version of SVT's news topic keyword ontology, which lists some 1,500 keywords in a hierarchical structure with ten top-level categories including economy, leisure, culture, medicine, and politics. Further metadata includes people and groups, location, time, and type (such as "who-what-when-where" news item, "why" in-depth news item, interview or debate).

In compiling the MyNews show, the system matches the interest profile of the current viewer with the metadata of recent news clips to compile a selection that fits within the allocated programming time (initially set at twenty minutes). If the viewer invokes More, Related, or the Increase Time or Decrease Time functions while watching, similar selection rules are invoked to change the composition of the news show on the fly.

The project results prompted consideration of potential improvements. First, the team concluded that the rigidity of the news genre makes a news show without an anchor somewhat unfamiliar. The archival publication on MyNewsMyWay (Lindstedt et al. 2009) speculates on how archived anchor sequences could be combined automatically with news clips to create a more familiar experience. Second, the team felt that the demonstrator's design favored interactive viewing at the expense of traditional, passive viewing, which could be addressed to some extent by providing one-click defaults for the More and Related functions.

Finally, the perennial issue of specifying personal-interest profiles was identified as a possible stumbling block for the chosen approach. Since the quality of the profile directly determines the relevance and significance of the MyNews show, it is crucial that the profile accurately portrays each person's interests, and that the profile can easily be modified when necessary. During the project, the researchers ended up proposing a rather complicated scheme for profile editing, based on the Topic keyword ontology underlying the demonstrator's selection mechanism. In retrospect, and based on how difficult it is, in practice, to make users edit personal profiles with precision and regularity in other application areas (e.g., Light and Maybury 2002), the approach proposed in the project must be deemed rather impractical. However, the OurNews-OurWays study was also initiated within the scope of the NM2 project (see chapter 6), and the tribal metadata mechanisms developed there illustrate how the same problem for a viewer of finding something relevant to watch can be treated more effectively by moving from the individual to the social realm of media consumption.

The MyNewsMyWay case represents a fairly typical collaborative media design intervention in a setting characterized by conventional, institutionalized media practices. The fundamental assumptions on division of labor between producer and consumers were never really questioned, and the work is most aptly characterized as an exploration of possible incremental transformations within a given institutional structure. Consumers should be able not only to time shift but also to shape shift their news and sports TV content, and this poses a set of new requirements on production tools and practices—but those tools and practices are still seen as firmly tied to the professional production environment. As pointed out earlier, it is instructive to compare the MyNewsMyWay case with the OurNewsOurWays case reported in chapter 6, which emanated from the same institutional structure but adopted a slightly more speculative perspective. In OurNewsOurWays, the assumption is rather that the future audiovisual mediascape will comprise material from many sources, professional as well as nonprofessional, and the resulting design consequently concentrates on tribal (nonprofessional) design-in-consumption and production-in-consumption.

More generally, the two cases together illustrate a useful approach in dealing with design interventions in institutionalized settings, where both long-term and short-term scenarios are addressed in order to clarify strategic visions as well as to probe initial steps toward such visions.

Substrate: From Distribution Channel to Collaboration Platform

Substrate is an ongoing story of institutional transformation, focusing on how an existing mass media institution approaches the challenges posed by collaborative media. Specifically, the mass medium under consideration is technical information, or product information: user guides, product manuals, operation and maintenance instructions, and the like. At the time of writing, the Substrate project is still running and the resulting new media products are not yet launched or validated broadly. In the case study to follow, the co-production of researchers and professionals as well as the artifacts coming out of the joint design work are read as vehicles for understanding how an established media institution may respond to the collaborative media challenge. The account is fairly detailed: in this case the key to understanding the dynamics of institutional structure transformation truly lies in the details.

Technical information is a substantial, albeit somewhat anonymous part of the media today. Its place on the map is actually somewhat difficult to assert, since technical information is produced for a variety of products, settings, and industrial segments. For instance, the folded page of diagrammed instructions on how to assemble a bookcase purchased in a flat package constitutes technical information—but so does the million-word collection of technically advanced information on how to install, configure, maintain, and troubleshoot a mobile network hub for an entire country. Technical information is ubiquitous in any field where man-made products and services are deployed for people's use. In some cases, such information amounts to visual communication and signage design for one-off instant use by virtually anybody, whereas in other cases it addresses a tiny population of highly trained and specialized technicians working for years on a custom configuration of a vastly complex technical system. This diversity also means that technical information belongs to several industrial sectors: Consultancies specializing in easy how-to guides for public places and services may be close cousins of communication agencies and consider themselves part of the media sector, whereas organizations developing the large bodies of bespoke information for complex technical systems typically need enough technical competence to be considered part of the industrial sector in question, such as manufacturing or ICT.

In spite of this diversity, there are still a few commonalities that tie the field of technical information together. One is that the information produced is needed and useful in many cases, even though the most common taunt known to technical information professionals is: "If the product design were good enough, we wouldn't need any technical information." It is certainly easy to find funny examples of superfluous or misguided technical information, often due to cost-saving automated translation ("keep out of children" for a kitchen knife) or legislative reasons ("not intended for drying pet animals" for a microwave oven), but generally speaking, any product more complex than a toothpick benefits from well-crafted technical information that may help the user understand the logic of the product and use it in more comprehensive ways. What is more, technical information ties in with customer support and similar functions to enhance the experience of the product.

Another commonality is that, broadly speaking, the technical information field's self-image is, largely, that of a traditional mass medium. In other words, the dominant sense within the field is that proper technical information is *produced* by information architects, technical writers, and other specialists, then distributed in its final form to be *consumed* by a large audience of product owners and users.

The view of technical information as a mass medium may seem increasingly obsolete, but it still holds commercial currency when it comes to the so-called business-to-business (B2B) segment of the market, where the products are often technically quite complex, the consumers of the information are professionals who work regularly with the products in question, and tasks often include configuration, operation, maintenance, and troubleshooting. However, when it comes to consumer products and business-to-consumer (B2C) technical information, it is clear that the everyday use of collaborative media has left mass-media technical information bleeding by the roadside. Home electronics, appliances, cars, and other consumer products are undeniably complex technical systems, but when a consumer needs to find out how to get something done the first instinct today is not to pull out the owner's manual (if it ever were) but rather to search the Internet. The reason for this, of course, is that we have learned such searches are often successful: we can easily locate accurate and timely information on open newsgroups, moderated chat logs and discussion forums, microblogs, editorial websites, and other online resources—and only rarely does the relevant information originate from the appointed technical information producers or the original providers of the product. Instead, it turns out that for most products, there are other users out there who are willing and able to devote time to answering questions, writing instructions, compiling product reviews, and curating insights outside the traditional production system of mass-media technical information.

It should be clear therefore that technical information as an institution is challenged by collaborative media in a manner strikingly similar to what happens in broadcasting and other mainstream media. Hence, one of this book's authors (Löwgren) found it appropriate to initiate a project together with an established technical information actor in 2009, in order to explore the nature and scope of the structural transformations that could follow from seriously considering collaborative media as a potentially game-changing development within the business landscape.

Sigma Kudos is a relatively large, international consulting firm within technical information and information logistics, counting some seven hundred employees worldwide. It originated in Sweden where there are offices in seven cities, and is represented in China, Hungary, Ukraine, and Finland with partner offices in India and Malaysia. It is part of Sigma Group, an international ICT conglomerate. The main source of technical information business for Sigma Kudos is B2B services for large customers in the ICT and telecom industries.

The Swedish branch of Sigma Kudos includes a small team working on tools and platforms for technical information in a somewhat exploratory way. Prior to 2009, the primary product of that team was the DocFactory tool suite, consisting of a production part and a consumption part for streamlining the development and distribution of technical information within a mass-medium production paradigm. The team had a mandate from management to continue exploring innovations that might open new markets and new positions for the company, and ideally to help shift the company's relations to their customers from reactive consultancy to a slightly more proactive stance based on projections of the future of technical information. The researchers, as noted, considered technical information to be a potentially interesting case of media structure transformation in response to the emergence of collaborative media. Thus, mutual interests existed and the collaboration was formalized in mid-2009 as the Substrate project.[1]

Initial steps of the joint work were mostly aimed at finding directions and challenges to be addressed within the project. The development of everyday collaborative media and its implications for B2C technical information were quickly acknowledged; however, the main motivations for Sigma Kudos were to be found in the area of B2B, due to the fact that it made up most of the firm's technical information business. The driving forces for the DocFactory team had been to make production, distribution, and consumption of technical information as efficient as possible within the mass-media mindset of specialists producing and users consuming. The DocFactory tool suite was designed largely around two main technical principles: *topicalization* and *faceted browsing*.

First, topicalization essentially means that technical information should be divided into self-contained topics, where the rule of thumb is that each topic is the answer to one question. In order to understand why this was a primary goal of pre-2009

DocFactory, it is important to know that production of technical information within Sigma Kudos and their customers at that point was largely structured around documents. The legacy of print was strong enough to structure also digitally distributed technical information in PDF documents with chapters and sections.

From a production point of view, this meant that updating a published set of technical information was extremely hard, time consuming, and error prone, since traditionally created documents have very little semantic structure. To simplify slightly, if the product is updated and the steps for completing operation X are changed, there is no way to update the technical information accordingly, short of manually searching the whole set of documents and making changes wherever operation X is mentioned. Moreover, the problems caused by the lack of semantic structure multiply when technical information is published in several languages.

There are similar efficiency arguments to be made from the consumption point of view. For instance, when a specific part of the technical information is published as one PDF file, the only reliable way to find information about operation X would be to search the document and sift through all the search hits to locate the most appropriate one.

Second, dividing the information into topics would be one necessary step toward achieving more efficient production and consumption of mass-media technical information, but not a sufficient one. In order to realize the benefits when a document is divided into hundreds or thousands of topics, it is necessary to augment the information with some form of semantic metadata that would enable efficient access to the right topics. The approach chosen by the DocFactory team was faceted browsing, which essentially entails tagging every topic in a number of specified dimensions (known as facets) and then allowing for conjunctive filtering on multiple dimensions.

For example, assume an information set with millions of news articles. A faceted browsing interface to that information set would provide filters for facets such as year, location, and person. The user would be free to engage those filters in any order and any combination to rapidly prune the current selection down to only the articles that concern, for example, music in Japan in 2006.[2]

The work invested in the DocFactory tool suite, and particularly the concepts of topicalization and faceted browsing, were important starting points for the collaborative work between researchers and Sigma Kudos. Much of the initial joint work was devoted to exploring the implications of collaborative media for B2B technical information. In these discussions, the researchers' experience from Kliv (discussion follows) was pivotal in understanding the idea that users can, and should, produce "content" for technical information that is sometimes more relevant and accurate than what a conventional production organization could provide. The project team agreed that the project should start exploring successors to the DocFactory tool suite that would support more collaborative forms of technical information production and consumption. Work started on designing the Substrate infrastructure.

Another foundational activity of the project concerned raising awareness of the collaborative media challenge in different levels of Sigma Kudos, and gaining support for devoting resources to addressing the challenge. The overall shape of that activity was somewhat top-down, in that the lead researcher was given the opportunity at an early stage to run a half-day workshop on collaborative media challenges at a retreat for the whole Sigma Kudos management group. Following that workshop, the managers participating in the retreat contacted the researcher directly to carry out training and creative sessions with the technical writers and information architects of their respective units.

In any consultancy, an important factor in influencing strategic decisions is what the customers want. Sigma Kudos was no exception in this regard. As another result of the early introduction to the management group, the lead researcher was also invited on several occasions to run or participate in creative sessions with key customers on strategic implications of collaborative media for technical information.

In retrospect, the business purpose of these sessions from the point of view of Sigma Kudos appears to have been twofold: to investigate future needs of customers in the direction of collaborative media, and to start projecting an image of a more proactive and future-oriented consultancy.

This image is also an important aim when it comes to the public perception of Sigma Kudos. Since the start of the project, the company has organized open seminars for customers and potential customers on a number of occasions, addressing the future of technical information. The challenges of collaborative media and the progress of the Substrate project have been key ingredients in these seminars, and it might be safe to conjecture that the seminars would not have occurred without the Substrate project. Similar activities have also been carried out several times as part of the larger business events organized by Sigma Group, such as the 2011 Camp Digital[3] that gathered several hundred participants in Stockholm and was later repeated at two other Swedish venues. Finally, with regard to public image, it must be mentioned that Sigma Kudos recently commissioned a broad national survey among customer and potential customer markets of technical information, aimed at gauging the current state of the art and future expectations. The intention is for the survey to be recurrent and for Sigma Kudos to establish itself as the national business leader in technical information, by publishing the results openly and thus demonstrating that the firm takes responsibility for the development of the field as a whole and its future.

The Substrate project primarily focused on designing new tools and infrastructures for collaborative technical information. The design story moves from initial exploration of ideas based on the business interests of Sigma Kudos and the knowledge interests of the researchers toward a synthesis into three main directions called Implicit, "Flickr" (short for the-direction-that-would-work-a-bit-like-Flickr), and Community (see figure 5.3).

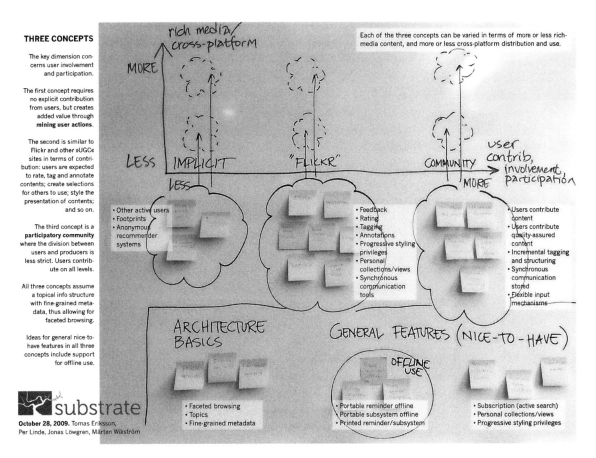

THREE CONCEPTS

The key dimension concerns user involvement and participation.

The first concept requires no explicit contribution from users, but creates added value through **mining user actions**.

The second is similar to Flickr and other »UGC« sites in terms of contribution: users are expected to rate, tag and annotate contents; create selections for others to use; style the presentation of contents; and so on.

The third concept is a **participatory community** where the division between users and producers is less strict. Users contribute on all levels.

All three concepts assume a topical info structure with fine-grained metadata, thus allowing for faceted browsing.

Ideas for general nice-to-have features in all three concepts include support for offline use.

substrate

October 28, 2009. Tomas Eriksson, Per Linde, Jonas Löwgren, Mårten Wikström

Figure 5.3
The three main directions identified in early concept development.

The key dimension for organizing the three main directions was user involvement and participation: The Implicit direction would not entail any explicit action on behalf of users beyond their traditional consumption, but the envisioned system would mine user actions during consumption to create added value in the form of, for example, footprints, anonymous recommendation systems, and other indications of user activity such as most-viewed selections. The Community direction would be a fully open collaborative-media infrastructure where the distinction between "users" and "producers" would be more or less eradicated, where any member could produce content, and where community mechanisms such as reputation points earned through voting would be used for validating contributions rather than structural mechanisms such as appointing some people to the role of "producer." The "Flickr" direction represented a middle ground, closely modeled on existing sharing sites, where users would primarily produce metadata such as tags, ratings, annotations, selections, and customized styling. In this direction, the actual production of primary content would still be seen as a privileged action and the role of "producer" would still be upheld to some degree.

The project team members decided, predictably, to explore the middle ground first in the hope that it would provide a feasible transition from current mass media notions of technical information toward more collaborative media. The concept was developed with primary focus on users and consumption to the point where a fairly detailed specification existed for the viewer side of a new technical information infrastructure, based on elementary ideas of collaborative media (see figure 5.4).

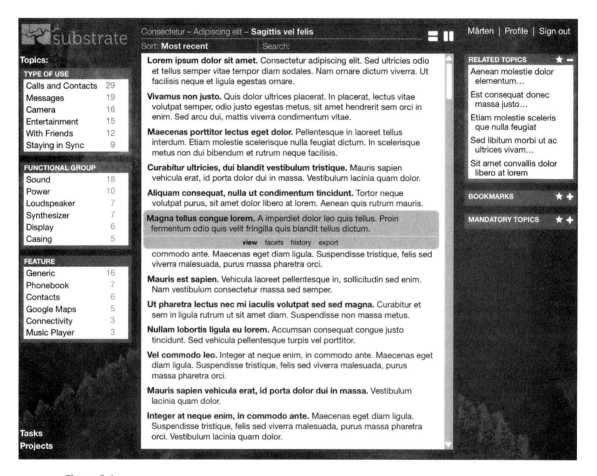

Figure 5.4
One of the detailed interface sketches for a technical information viewer providing facilities for production-in-consumption.

However, there was a sense that this direction of work, albeit generally important and full of learning opportunities, would not provide enough of an incentive to motivate Sigma Kudos to commit deeply.

The design process was revitalized in early 2010 when the Sigma Kudos team members moved to shift the focus of the work from consumption to production. Specifically, the idea came up to concentrate on the transition from document-based to topic-based production and how to facilitate it. The core of the idea was the observation that collaboration in technical information production is not always smooth and effortless. On the one hand, version management and consistency are perennial challenges in a document-based production approach, and existing enterprise solutions were perceived as heavy, inelegant, and inefficient. On the other hand, existing open solutions such as Google Docs were deemed irrelevant for reasons of business security. The idea as originally proposed was to create a lightweight, flexible, state-of-the-art tool for sharing documents—but to build the tool on an architecture that would be designed for sharing topics. The tool would treat documents, such as Word and PDF files, as special cases of topics and it would support semantic metadata and faceted browsing to make sharing convenient and efficient. If such a tool existed, it could become a useful lever to facilitate the production-side transition from documents toward more fine-grained topics.

The orientation phase of this new design direction was relatively short and goal oriented; a few rounds of concept ideation focused on streamlining the sharing, followed by exploration of an application where social features of sharing were foregrounded. The underlying architecture would be server-based, where documents as well as topics would be stored with appropriate semantic metadata, but where editing the contents of the documents or topics would be handled outside the sharing core. The concept was summarized in relation to the previous approach; the key direction was that the new design would serve as a lightweight interface to the previously designed, more comprehensive infrastructure. Easy and efficient sharing was seen as the transitional route from existing, document-based management of technical information toward topic-based approaches and faceted browsing. The new design was named SmartShare (see figure 5.5) and it was intended to address both the production and the consumption side of technical information.

At this point, production of a prototype was prioritized and resulted relatively quickly in a standalone application capable of storing documents and sharing them among a specified group of authorized users. The first prototype emphasized an architecture that would be flexible and resilient enough for deployment, including issues such as sharing rights for users, server administration mechanisms, and provisions for some sort of history or version management to be designed later on. In a sense, although the impetus for SmartShare was the user experience of lightweight sharing, these stages of the work were geared toward a general, comprehensive platform for storing and accessing documents as well as topics.

The "Topic" menu contains
"Upload" plus the context menu
alternatives for selected topic.

3. The main application window
when a topic is selected in
the list.

Facet values and tag values of the
selected topics are indicated in
the left-side boxes, much like in
the Substrate sketches for the CAT
application.

A large button appears to the left
of the selected topic to invite the
user to engage with the metadata
of the selected topic. The button
invokes the "SmartShare" function
to present the metadata drawer.
Suggested keyboard shortcut is
<SPACE>.

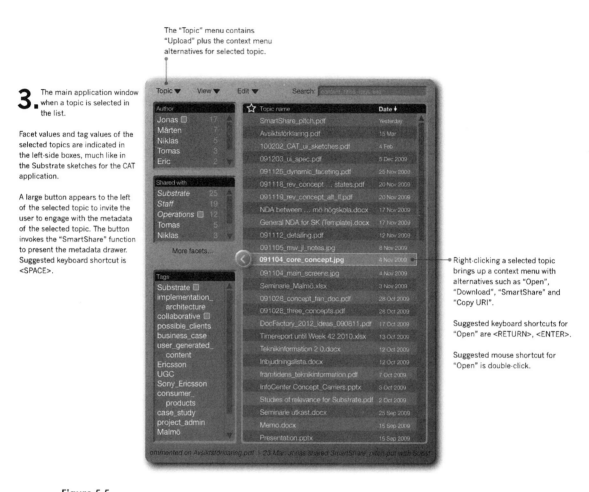

Right-clicking a selected topic
brings up a context menu with
alternatives such as "Open",
"Download", "SmartShare" and
"Copy URI".

Suggested keyboard shortcuts for
"Open" are <RETURN>, <ENTER>.

Suggested mouse shortcut for
"Open" is double-click.

Figure 5.5
Detailed interface sketch for SmartShare.

When the broad strokes of the platform were in place, work shifted to the user interface and features. The central concept of the interface design was a list showing all topics that the current user had the right to view, and a small set of facets for filtering the topic list. In the first set of interface designs, it is clear that the focus was on sharing documents; the facets were more or less automatically generated document metadata such as file types and author names. The only genuinely collaborative feature found in the sketches at this stage was tagging. This design was quickly revised to address the issue of collaboration more thoroughly, including favoriting and annotation.

After this step, subsequent work on SmartShare can best be described as incremental prototyping. Several versions have been released, and after each new release the team discusses the roadmap for next and future releases. In those discussions, three categories have emerged for talking about new feature ideas: (1) in the next release, (2) on the roadmap for future releases, and (3) not on the roadmap. The main reason for these categories is that SmartShare has been taken to the market, and when discussing customers' feature requests it is important to know their relation to the roadmap in order to be able to set the price for the requested feature (if something is not on the product roadmap, it has to be more or less fully funded by the customer placing the request).

To summarize, the main developments so far are that the spring 2010 SmartShare concept is largely implemented: document sharing on a deployment-strength server architecture, including tools for user and server administration; annotation and tagging features; informal coordination and curating; and tools for editing facets and facet values. It has been broadened to three deployment platforms, including a web service and a mobile app as well as the original standalone application. An early version was launched internally within Sigma Kudos in the spring of 2011, starting with the management group. The hope was not only to gain visibility and acceptance for the ongoing work in the project, but also that members of the management group would use the tool for sharing their internal management documents and thus be convinced of its qualities and facilitate its further dissemination in the organization. This strategy was not entirely successful, even though some members of the management group have demonstrated subsequent awareness of SmartShare and introduced it into the discussions with their respective customers.

More important, the Sigma Kudos project team members started relatively early to include SmartShare in their own repertoire for customer contacts. The effects of this move have largely been twofold. First, as mentioned earlier, much of the existing B2B market is oriented toward the production side. Discussing a SmartShare approach in such contexts has led Sigma Kudos to reintroduce the distinction between production and consumption. Much effort has been devoted to exploring how SmartShare can be rapidly deployed with different interfaces to make custom information-viewers tailored both to aesthetic demands and to functional needs of different customers. Those custom viewer skins typically focus on faceted browsing and other ways of efficient information consumption, and they can be constructed using the SmartShare core in a matter of hours. In the context of such demonstrations, the standard (full-featured) SmartShare application is most often described as the production environment.

Second, it turns out that the SmartShare concept of lightweight sharing not only appeals to intended customers in the area of collaborative technical information, but also lends itself to application in other areas of collaborative information logistics. This is certainly testimony to the generality of the underlying topicalization plus faceted browsing approach; however, what it also means is that the focus of the ongoing product development process is diluted, and the need for measures such as the aforementioned three categories of feature requests is highlighted. More generally, it is fair to say that the product strategy for SmartShare and potential follow-ups is still very much work in progress within Sigma Kudos and the Substrate project.

Stepping back somewhat, it is time to ask what the ongoing Substrate case can tell us about the transformation of institutionalized media structures in the face of the collaborative media challenge.

The high-level, strategic activities within Sigma Kudos reflect a certain sense of urgency and imminent change when it comes to the (collaborative) future of technical information. On this level, there is a clear direction toward a more proactive stance with significant strategic consequences. It is interesting to note, however, how this more rhetorical level compares with the parallel design project, which is more directly exposed to the current realities of technical information production on the "shop floor" and of existing customers and possible existing markets.

In the first phases of concept development for the collaborative technical information platform, it is no coincidence that the key dimension used to organize the three main directions was user involvement and participation. This is a strongly producer-centric perspective, where the norm is that specialists produce and the degree of deviation from the norm is measured in how much the "others," the people formerly known as users, will be involved and participate. This observation is not imposing a value judgment, but merely reflects the fact that the joint design project started from Sigma Kudos's existing strengths and significant investments in a technology base and an established practice of specialists producing technical information. Furthermore, Sigma Kudos is fundamentally a consulting firm rather than a product development company, and it has no dedicated R&D budget. For reasons of business prudence, the dimension of how to deploy and sell the results was always present as the project developed, which means that customer priorities come into play—and many of Sigma Kudos's customers consider technical information to be worthy of relatively little attention and investment, compared to the products themselves.

A similar observation concerns the turn in the design process in early 2010, when the focus of the explorative design work moved from consumption to production. In retrospect, it was clear that this move increased the momentum of the design project toward prototypes and eventually launchable products. Again, the team found that a more producer-centric perspective provided more internal leverage and commitment at the level where the actual work was done. The explanation again resides with the habitual practices of Sigma Kudos, its professionalism, its existing customers and markets.

The overall conclusion at this point is, unsurprisingly, that changing the existing tends toward starting from what exists. Sigma Kudos is a relatively large, stable, and financially quite successful company. The "collaborative media challenge" is certainly a reality for its key stakeholders, but at the same time it can be easily circumvented for the time being by concentrating on large B2B customers where the legacy of mass media technical information is as strong as within Sigma Kudos. In such customer relations, proposing incremental changes is enough to be perceived as proactive. Moving toward topic-based information and faceted browsing for efficiency reasons, taking off largely from within the existing producer-consumer framework, is a feasible way for Sigma Kudos to move forward while capitalizing on existing investments in DocFactory.

From this point of view, the Substrate project adds two critical components—the technical infrastructure and the organizational intervention—that are both geared toward connecting the present with a strategic future. In other words, the activities of the project aim to put Sigma Kudos in a position where steps toward production-consumption efficiency within a mass media mindset can be followed seamlessly with further steps toward more collaborative technical information, and thus to some degree unify the incremental with the more radical.

This strategy apparently works in relation to the business realities that dictate the working conditions for consulting firms such as Sigma Kudos; it also makes sense from a research point of view as the infrastructure is being designed to accommodate more genuinely collaborative approaches to technical information. For the researchers, a top priority at the time of writing is for the Substrate project team to identify a case involving a potential new customer, where *collaborative* technical information is a meaningful proposition, and to start experimenting with SmartShare in that setting, in order to study potential outcomes and to inform the ongoing design process.

The challenge for Sigma Kudos is to balance incremental transformation from mass-media perspectives in existing B2B markets, where the reliable revenue is generated today, with collaborative technical information in new and emerging markets that are characterized by high risk and uncertain earnings—but at the same time may be the forerunners of the future of technical information. The sense in the project at the time of writing is that the most promising market for this kind of move is software, where topicalization of technical information integrates naturally with the production of labels, help texts, and so on, in the products themselves.

Another consideration of strategic relevance for Sigma Kudos is how to use the company's standing, its brand, and its expertise in technical information production in a possible future where most of the actual writing is done outside the company. This is already happening to a significant extent in the B2C sector of technical information, and it is clear that new roles emerge in such communicative practices beyond the writer and the reader. Some of these new roles include facilitators, editors, and curators—and Sigma Kudos has the opportunity to start preparing to fill them.

Kliv: Participatory Design of Workplace Media

The Kliv system was an early and seminal example of designing collaborative media in a workplace setting. One way to understand it is to look at the final result: a system where medical staff at the intensive care unit of Malmö University Hospital could share and develop their joint body of practical knowledge on how to carry out various work tasks, often concerning less frequently used medical equipment. The system was deployed around 2002 and is a sociotechnical one in the sense that its components consist of digital media technology as well as work practices and procedures.

More specifically, Kliv is based on the idea of staff members creating short video instructions for tasks they are familiar with. The video is recorded by a colleague using a simple consumer-grade video camera, and sometimes takes several attempts to get right (see figure 5.6). There is no editing apart from what the camera itself affords. When a video is recorded, it is reviewed by colleagues for quality and relevance.

If the video is found useful, it is given a unique barcode, which is printed on paper and placed in the work environment at a spot mentioned in the video. Staff members carrying handheld computers (PDAs) augmented with barcode scanners can now play back the video as needed, at the exact location where they need it (see figure 5.7).

The Kliv system was successful in many ways. First, it was used for several years after deployment: Staff members at the intensive care unit referred to the videos through their PDAs when they needed reminders on, for example, how to operate an unusual type of ventilator. New videos were created and added to the collection. Many colleagues engaged in reviewing and collaboratively improving the quality of the video material. This may seem like the obvious outcome, but the reality of so-called knowledge management systems is different: there are many examples of systems intended

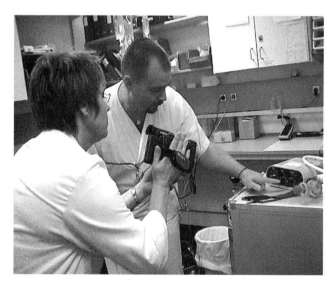

Figure 5.6
Recording a Kliv video.

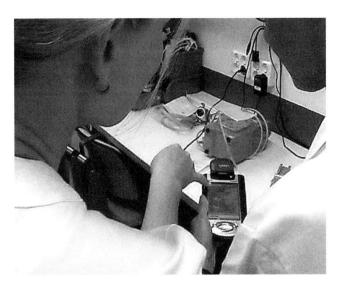

Figure 5.7
Watching a Kliv video.

to support knowledge management in an organization, but which are never integrated by the users into their daily routines once the development phase is over and the dedicated project resources are exhausted.

Second, the externalization through Kliv of previously tacit practices led to collaborative reflection on how work was done at the intensive care unit, and how it could be improved. Professional learning was taking place, on individual as well as collaborative levels.

Third, Kliv was recognized by professional communities as a landmark concept. It was awarded the *Dagens Medicin* ICT prize in 2002 as well as the first prize in the 2003 Users Awards contest. Following a fair amount of journalistic coverage, several hospitals in Sweden and Denmark initiated projects to explore the feasibility of implementing Kliv-like systems in their own practice.

For the purposes of this chapter, though, it may be even more interesting to consider Kliv as an example of (design-oriented) research into collaborative media in an institution—in other words, to study the participatory design process that led to the sociotechnical system described in the previous paragraphs. This process "merely" represents a standard case of well-executed participatory design practice; what is relevant for our purposes is how it can also be read as illustrating salient aspects of collaborative media interventions.

The Kliv project was a joint effort between Malmö University, Interactive Institute, and Malmö University Hospital. It was run by Erling Björgvinsson and Per-Anders

Hillgren,[4] who acted as designers in the conventional participatory-design sense of the word, planning and facilitating a design process in which members of the medical staff at the intensive care unit participated over a sustained period of time.

The project started when the intensive care unit invited Björgvinsson and Hillgren to work with them as researchers/designers on ideas in the area of ICT support for competence development. Initially, the intensive care unit was envisioning some sort of interactive training material, but the researchers were given free rein to start from scratch. After a phase of ethnographically inspired studies to familiarize the researchers with the environment and practices of the intensive care unit, they carried out a *dialogue* phase involving several workshops with the medical staff.

Some of these workshops entailed playing metaphor games in order to foster reflection on the work and to create "generative collisions" between the designers' observations and the staff members' everyday practices. Another workshop was focused on technical possibilities, packaged as generic building blocks within a game set in a hospital ward. The building blocks were inspired by ubiquitous computing, and since the researchers had noticed that the knowledge culture of the intensive care unit was largely oral, there were also building blocks that had to do with digital audio and video. It turned out that the workshop participants considered the idea of linking digital information to the physical space to be the most promising one, and it was decided to move further in the direction of digital video and physical tags overlaying digital information on the physical workspace (i.e., what would today be called location-based information).

The next phase involved a range of *explorative experiments* in the workplace. In order to explore the idea of location-based information, a few staff members agreed to carry mockups of pocket screens during their regular work in order to come up with ideas on where and when they could use digital information on the fly.[5] This experiment showed, among other things, the need for information on how to operate pieces of equipment that were only rarely used.

Another set of experiments involved staff members who were considered particularly good at handling certain pieces of equipment. The researchers made a few videos of these staff members talking without any special preparations about how to use the equipment in question. A large group of the medical staff viewed the videos and the general reaction was pleasant surprise at how good they were.

Combining the insights, another experiment was conducted in which a nurse was asked to assemble a piece of equipment that was new to her. She was given a hand-held computer (a brand-new Ipaq—the first commercially available PDA that could play video) with videos stored locally on it, in which her physiotherapist colleague explained the assembly procedure and talked about her own experience using it. It turned out that the nurse preferred the video format to written instructions and the PDA's small screen proved to be valuable because she could easily hold the device next to the real thing for comparison.

As the design team agreed that location-based videos featuring colleagues would be a valuable resource, the work proceeded into a phase of *implementing* the concept in the everyday organization and practices at the intensive care unit. The first task to be addressed was the production of the videos. The researchers recorded a collection of video clips showing staff members improvising the sharing of knowledge on various work tasks, and then spent time in the staff lounge of the intensive care unit editing the material. Thanks to this move, staff members noted how successful the results were and learned about the production guidelines that the researchers had discovered, such as cutting only in the camera, avoiding the zoom button and instead moving the camera close, letting the people being filmed tell their stories at their own pace rather than interrupting with questions, and so on. The stage was thus set for staff members to take over the recording, and it was found that this handover led to several additional benefits: joint dialogue and reflection between recorder and subject on what the clip should contain; the recorder knowing the work and being able to capture its tangible aspects better on video; and a sense of comfort and security for the person being recorded when the recorder was a well-known colleague. The researchers moved on to organize meetings where the staff-produced videos were reviewed and commented on by colleagues.

Another implementation aspect was to create accessible tools for everyday use. Barcode scanners were purchased and connected to PDAs, and student programmers were enlisted to create a program to connect barcodes to video clips. In order to facilitate socialization of the specific technology into the organization, the researchers organized a training activity during which the majority of the medical staff learned how to make videos and access them by scanning barcodes.

Finally, the design team determined that a sustainable implementation would require organizational support. Even though the idea was that all staff members should be able to make a video, it was deemed necessary to assign formal responsibility for certain aspects of content production. Thus, a review group was appointed with the task of asserting the medical appropriateness and correctness of the videos. Moreover, a deployment group was made responsible for transferring videos to the PDAs and for producing barcodes.

At this point, the researchers withdrew from the process at the intensive care unit and, as indicated earlier, the Kliv system took on a successful and comparatively long life of its own. In many ways, the project was a textbook example of conventional participatory design at its best. Specifically, the researchers played the conventional designer role in that they facilitated the design process, managed its progress and planned next steps concretely, created design artifacts such as games and experiments to tease out the locally-specific knowledge of the medical staff members, and contributed their own knowledge from the fields of interaction design, ubiquitous computing, and digital media technology.

Medical care represents an institution of society in many ways, and this is often reflected also in how ICT enterprise support, knowledge management, and staff training are viewed. On one level, the Kliv case illustrates the emancipatory and empowering capabilities of traditional participatory design to unfreeze an institutional structure (Björgvinsson 2007) and put the practical knowing of shop floor workers into play.

At the same time, hindsight makes it possible for us to see how the specific approaches explored and implemented in Kliv represent a highly prescient case of a collaborative media design intervention, even though the notion of collaborative media was hardly recognized at the time the work was done. For us, Kliv constitutes a seminal example of what a collaborative media design intervention at the grassroots level of a strongly institutionalized structure can be like when the tools and the values of traditional participatory design are employed in a skillful way.

Hacktivism: Making People Fashion-able

The final case in this chapter deals with fashion design and fashion theory, and specifically with Otto von Busch's work on developing a new role for the designer where fashion practice is seen as a form of social activism (von Busch 2008, 2012).[6] This may seem like an awkward choice for a book on collaborative media, but as we shall see, the case is apt for our purposes in more than one way.

Analytically, fashion is increasingly seen as an expressive form for social communication and communality—in short, a *medium*. And like the more conventional media, fashion has an established, hegemonic structure where the haute couture and the leading fashion houses act as *auteur* directors in dictating the trends and directions. Secondary levels of production and distribution, including the retail industry, are responsible for bringing the trends into mass consumption. Consumers, finally, are assigned the eternal state of "interpassivity" (Zizek n.d.) or "radical mediocrity" (Oosterling 2007) in that whatever creativity and expressiveness there is for them to exercise consists of choosing between endless minute variations of the same trends.

The analogy should be quite clear with conventional broadcast media where producers own the means of production and distribute a large number of intersimilar variations for the broadcast consumers to choose from. In the conventional media, there is an obvious critical position to be explored which is motivated by the growth of collaborative media and which, simply put, consists in demanding more participation, empowerment, engagement on behalf of the people formerly known as consumers. Von Busch explores a similar critical position in his work, and thus we find his experiments and findings to be highly relevant for our purposes. More specifically, the critical strategies and practices explored by von Busch for fashion design are directly applicable also to design situations concerning more conventional media forms, such as news, film, and music. The best way to start exploring those connections is to move on to an introduction of the case.

Von Busch has carried out a series of experiments to explore how fashion can be opened up to participants outside the conventional producer structures as a form of social activism. An early step was to develop a series of do-it-yourself manuals illustrating in images and short descriptions how to modify old clothes into new forms (see figure 5.8).

The manuals were modeled on cookbooks rather than assembly instructions, in the sense that they were intended to encourage creative experimentation and improvisation. The notion of an action space is important for von Busch, and much of his efforts were directed at opening up the action space and enabling people to engage in experimental craft (as opposed to reaching a guaranteed and predictable end result). Hence, the manuals focused on methods for creating specific effects or solving typical problems. Since the images in a manual depict a specific piece of garment, and it is unlikely that the interested users will have exactly the same kind of model lying around their wardrobes, the final result will necessarily be a unique creation: inspired by the manual but not determined by it.

The modification manuals were packaged with other do-it-yourself kits and were quite well received by the established fashion industry, to the extent that they were distributed for some time by a fashion company and sold at conceptual fashion stores and art-and-design bookstores. However, they never seem to have catalyzed much of a grassroots uptake, but rather to have been neutered by appropriation into established structures.

Moving on, von Busch initiated and facilitated a series of more participatory experiments where, for example, clients at the textile studio of a rehabilitation center and mental health facility in Estonia were engaged in producing fashion garments in collaboration with local design students and an art association. The results were photographed in the visual vernacular of fashion photography and exhibited at a gallery. Other experiments involved the production of a fashion fanzine that would be shop-dropped into retail copies of high-end fashion magazines, open workshops where artists and designers share and develop their methods in collaboration with nonprofessional participants, and a clothes swap and redesign event with over five hundred participants.

Another line of inquiry in von Busch's work concerns how the hegemonic structures of the fashion industry can be challenged by new collaborative practices, bringing the different links in the value chain—creation, production, distribution, consumption—closer together. One experiment illustrating this is the Dale Sko project, where a century-old and financially challenged shoe factory in a small Norwegian town was used as a forum for collaboration between craft workers and established fashion designers. In a way reminiscent of the Arts and Crafts movement, designers would engage with the factory workers to explore new ways of using and "mis-using" the industrial shoe production processes for creative purposes (see figures 5.9 and 5.10).

PUFF-JACKET

a method for remaking a suit jacket and
matching pants into a new combo

a *>SELF_PASSAGE<* method

© copyleft by *>wronsov<* Oct 2007

1. take an old suit jacket.

2. take a pair of matching pants, cut off legs just under the waist line.

3. unstitch side pockets and cut off arms just above the shoulder seam.

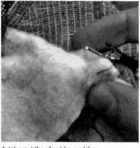

4. take out the shoulder padding.

5. put the legs as sleeves, start pinning at top and bottom seams of the armhole.

6. make seam straight at front., let a part of the pocket still be seen.

7. pull together excess fabric into pleats close on top of the shoulder. attach the new sleeves.

8. make the sleeves slimmer.

9. cut out a part of the front.

10. make channels in the back to create a slim fit. move front buttons to fine adjust.

11. your new silhouette - your new self.

Figure 5.9
Designers and factory workers side by side during the Dale Sko intervention.

It turned out that the contributions of the designers inspired recombination of existing materials, models, and practices of the factory into new results that were quite successful, artistically as well as financially. In another experiment, the aim was to connect creative do-it-yourself impulses with an existing upscale fashion brand and thus to study the possibilities of questioning the whole system of fashion production. This experiment failed in the sense that the intended patterns of collaboration and influence were more or less buried in the details of business-related issues, but it was still seen as an important first step toward creating exchange and dialogue between two fields that are normally not on speaking terms.

The experiments in fashion were carried out within the academic framework of artistic research, and in many ways they form their own results for other researchers/

Figure 5.8 (at left)
A manual for making a puff jacket out of an old jacket and an old pair of pants.

Figure 5.10
Image from the Dale Sko designer intervention.

designers and researchers/artists to appropriate and incorporate into their own creative practices. However, von Busch also offers a slight abstraction by presenting a set of conclusions on the role and responsibilities of a designer who wants to approach fashion as social activism.

First, the designer is characterized as an *intensifier* and *hacktivist*. For von Busch, intensifying entails the capability to spot and reveal existing potentials and initiatives that are then supported and amplified through workshops and other interventions. This requires facilitation on social levels, as well as material skills in terms of providing tools and teaching craft. Being a hacktivist means, among other things, the ability to reverse engineer a system and use its parts to create better potential for change. The do-it-yourself manuals mentioned earlier illustrate how the professional practice of sewing clothes can be "hacked" using comparatively simple methods and tools, and thus is transformed from something owned by the established producers into something amenable to anybody interested in engaging with exploring fashion.

Von Busch further characterizes the practice of an intensifier hacktivist fashion designer as follows:

Reawakening a spirit: Inspire and boost the thirst for exploration and emergence, expanding action spaces through simple examples, workshops, and manuals to form new forms of attention and awareness.

Giving voice to the silent: Create a language of practice and encourage experiments in visual expression to develop a critical usage of existing media channels while creating new ones.

Going through informal channels: Bypass gatekeepers; find your own, low-level paths of action.

Building self-reliance: Teach simple modular methods or subsystems that can easily be expanded into other interventions and creations, developing a trust and courage in one's skills.

Mobilizing resources: Reorganize production, open new action spaces by re-circuiting the existing ones. Use the possibilities of what is considered as junk, making the leftovers of society your pool of treasures.

Provoking what is taken for granted: Help to make the virtual or possible imaginable and discussable. Make models and visionary prototypes. Challenge the participants' imagination.

Making microplans: Think in small steps, plan small, but be open to serendipity. Make examples of how the single informal action might be turned into a stabilized activity and a sustainable project or business, at least resulting in richness of dignity and self-respect. Map relations and prototype protocols.

Forming alliances: Engage participants, share resources and skills, collaborate and build assemblages together. Be a rhizome, a pack of wolves, a swarm of rats. But be conscious of the risks it involves and take seriously the responsibilities it demands.

Intensifying the power: Plug the project into a larger energy system, use its potentiality, connect with other lines and ride their shared power, boost the flows, accelerate the participation, celebrate a shared re-engagement. (2008, 54–55)

This amounts to a designer's manifesto of sorts. We would argue that it captures quite accurately the essence of collaborative media design interventions and the intertwined yet distinct moments of design and production, as well as the new challenges for designers to catalyze rather than to determine. This position, which justifies the inclusion of the Hacktivism case in a book on collaborative media, is not only based on process isomorphism but also on the fundamental assertion that fashion is not only medialized, but to a certain degree actually should also be seen as a medium in itself. Thus, the kinds of collaborative fashion-design interventions that von Busch explored equally constitute collaborative media design interventions.

The Hacktivism case, like the others in this chapter, is set in a highly institutionalized environment: the fashion industry. Like the Kliv case, it concentrates explicitly on grassroots emancipation within the institutional structure, rather than the incremental transformations illustrated in MyNewsMyWay and Substrate. What sets it apart is mainly its activist flavor of moderate subversion; even though the emphasis on empowering action is similar, the main difference is that such action in Hacktivism is fundamentally read as critical—and expected to be performed in a critical mode of operation—whereas the action anticipated in Kliv is, ultimately, constructive.

Accepting our assertion that the Hacktivism case does represent collaborative media design interventions, then, means that the case provides valuable insights into the anatomy of activist interventions that are relevant for the whole field of collaborative media and our understanding of it.

6 {{{{{ Collaborative Media and Tribes

The collection of cases in this chapter concentrates on tribal settings: social structures engaged in collaborative media practices of design, production, and consumption, and characterized by a relatively high degree of communality. A tribe typically is fairly small, its members typically have something in common, and they typically exhibit a sense of belonging to the tribe and a certain amount of altruistic behavior, in that a tribe member "donates" effort, skill, or other valued resources in the best interest of the tribe (while expecting to benefit fully from the altruistic donations of other tribe members).[1]

The first case, OurNewsOurWays, concerns an explorative design concept on the topic of what to watch on future television. The starting point of the work is the assumption that the volume of available and potentially relevant audiovisual material is growing explosively in collaborative media, and the concept illustrates a tribal approach to consumption where design-in-consumption and production-in-consumption are meaningfully embedded to facilitate the tribal joining of forces.

The second case deals with the open-source hardware platform known as Arduino. This healthy and rapidly growing community entails a number of tribal structures, which are examined in order to elicit insights that will be increasingly significant as the infrastructures of collaborative media grow to include the physical medium known as the Internet of Things.

In the third case, Malmö City Symphony, we focus particularly on gestation processes of tribal structures in a collaborative media design intervention that is place specific and cuts across online, broadcast, and event media.

The selection of cases in this chapter thus aims at spanning a rather broad palette of tribal practices and structures in collaborative media, with the intention to highlight differences as well as similarities.

OurNewsOurWays: Social Navigation in a Sea of Media

It is rather late at night. You know you should go to bed, but somehow you don't quite feel like it. Way too tired to stay on the computer, though. Maybe a bit of TV. Thank God those new media people have finally learnt that most normal guys don't always want to hunt, search and browse—sometimes it feels good to simply sit back and idle to whatever is on. Within reason, mind you. Best way to watch TV by far is to watch with your friends, seeing as they all have such impeccable taste ;-).

Nothing on the front page that really catches your eye, so you settle for a live hockey game and come in towards the end of the second period. Adam is on as well and he seems to be just about as indifferent to the game as you are. As you chat casually to him, you can hear that he is a little more alert than you, looking around for other stuff to watch. He talks about these new streetskating clips, and after a while you ask him to zap you in. It is actually not half bad. But then the phone rings, and when you get off the call it is definitely time for bed.

Next day is sort of slow, so you check back on Adam's clips. One of the skaters is particularly wicked and predictably, Katie has a bunch of other clips on him. As you watch a fairly recent interview, you learn that he is actually planning to compete in the festival games in your city in only a few weeks. Surely Adam will be excited to find out about that.

This vignette, written as part of the OurNewsOurWays design process, illustrates how a near-future "user" might perceive OurNewsOurWays, a design concept that explores social navigation of audiovisual media. The work was reported in Lindstedt et al. 2009 as a part of MyNewsMyWay, a larger project mainly oriented toward innovation on the production side of TV broadcasting. MyNewsMyWay was reported in chapter 5 as a case study on the institutional level; here, we focus on OurNewsOurWays because it was intentionally designed to be a tribal platform. In a nutshell, the main difference between the two cases is that MyNewsMyWay concentrated on incremental transformation of institutionalized media practices, whereas OurNewsOurWays represented a more speculative long-term scenario.

At one level, it is clear that TV broadcasting implies a solid range of *established consumption practices*, many of which, on the one hand, focus on the typical living room scenario in which consumers sit back and are broadcast to, within the localized social context of family and friends (the larger social context serves mainly as a backdrop). The emerging practices concerning online audiovisual media, on the other hand, can be characterized as demanding more engagement and taking place in larger, more heterogeneous social contexts. The means of production and distribution generally are more available; the publication of audiovisual content through blogs and video sites generally addresses an anonymous "public"; the "consumption" of online audiovisual media generally requires a fair amount of searching and browsing as soon as anything more than the latest video-gone-viral is sought.

Even though TV and online audiovisual media can be seen as two very different genres in terms of the expectations they set up for their "consumers" and consumption practices, there is also a technical sense in which the distinction between the two is rapidly becoming futile. As TV moves toward digital production and distribution, there is essentially no difference between watching a TV broadcast and watching a YouTube clip: in both cases, we are streaming an MP4 file to a screen. So far, the TV industry has treated this technical convergence mostly as an opportunity to offer time shifting in the form of affordable equipment for digital recording and on-demand ("play") services that make TV material available online after its initial broadcast for later viewing (in its original broadcast form).

However, the technical convergence between broadcast TV and online audiovisual media has more far-reaching implications. Most notably, it is likely that TV will evolve from a separate broadcasting infrastructure to becoming part of the domestic digital media platform, meaning that what is shown on the TV screen in the near future is not limited to broadcast TV material but may include all manners of online audiovisual media. If and when that happens, we will end up in a situation where huge amounts of freely available online audiovisual media are available alongside TV material from established broadcasters and other archives. A design challenge for this hypothetical platform of future television is the two sets of genre expectations that would be in simultaneous play—expectations that are incompatible to some degree.

The brief of the OurNewsOurWays study was to explore the design possibilities of future television based on the assumption that both TV practices and online media practices will shape the expectations, preferences, and actions of the people formerly known as consumers and users.

When this hypothetical future TV goes from a professional broadcast service to a vast sea of online audiovisual media, the volume of available and potentially relevant material will grow by several orders of magnitude. Moreover, when this occurs, conveniences such as structured metadata, ontologies, editorial work, and professional curation can no longer be assumed. It is obvious that we need to explore alternative ways for people to find worthwhile, valuable, rewarding, and entertaining material—in short, something worth watching. Existing work in online audiovisual media tends to focus on powerful search methods, automation, and collaborative structures demanding high levels of user effort. Since the TV genre traditionally draws on rather low-effort paradigms of engaging with the material, such as viewing, skimming, browsing and personal recommendations, we felt that the most interesting design space to examine is one more strongly influenced by *traditional TV practices*. Further, this choice of direction for us implied a focus on localized social structures and a fundamentally *tribal* approach to the project brief.

One author (Löwgren) teamed up with Amanda Bergknut and set out to explore the design space of "what to watch on future television." The method of the study was *design-led exploration*, aiming at creating concrete envisionments of possible partial futures. The idea behind such methods is, simply put, to be able to envision experiencing new products and services long before costly decisions are made to invest in building and deploying them. The work entails explorative phases of *ideation*, detailing of ideas in *representations* that envision what it would be like to use the intended products or services, and various forms of *formative evaluation* whereby potential stakeholders assess the envisioned ideas and conclusions are drawn on directions for further exploration. In design-led exploration in general, the most imminent risk is ending up in blue-sky scenarios that essentially lack significance as knowledge contributions since they draw on technological or societal assumptions that are unrealistic. This risk is customarily counteracted by actual experimentation, in order to avoid infeasible directions, and by basing the creative work on a strong body of knowledge on what is realistic technically as well as socially.

The OurNewsOurWays study started with a phase of divergent ideation and research on trends and possibilities in TV, news, media, and society. Based on the assembled material, five main concepts were synthesized as follows (see figure 6.1):

Broadcast 2.0   A stream of new material from producers, including established broadcasters, passes by the audience and lands in the archives. The audience has access to socially grounded filters to catch things in the stream and socially grounded search methods to retrieve things from the archives. Typical stream functions would be news monitoring and location-based current information.

Many small tribes   A group of relatively few members, who know and trust each other, takes on the shared task of handling a huge archive. An open ambient audio channel with automatic metadata is a suitable interaction form for the intimate character of the group. Other central functions include footprints of group member activity, monitoring based on the actions of group members, and increasing social network visibility. Socially qualified members may earn the right to disseminate material outside the group.

The common construction   A relatively small community produces a growing and living document combining nuggets from media archives with self-produced material. Connections to digital storytelling and folklore, perhaps a flavor of cultural heritage, can be a communicative tool for a dispersed community.

Wayne's World   Obviously homemade productions are made by fans for fan communities, and involve digging deep into the archives, finding trivia and clips that have never been seen before. Video collage tools may be crucial.

Picture-in-picture opinion   Opinion makers and activists connect their own material to archive material, packaged as free channels, and typically presented as picture-in-picture visuals where own material is superimposed on archive material. Video collage tools may be crucial.

These five concepts formed the basis for a workshop with stakeholders from TV broadcasting and the online audiovisual media field, leading to the formation of a direction based on a combination of two of the initial concepts: Broadcast 2.0 and Many small tribes (see figure 6.2).

The final concept illustrates how a tribe member navigates and accesses relevant audiovisual material from a vast pool of sources, including established broadcasters as well as nonprofessionals.

Figure 6.1
The five main concepts (handouts from the workshop).

Figure 6.3 shows ours lead character watching OurNewsOurWays with a fellow tribe member who is remotely present through an ambient audio channel. The front page of the service presents suggestions for what to watch, based primarily on *social metadata* (details follow). The interface as a whole is designed to be navigated with a conventional remote control, in the spirit of favoring TV practices over online audiovisual media practices.

While watching a clip, tribe member lists and communication functions are available as shown in figure 6.4. The member lists include friends as well as *pathfinders*—recognized and interesting people who have agreed to be followable on an asymmetric

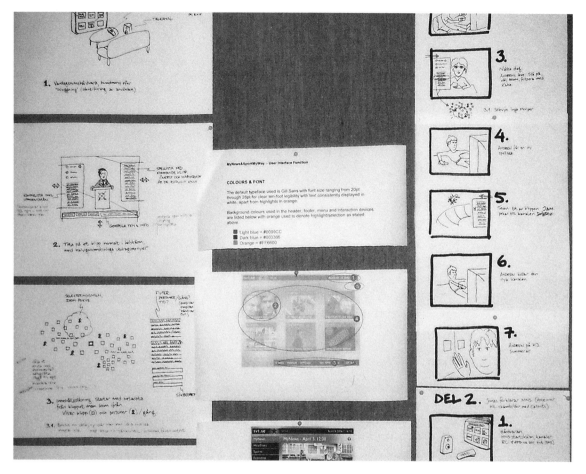

Figure 6.2
Storyboarding the final concept to be realized as a video scenario.

basis. The menu also illustrates basic shape-shifting functions such as limiting content selection on desired viewing time, retrieving more material on the current topic, and retrieving material on related topics. Social metadata from the tribe are the key source for relevance assessments in all of these functions.

Another way to locate relevant material, as shown in figure 6.5, is to explore the relations among tribe members, and particularly which material they consider relevant. Using knowledge of the other members' preferences, interests, and idiosyncrasies, the location of new material worth watching becomes more feasible and predictable.

The key to the OurNewsOurWays concept is the notion of social metadata. As we observed earlier, it would not be relevant to assume complete and correct metadata

Figure 6.3
Watching OurNewsOurWays with a remotely present friend.

for all audiovisual sources, or even for a significant proportion of them—which would seem to make the task of locating relevant material virtually impossible. However, given the tribal nature of the groups roving the archives, and specifically the assumption that tribe members will be prepared to share with other tribe members, we can mine metadata from a particular tribe's use of each clip, including links that have been made to clips (indicating that the clip was of interest to the link maker), text and audio comments on the clips, and the amount of activity that the clip has received from the members of the tribe. By keeping track of the tribal structure through lists of "friends" and "pathfinders," we can assure that reasonable integrity requirements are met. In cases where clips have conventional metadata such as content annotations or information on date, time, and location, they will obviously be used by the retrieval mechanisms alongside the social metadata.

Recent research into the social uses of interactive TV lends some support to the OurNewsOurWays concept. For instance, Bernhaupt et al. (2008) demonstrate through ethnographic studies the significance of shared experience in the context of families (which may be said to have certain social characteristics in common with tribes) and the related privacy issues thereof. The metastudy by Cesar et al. (2008) similarly indicates social communications as one of the top priority items on the research agenda for interactive TV (even though they settle for the conventional conceptualization of asynchronous/synchronous versus co-located/distant, without looking further into the nature of the social structures and communications they call for). Finally, and supporting one of the more detailed design choices in OurNewsOurWays, the prototype

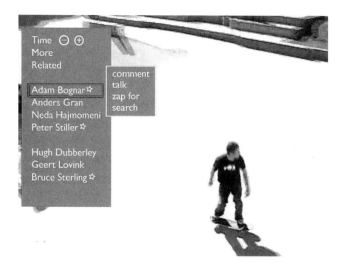

Figure 6.4
Tribal functions available while watching a clip.

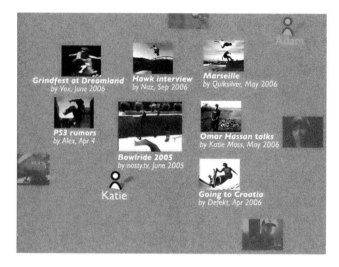

Figure 6.5
Finding interesting clips through tribal relations.

testing and focus group studies of Harboe et al. (2008) suggest a high perceived value of always-on audio channels for distant, simultaneous TV viewing. Specifically, they find strong empirical support for the possibility of "geeking out over a common interest," which seems to suggest that tribal structures are well served by synchronous audio links. Further, their studies show that conversation management is generally smooth and that always-on audio fosters a pleasant sense of awareness: "It felt like she was in the room." Harboe et al. fail to find any support for added benefits of video links as opposed to audio-only communication.

In terms of existing products and services, the website hearsay.it to some extent represents an implementation of the OurNewsOurWays concept for the area of online news. Basically, it aggregates a fair number of online news sources and blogs, and users share what they read through the aggregation for others to follow. Sharing is accomplished through a friend structure based on explicit signup. Thus, the basic approach of harvesting social metadata is similar to what OurNewsOurWays proposes, but at the time of writing it seems that hearsay.it is failing to attract significant interest. In our analysis, the main difference lies in the fact that hearsay.it addresses a medium that is already starting to grow a set of specific practices, but it is designed in a way that fails to blend with those practices. In other words, if you were to decide to adopt the service you would have to change your habits to some extent—and that is most likely a poor strategy in cases where success hinges on reaching critical mass through organic/viral growth. From that point of view, it could have made more sense to turn the approach inside out: instead of designing a new standalone substrate for communication and sociality around news, it could have been more relevant to design the service as a Facebook app drawing news reading into a user's existing social structures and media practices. What Facebook does do, in this respect, is to draw together notifications from separate news apps to achieve a similar effect.

To take the discussion to a slightly more general level, one of the most obvious observations about collaborative media—compared with traditional mass media—is that the amount of available "content" grows by many orders of magnitude when virtually everybody can produce and distribute online material.

Moreover, the growth is not equally distributed among media forms. The Internet was always a text-first medium, with email, chat, and discussion forums forming the backbone for various communication practices. The last ten years, however, have borne significant developments in bandwidth and mobile connectivity, together with continuous improvements in portable digital recording devices for image, audio, and video. What this means in practice is that the rate of growth for online material is proportionally much greater for images, audio, video, and other "rich media"—which happen to be exactly the media forms for which we don't have very powerful search and filtering technologies.

Consider the relatively effortless and elegant way in which we can search and browse our way to useful and reliable text information for almost any purpose from writing a school paper to deciding which washing machine to buy. We tend not to think very much of it, but it is in fact a remarkable performance considering the huge number of hits that any Google text search yields. And the quality of the performance is in part due to the sophisticated technologies for text search and retrieval that underpin Google's apparently simple search interface.

Now compare with the experience of locating a useful, visually appropriate, and legally accessible illustration for the school paper, or for your next conference presentation, for that matter. It is clear from this little thought experiment that the tools and technologies available to us for searching and accessing rich media are having a hard time coping with the growing amounts of available material. It should be apparent how this observation extends to the medium of "future television."

From the perspective of an individual participant, it is no wonder that handling the amounts of available information feels like trying to stay afloat in a rough sea. And the field of search and access technologies doesn't seem quite ready to provide the needed lifejacket. What tends to happen in collaborative media, then, is that people collaborate and rely on each other to get the material they want and need with moderate effort.

The most obvious contemporary example of how individual information access is turned into a social task is, of course, the Facebook Like function. In some constituencies, the use of Facebook can be more or less taken for granted (see chapter 1). This means that Facebook becomes a communication platform with enough reach to be regarded as a backbone platform. Unlike previous backbone platforms such as phone and email, Facebook provides the necessary tools to surpass the threshold of spontaneous sharing: the Friends network and the Like button that can be integrated in other online environments. The net result is that when you read a blog post that you like, clicking the handy little thumbs-up icon is effortless and spontaneous. In doing so, you make a contribution to the shared task of filtering the media landscape that you and your Facebook friends engage in constantly. You provide a recommendation to your friends, and they can judge its relevance and appropriateness based on what they know about you, your tastes, and your recommendation habits. Moreover, you expect and get reciprocity in that when you check your Facebook, you will find recommendations from your friends that you can similarly assess and possibly enjoy. This is a very simple example, yet it illustrates how a highly complex process of social dynamics is put into play to address the virtually insurmountable task of finding value and meaning in everyday collaborative media.

This survival strategy of joining forces is the foundational mechanism underlying many contemporary collaborative media practices, such as tweeting a link, embedding a video, sharing a photo, and other similar sharing mechanisms. There is a general distinction to be made, however, between anonymous and named sharing. The infamous "People who bought X also bought Y" feature of Amazon.com (Linden, Smith, and York 2003) is an example of anonymous recommendation, presumably useful to facilitate serendipitous finds and impulse sales, yet lacking in the social richness of knowing who recommends Y and thus being able to assess the value of the recommendation. This extends also to more innovative social navigation strategies, such as being able to follow the footprints of others. Anonymous footprints—showing, for example, how many times a certain news article has been read—are nice, but they can't really compare to the possibility of browsing the exact articles that your knowledgeable colleague spent the most time reading earlier today. This distinction, which is in many ways the defining characteristic of a tribal approach, is quite clearly illustrated in the OurNewsOurWays concept.

Further, when talking about finding information online, the topic of metadata is generally a key consideration. Scholars like to say that metadata are data about data, or information about information. For example, if you find a video clip online it will have a title, a screen name of the person who uploaded it, a date, a few keywords, and a summary. Perhaps there is also information on how many times it has been viewed, and a few comments by viewers. All of this is metadata that help you search and access the video clip.

As OurNewsOurWays demonstrates through the social metadata construct, when it comes to collaborative media, it turns out that social strategies are the keys also to successful metadata. Scholars in library and information science have debated for many years on the merits of ontologies vs. folksonomies (e.g., Gruber 2007), which refers to comparing professionally produced categorizations and indices with metadata in the form of unstructured tags provided by the "users." With the explosive growth of available material online, the debate has lost most of its relevance—it seems rather obvious that producing and overseeing professional category structures and indices for collections such as YouTube would require impossible amounts of editorial resources. Instead, the focus has shifted to finding appropriate tools to empower people to take part in the creation of useful metadata. Simple examples include the ways most upload sites encourage you to choose from previously used tags when tagging a new item (in order to make the tags denote meaningful subsets of the information collection, rather than single items), or how tag-oriented services like Delicious introduce concepts like bundles to help you structure tags and tag-based access to the right material (Smith 2008). Making it easy and attractive to comment on material is another way to encourage people to provide useful metadata. The OurNewsOurWays concept takes this one step further by collecting social metadata as beneficial side effects, through mining the actions of fellow tribe members. The intention is to leverage consumption—which is the main motivation for engaging—to provide implicit design-in-consumption changing the infrastructure for other tribe members.

Overall, we find that joining forces in consumption is a more or less inevitable survival strategy in the face of the explosive growth of available and potentially available media texts. Sharing and other forms of informal curating are key practices, corresponding to what we called production-in-consumption in chapter 2. Similarly, we argue that design-in-consumption is beneficially realized through the side-effects approach of eliciting social metadata from acts of consumption and production-in-consumption. Most important, all of these practices are facilitated by a tribal approach whereby the atomic social structures are marked by a certain degree of coherence, communality and altruism.

In terms of predictive accuracy, the OurNewsOurWays case takes off from a media consumption situation in which the established collaborative practices today are essentially off-channel (Twitter while watching TV, on-demand services on the computer outside the "TV sphere" of the living room and the remote control, etc.). The OurNewsOurWays concept represents a vision of within-channel, low-engagement practices of tribal collaboration; it is possible to imagine a scenario starting in current TV technology and leading to the deployment and uptake of an OurNewsOurWays-like "future TV" platform. Key milestones of that scenario would be the commercial standardization of Internet-based TV broadcasting and on-demand services, then the emergence of low-engagement practices in the TV sphere of the living room where channel surfing is gradually complemented with on-demand services and content navigation based on interaction idioms that are more backward-leaning than current on-demand TV offers on the computer.

The final step involves the growing recognition that tribal efforts are needed to cope with the growth in accessible audiovisual material and to enhance socially meaningful TV experiences. We find this to be a likely course of development, in keeping with the strongly emerging social structures in collaborative media of many small tribes sharing the same platforms but leading more or less parallel lives. At the risk of bordering on evangelism, we would argue that the level of altruistic support offered by tribal structures is a necessary complement to professional curating in coping with the sheer volume of potentially available material in the collaborative media landscape. OurNewsOurWays is one possible envisionment of how such structures could play out in the realm of "future television."

Arduino: Designing the Infrastructure of Material Media

The story of Arduino starts in the early years of this century, when ideas of merging the physical and the virtual worlds were starting to gain a foothold in academic institutions of ICT and design. Concepts like tangible interfaces, place-specific computing, and physical interaction were seen as promising steps toward a more ubiquitous or pervasive view, where computing would escape from desktop boxes and into our everyday engagement with the physical world.

Interaction design schools were paying attention to these developments and to how they could be integrated into advanced curricula; two such schools were Interaction Design Institute Ivrea, in Italy, and the School of Arts and Communication at Malmö University, Sweden (the affiliation of this book's authors) where Massimo Banzi in Ivrea and David Cuartielles in Malmö independently experimented with teaching methods and tools. They both found that physical computing was difficult to teach, since the prototyping tools needed for students to experiment were very costly and hard to use. Casey Reas, Banzi's teaching colleague at Ivrea, had earlier designed Processing (Reas and Fry 2007), a very successful programming environment for visual designers and other nonprogrammers. Hernando Barragan, a master's degree student at Ivrea, embarked on a project called Wiring with the aim of creating an electronics prototyping environment that would be as easy to use as Processing is for software. The key ideas of Processing, which were carried over to Wiring, were as follows: a simple, flat conceptual model of the program; the ability to try out a program under development with a single click to compile and run; encapsulation of more difficult coding tasks into reusable libraries; and community-driven development of coding examples and libraries under open source licenses.

Based on Barragan's work, a small team formed around the idea with Banzi and Cuartielles, David Mellis who was then a student at Ivrea, Tom Igoe who had been teaching physical computing at ITP in New York for a long time, and Gianluca Martino who came from a background in electronics engineering and manufacturing. The prototyping environment was designed around four major requirements (Banzi 2009):

1. Inexpensive: The price to get a personal experimentation platform should be equal to that of a meal.
2. Packaged with a so-called Integrated Development Environment (IDE), which includes all you need to be able to write and run programs. The IDE would be very closely modeled on the successful Processing environment.
3. Programmable via USB, since many design students were using Apple computers and existing tools for electronics prototyping would require complicated fixes to run on anything other than a PC-style serial port. The new tool should be plug and play.
4. Supported by a community, again inspired by the way the Processing community had demonstrated the possibility of far-reaching dissemination and creative power. The choice of an open source approach was based on experience from previous development projects and a desire to maximize the chances for dissemination and community uptake (Cuartielles 2012b).

The project got the name Arduino after a bar in Ivrea (Bar di Re Arduino) that in turn is named in honor of Arduin, a minor king who ruled northern Italy between 1002 and 1004. The original Arduino consisted of a board with a microprocessor and some other electronics, a programming environment, and documentation (see figure 6.6).

The board has a number of analog input pins and a number of digital input/output pins. Put simply, you connect it to various sensors and actuators, then write a program on your computer that runs on the Arduino processor to decide what it should do.

To take an example, consider one of the earliest student projects made with bits and pieces of what would later become the full Arduino environment: an alarm clock hanging from the ceiling. If you hit the snooze button when the clock rings, it would climb partway up its suspension wire and then ring again after the snooze period, eventually forcing you to get out of bed to reach it. To realize this idea, you would essentially connect a time display, a loudspeaker, a snooze button, and a motor to an Arduino board and then write a program like this:

1. When present time equals alarm time, start making the alarm sound.
2. If the snooze button is pressed while making alarm sound, stop alarm sound, add snooze time to alarm time, and activate motor for a while to climb partway up the suspension wire.
3. Go to step 1.

When you get that program to run on the Arduino board, you essentially have a prototype of an innovative and annoyingly effective alarm clock. There would have to be controls for setting and clearing the alarm, and perhaps you would give your clock a distinctive physical form by building a custom case to house the components, and so on—but the general point is that an ordinary industrial design student using Arduino would be able to create a working prototype in a matter of days after relatively brief

Figure 6.6
One of the original Arduino boards, with the USB cable soldered straight onto the connectors.

initial training, and at a cost that is less than what students normally pay for textbooks for a single class. (It is amusing that one can find alarm clocks like this in gadget shops today [for example, see figure 6.7]. Whether the clocks originated with the student project mentioned here is not known.)

The first manufacturing run of Arduino boards in 2005 was for a batch of three hundred, funded by Banzi and Cuartielles. The price was set at 20 euro each, which may be a little high in relation to a student meal, but was still within reach and far below the price of equivalent tools such as the BASIC Stamp microcontroller. Concerning the community and open source aspect, the intellectual property (IP) model for the software was modeled directly on existing open source software (specifically, the Gnu Public License) and the documentation was placed under a Creative Commons license. But what about the hardware? Traditionally, open source is based on the ability to copy software at no cost, at original quality, an unlimited number of times. Hardware, on the other hand, carries a cost for every copy. The solution was to make the design as cheap and generic as possible in terms of required components and then place the immaterial IP, such as design documents and specifications (where the real creative effort lies) in the public domain as open source. The notion of open source hardware put forward in the Open Source Hardware (OSHW) statement of principles echoes this idea:

Open source hardware is hardware whose design is made publicly available so that anyone can study, modify, distribute, make, and sell the design or hardware based on that design. The hardware's source, the design from which it is made, is available in the preferred format for making modifications to it. Ideally, open source hardware uses readily available components and materials, standard processes, open infrastructure, unrestricted content, and open-source design tools to maximize the ability of individuals to make and use hardware. Open source hardware gives people the freedom to control their technology while sharing knowledge and encouraging commerce through the open exchange of designs. (OSHW n.d.)

OSHW is not an Arduino concept, but Arduino and similar projects have fueled its development. In reality, however, the goals of OSHW are not entirely coherent with the Arduino aim of developing prototyping tools for creative people without formal engineering training. Early attempts to give students blank boards and a bag of components together with assembly instructions basically showed that electronics assembly is a craft that requires some skill; if soldering is poorly done, for example, the resulting circuits behave in erratic and unpredictable ways. Thus, it was concluded that the basic Arduino board should be available in assembled form. A specific decision was to make the inputs and outputs female connectors, since the project team felt they would be more approachable and open to tinkering than male pins.

News of the inexpensive and approachable prototyping tool for physical computing spread in design schools as well as in other parts of academia, and in art and design firms and studios. In 2006 it was introduced to the DIY/hobbyist community by the widely circulated magazine *Make*. The number of online resources grew quickly,

Figure 6.7
The TimeBomb, a climbing alarm clock found in a Malmö gadget store in early 2012.

including information, documentation, and inspirational examples of Arduino projects, as well as retail availability of boards, kits, and accessories. An international community formed and grew rapidly, with additional jumps in the curve for particularly influential publicity such as a *Wired* article in late 2008 (Thompson 2008). At the time of writing, the official Arduino community at arduino.cc has 70,000 registered users and logs over 60 million page views per month. The current list of board variations and accessories extends to more than thirty Arduino models for different needs and application areas.[2] It is estimated that some 450,000 Arduino boards have been made. In addition, there are at least a handful of clone projects such as Freeduino and Pinguino following suit with an unknown number of Arduino-like boards.

More details on the history and current state of Arduino can be found in Schwartz and Laporte 2009, *Arduino: The Documentary* (2010), Kushner 2011 and Cuartielles 2012a. It is safe to say that Arduino represents a success story, as evidenced by large uptake and third-party interest. Arduino has been the target for elaborate sponsored tutorials (Blum n.d.), the springboard for corporate innovation investments and, most notably, selected by Google as the official basis of their development kit for Android accessories (Melanson 2011). In the following pages, we will examine four particular aspects of the Arduino community with an eye toward better understanding its tribal character and dynamics, and ultimately its significance for our approach to collaborative media. The four aspects are hacker culture, art and design, hobbyism, and the developing world.

Arduino has always had strong connections to the *hacker culture* and ethics, including the open source treatment of intellectual property and the strong emphasis on creative grassroots collaboration as well as the empowerment rhetorics focusing on helping people understand and regain control of the world we live in (where there are more computers than people) by giving them tools and knowledge to take apart, rebuild, and create (*Arduino: The Documentary* 2010). There is a sense in which the Arduino aim of turning consumers into co-producers relates to core hacker values for which knowledge is the ultimate power and the key to survival lies in hacking the large technical systems (and, if necessary, subverting them).

Other hacker values that pervade the Arduino community include the notion that information should be free and grows in value from sharing, that activism based on sound technical reason may overtake common assumptions and sometimes even law, and that quality of work stems from intrinsic motivation and an urge to explore and learn. The tone of avant-garde elitism and meritocracy can also be perceived in places. (For more on the general characteristics of hacker cultures, refer to Raymond 1999 and Himanen 2001.)

From a media studies point of view, this is an interesting opening to elaborating the notion of produsage (Bruns 2008). It can be argued that the produsage concept suffers from being foreign to the fine details of technology. Combining Bruns's view with our notion of infrastructure as forming one of the two essential components of media materials, we can see that produsage is not limited to production-in-consumption but that it also, and perhaps more important, entails design-in-consumption. In other words, hacking the infrastructures is every bit as integral to produsage as are creating and disseminating new texts.

Arduino originated as a tool for prototyping human–machine interaction, but increasingly is turning into a tool for prototyping collaborative media. This development toward "material media" will be elaborated further in this chapter; what it means here, though, is that what we can learn from the tribal aspects of collaborative creation in the Arduino community is also relevant for better understanding design-in-consumption in collaborative media in general.

As argued by de Paoli and Storni (2011), it is essential to address the notion of skills to understand the dynamics of the Arduino community. In spite of the initial intentions to create an approachable platform for artists and designers, it is significant to note that four of the five members of the original Arduino team have various amounts of educational background in computer science and engineering, and the fifth member (Igoe) has an impressive track record of teaching physical computing and interactive telecommunications. It is safe to say that Arduino originated in a culture of master-level skills in programming and electronics. For example, when the first Arduino classes were given, students received blank boards, bags of components, and a set of instructions. The first task was to assemble their own Arduino circuits, in order to foster a sense of ownership and empowerment. It turned out, however, that the students' assembly skills were unreliable, resulting in hard-to-find technical problems when students used their homemade circuits in design projects. Moreover, de Paoli and Storni (ibid.) point to the simple fact that soldering and other activities involved in assembling electronics require equipment and facilities that are specialized to some degree. Even though soldering, for example, is more or less taken for granted as a completely accessible makeshift activity in the core Arduino culture, comparable to pencil sketching, it can also be understood on more institutionalized levels as a highly excluding frame.

Now, one of the credos of any hacker culture is "Don't complain, fix it" and it is no surprise that the Arduino community responded to this situation by fixing it. Specifically, de Paoli and Storni point to the example of using a so-called breadboard that fits on top of the Arduino board and that offers a way to connect the Arduino to other components using simple wires that can be attached and removed without the need for soldering. Thus, the breadboard makes experimentation and prototyping more approachable for nontechnical users, at the cost of robustness and compactness: breadboard constructions are considerably larger and bulkier than soldered circuits, which may be a problem if you make something that needs to fit inside a small space, and they are also not as durable as a soldered circuit. Either way, the soldering requirements and the breadboard response demonstrate how the Arduino infrastructure itself transforms in the hands of its community.

The Arduino community is rife with examples of hacker-flavored projects. One that has gained relatively widespread attention is the ZPM espresso machine (zpmespresso. myshopify.com), a startup project by two Russian-American engineers who wanted good coffee but couldn't afford to buy a machine of high enough quality. Instead, they analyzed the process of coffee making in minute detail and then designed a new machine that retails for less than half the cost of existing high-end coffee machines on the market. In their new design, a core component is an Arduino-implemented and quite sophisticated control algorithm that apparently gives results comparable to the high-end machines. Another spectacular example is Photoduino, which is a controller based on an Arduino board that connects to a regular digital single-lens reflex camera and enables fine-grained control of flash and shutter, thus making it possible to create photographs that would ordinarily require specialized (and very expensive) equipment for high-speed photography (see figure 6.8).

It goes without saying that these and thousands of other Arduino projects are made openly available under open source licenses, thus in effect extending the infrastructure by making new devices and designs available for others to use and build further upon.

Moving on, we might recall that the original design requirements for the Arduino project were to some extent motivated by the urge to empower design students to

Figure 6.8
Image taken using a Photoduino-controlled regular DSLR camera.

create in digital media. Thus, it may come as no surprise that parts of the *art and design* world have embraced and appropriated Arduino.

Just as design culture has spawned a digitally oriented branch into interaction design, there is an active art culture interested in exploring the possibilities of digital materials. Gibb (2010) does a useful job of surveying the use of Arduino in what she labels "new media art and design," interviewing thirty-seven artists and designers on their creative practices and their uses of Arduino. Her main finding, which in some ways echoes the practices of the Arduino hacker community, is how artistic considerations of form and function are allowed to influence the actual development of the infrastructure—the Arduino components—due to the open and collaborative nature of the community. The primary example of this is the development of the LilyPad Arduino.

LilyPad is a version of an Arduino board designed for use in wearable computing, smart textiles, and the like. For this project the physical design of the board itself was considered from an aesthetic standpoint, which is more or less unheard of in the field of electronics, but was deemed necessary for the LilyPad application. The creator of LilyPad is Leah Buechley, who was teaching the design of electronic textiles. She found that it was hard to work with microcontrollers prior to Arduino; put simply, they were too large to hide comfortably but too ugly to display on the surface of garments. Working with Arduino community member Jean-Baptiste Labrune, Buechley designed a surface-mount circuit board holding the processor, connectors, and all the other components of an Arduino board but with very different physical properties.

The LilyPad is circular and thin and its color and text are intentionally designed for a distinct visual appearance—thus making it a decorative element of a piece of electronically enhanced clothing and textiles (see figure 6.9). Equally significant, the LilyPad connectors are designed to be connected via conductive thread rather than soldered wires. In other words, when designing a piece of electronic textile using the LilyPad, the assembly consists of sewing rather than soldering. One might speculate that not only does this result in more supple and wearable products, but also that the creative process from the artist's or designer's point of view is more coherent and closer to the material qualities of textiles as such. Gibb (2010) cites an artist who feels that the LilyPad "helps artists to be less intimidated by microcontrollers because it looks different than other electronics."

However, the majority of art projects based on Arduino do not involve any collateral changes or extensions to the material as such, but rather represent the use of functions that Arduino offers in the service of artistic expression. One typical illustration is the label printer that was created as part of the I Am Poem project.[3]

One of the authors (Löwgren) cotaught with Erling Björgvinsson an interaction design project on collaborative media in 2011, for which students' brief was to work with a group of poets interested in exploring new media and digital forms of expression. One of the student groups (Marcus Ghaly, Scott Meadows, and Baris Serim)

Figure 6.9
Lilypad Arduino as part of an interactive embroidery, varying its light and sound output depending on the amount of ambient light in the room (detail).

teamed up with poet Pär Thörn to create a dynamic poem called "I Am," involving a piece of software that would continuously monitor Twitter, filter out all tweets starting with "I am," and present them sequentially. This idea has strong conceptual similarities to the rather well-known 2006 visualization "We Feel Fine," for which "I feel" statements were aggregated from blogs and web pages (Kamvar and Harris 2011); the "I Am" design team apparently discovered the concept independently.

Irrespective of intellectual genealogy, the simple and compelling idea for "I Am" turned out to produce captivating results. However, the group felt that it could be elaborated—for exhibition purposes as well as out of curiosity. The slow, steady, never repeating flow of tweets inspired the group to think of an endless strip of paper, printing the poem and thus preserving it but at the same time indicating its nonarchival and disposable status (so to speak). An outdated label printer was repurposed through the use of an Arduino board that served as controller and provided contact with the Internet. The resulting piece articulates a collective stream of consciousness, the "I" of the Internet, in a way that works well to bridge the virtual and the physical of the collaborative media (see figure 6.10).

Hackers, artists, and designers are certainly different in many ways, but from a cultural standpoint they can all be said to represent avant-garde currents. The corresponding mainstream of the Arduino community is arguably represented by *hobbyists*.

The hobbyist take on Arduino was established early on in the history of the project, as wide-circulation DIY publications such as *Make* magazine started writing about Arduino, for example, publishing how-to instructions for sample projects and offering beginner kits of Arduino boards and useful components for sale online.

It is certainly difficult, perhaps even pointless, to draw sharp boundaries between hackers and hobbyists, between avant-garde and mainstream. To the contrary, there is an ongoing and dynamic exchange of people, ideas, and projects; hackers contribute to

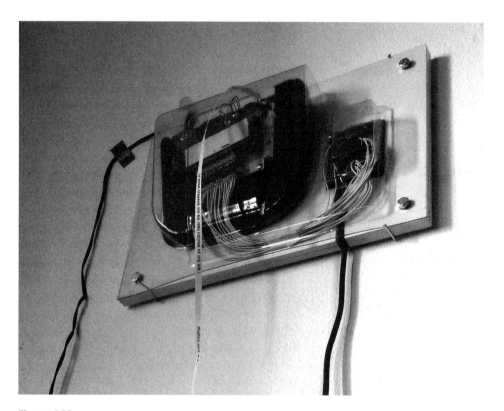

Figure 6.10
The I Am label printer in operation.

hobbyist publications, hobbyists perform work that is acknowledged among hackers, and so on. Nevertheless, it seems to us that there is a difference of degree between hackers and hobbyists in terms of creating innovation and collaborating toward improving the common good that is the Arduino infrastructure. In our reading, hobbyist Arduino work is slightly more oriented toward supposedly practical as well as playful and frivolous uses of the infrastructure. The hobbyists' production is that of "geeks, but a different kind of geeks" in the words of Arduino co-founder Massimo Banzi (Schwartz and Laporte 2009).

Examples of what we would consider typical hobbyist Arduino projects include a biker vest showing the wearer's speed, intended for informing surrounding drivers when cycling at night and thus reduce the risk of right-turn accidents, and a Rube Goldberg-esque machine for blowing soap bubbles.[4]

What hacker and hobbyist cultures undoubtedly have in common is the rhetoric of empowerment and of seizing control of the technology-pervaded world we live in by learning to disassemble something, tweak it, and repurpose it. Designing and building is necessary for learning and mastering the complexity of our life-world, and the Arduino community provides the necessary means to disseminate such a stance broadly.

A particular point that is often made about Arduino is how it enables creators to bridge the virtual and the physical worlds. This is to be understood in multiple senses, including how the virtual notions of programming and open source are translated to electronics and hardware as well as how Arduino enables the transfer of sensor data from the physical world into the virtual world where it can then enter into all sorts of mediated communicative practices. Williams et al. (2012) dub this development the "tangible turn" of digital DIY and hobbyism, and the implications of that turn are significant, at least in the eyes of some Arduino advocates: "That type of creative community of young people is going to change everything" (*Arduino: The Documentary* 2010).

Nowhere is the emphasis on physical-virtual bridges more clearly articulated than in the field of 3D printing. MakerBot is an Arduino-powered project providing open source drawings and components to create a simple 3D printer for home and hobby use. Basically, 3D printing is a collective name for a family of technologies with the same purpose: to automatically create physical forms from computer-generated 3D drawings. Software tools for creating models and drawings of three-dimensional forms have been around for many years, starting with advanced computer-aided design (CAD) systems for industrial use in engineering and architecture, and then spreading to domestic and leisure settings as desktop computers gained in processing power. Today, more or less every computer user has access to sophisticated tools for creating and sharing 3D models and drawings.

Taking the three dimensions from the screen to the physical world has been considerably more challenging, however. Less than ten years ago, machines for milling, casting, or depositing a physical form from a 3D model were extremely costly and advanced, and were being used exclusively in high-end engineering and product design firms. This is now changing rapidly, shifting toward mass-market use, and the MakerBot project is an illustration of that development. You can get a MakerBot kit for around $1,000 that you then assemble into your own 3D printer, capable of printing any model that is created using 3D drawing software. In keeping with the open source philosophy of the project, the 3D printer itself is complemented with a popular website where 3D models are shared and collaboratively improved on among MakerBot users (see figure 6.11). To some enthusiasts, the MakerBot project community is the forerunner of another cultural revolution on the same scale as Gutenberg's invention of movable type (*Arduino: The Documentary* 2010).

Finally, it is relevant to mention the issue of dissemination and basic values among core Arduino community members. David Cuartielles, who is one of the Arduino cofounders as well as a colleague of this book's authors, is responsible for dissemination and for the online community www.arduino.cc. He has facilitated hundreds of workshops, teaching

Figure 6.11
"A little tool that makes it easier to attach apple pieces to your birdcage," shared through Thingiverse (http://www.thingiverse.com, accessed March 21, 2013) and 3D-printed.

the use of Arduino through hands-on experimentation, and his main concern is what role Arduino can play for *empowerment in developing countries*, where resources that we take for granted, such as electricity and Internet access, are scarce.

In a recent talk, Cuartielles (2012a) describes an Arduino workshop with a group of Mexican craftsmen who are in the business of making mirrors. The participants are highly skilled in traditional carpentry, but have little or no previous experience of using computers (five of the participants didn't know what the Internet is). Their business model is to invite artists to design a new mirror, then make five copies of each new design with the artist's permission and sell them at rates sufficiently high to make enough money to sustain sixteen families.

Concepts for Arduino-enabled mirrors were designed in the workshop, including frames with dynamic lighting as well as a sensor-enabled mirror that offers dubious spoken compliments to the person standing in front of it. One of the main lessons for the Arduino community, though, appears to be that the fundamental mechanics of the community turn on the ubiquity of online media. An example mentioned by Cuartielles (2012a) is the documentation, which extends to over seven hundred documents with examples and tutorials that are all useful resources in learning and mastering Arduino. The documents are available online as a matter of course, making them searchable and their maintenance and translation convenient and crowdsource-able tasks—as long as online access is ubiquitous. What the Mexican experience does is to serve as reminder of how much has been taken for granted, and how the ways of the Arduino community are challenged in situations where such assumptions do not hold.

To conclude, it might be remarked that Arduino represents a successful case of open innovation, perhaps even a fascinating story of grassroots creativity and how to facilitate it—but why is it featured as a case study in a book on collaborative media? There are two distinct reasons for this decision.

First, as indicated in chapter 2, the nature of the media under consideration is changing. It is certainly true that Arduino started as a tool for prototyping interaction between people and machines—and it remained that way until 2009 when an auxiliary Arduino component called the Ethernet shield was introduced to facilitate the prototyping of Internet-connected objects. At that point, Arduino stepped into a much larger realm of discourse that has pervaded the ICT industry for over ten years: the Internet of Things. This concept started as a research vision in the late 1990s. It refers to a scenario of future technology where every device is connected to the Internet—including many things we would not think of today as connected devices, such as furniture, price tags, clothes, and coffee mugs. Following the successful penetration of mobile Internet in the Western world in the late 2000s, the Internet of Things concept has entered public consciousness, including in predictions such as the infamous "50 billion connected devices in the year 2020" meme from telecommunications provider Ericsson.

The technical story in itself does not mean much for our purposes—expectations of unbroken progress in terms of more, better, and faster have been with us for as long as there has been industrialism. What we do find significant, however, is the realization that if the technical infrastructure of the Internet of Things starts to materialize, then the big questions are going to be: What can people do with this new infrastructure, how can they do it, and why should they do it? And this is where the changing face of information technology in recent years comes in. Computers used to be individual tools for people to do information manipulation tasks, but now—for most of the people, most of the time—computers are media: digital infrastructures for communicating and collaborating.

If this analysis holds true, then it is wise to start preparing to conceptualize collaborative media increasingly as material media: communication infrastructures spanning the virtual and the physical. And from this perspective, Arduino becomes an important piece of the emerging material media puzzle. A characteristic example is to be found in the aftermath of the tragic Fukushima nuclear accident in the spring of 2011, when it became exceptionally relevant for earth citizens near and far to monitor radiation levels. Geiger counters are generally hard to come by, and immediately after the accident they were virtually unavailable. Japanese authorities were perceived as selective and secretive in their reporting on radiation levels and other post-disaster effects. What happened was that several grassroots initiatives coincided to form a crowdsourced radiation data repository called RDTN (later renamed to Safecast) collecting measurements from people using mobile and stationary home-made radiation measurement instruments, often constructed using Arduino (Gertz 2011; Howard 2011). Instructions on how to make a Geiger counter using an Arduino board were disseminated widely and enabled many people to contribute to the compilation of a big picture of radiation levels, as actually measured on the ground (see figure 6.12).

This and other examples add a dimension to our understanding of what media infrastructures mean as the material infrastructures develop. It also leads to the second reason for addressing Arduino as a case study here. We expect the development toward material media to lead to increasing convergence between the physical and virtual in collaborative media, and the hardware and electronics represented by Arduino are going to increasingly become part of collaborative media's infrastructures. The history of Arduino and the way its community operates can thus be read as valuable insights into the design, design-in-production, and design-in-consumption practices of collaborative media where infrastructures take shape in a tribal context.

Malmö City Symphony: Initiating a Place-Specific Collaborative Media Production

In 2008, one of the authors (Reimer) received a grant from the Swedish Knowledge Foundation for a research project called "Designing for Collaborative Cross-Media

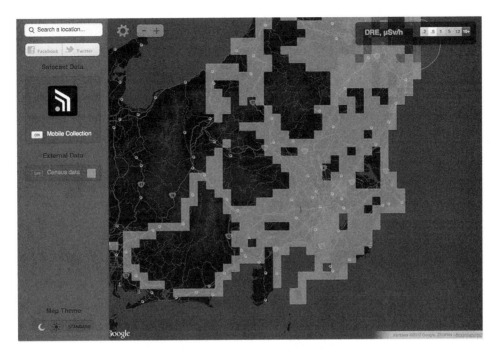

Figure 6.12
Screenshot from the radiation data aggregation site Safecast (http://safecast.org), showing radiation levels over Japan in April 2012.

Production and Consumption." The objective of the project was to experiment with new media formats, to create prototypes for new media production tools, and to develop new ways of producing collaborative media. The project was carried out with a number of colleagues at the School of Arts and Communication at Malmö University along with external actors, both professional media producers and cultural organizations.

One subproject, led by Erling Björgvinsson and Richard Topgaard from the School of Arts and Communication, consisted of creating a collaborative media production portraying an urban city landscape. The project took its point of departure in the following four points:

1. The project should involve both professionals and amateurs.
2. The production should have an open-ended character.
3. The content of the production should have a location-specific character.
4. The project should include a location-specific, physical event.

Given these points, the decision was to work with the documentary genre of *city symphonies*. The idea behind the genre is to portray a specific city during a specific point in time, using a diverse set of images. The genre is primarily tied to the 1920s, when films such as *Manahatta* (Paul Strand and Charles Sheeler, 1921), *Berlin: Symphony of a Metropolis* (Walter Ruttman, 1927) and *The Man With the Movie Camera* (Dziga Vertov, 1929) were made. Films are still made within the genre, however. A later example is *Finisterre* (Paul Kelly and Kieran Evans, 2005), about London and with music by Saint Etienne.

The reason to focus on, and update, this particular genre is that it addresses the meeting point between an experimental media form and a specific, physical location. And just as experiments with the cultural form of film, especially concerning the use of montage, were crucial in the 1920s, experiments with collaborative media productions can be said to be crucial today. The city chosen for portrayal was Malmö, Sweden.

In order to move forward from the notion of the lone director using his or her vision in order to create a particular picture of a city to the notion of using competencies from a large number of actors, most of whom are unknown to each other, a production model was designed: the idea was to start by gathering as many video clips as possible about the city of Malmö from anyone wishing to take part in the collaboration, then to create one specific production out of the clips while also making them available for anyone else who wanted to create their own production from the material.

Interested Malmö citizens (and others) were invited to take part in the production by uploading clips made with a video camera or a mobile phone onto a webpage. The clips could be any length. No sound was required. The topic was the city of Malmö. Three themes were suggested—"Uncomfortable Malmö," "Beautiful Malmö," and "Uncensored Malmö"—but it was not necessary to focus on any of them. Once the clips were uploaded, they were made available for other people not only to watch but also to remix (through P2P technology with The Pirate Bay serving as the distribution platform). This part of the production lasted for six weeks. About forty people had signed on to the webpage and contributed to the production, and sixty video clips were uploaded altogether. The relationship to the three suggested themes was fairly weak in general; people uploaded material they felt was interesting and relevant, no matter the connection to the themes, but the material unquestionably concerned the city of Malmö. Most of the clips portrayed public spaces, and many of them showed Malmö landmarks such as Folkets Park, the city's amusement park, and Santiago Calatrava's skyscraper "Turning Torso," the tallest building in Scandinavia. Another group of clips consisted of images signifying urbanity more generally, depicting, for example, city streets filmed from the window of a moving train on its way to the station.

In early May 2009, soon after the first part of the Malmö City Symphony project was finished, a live event took place at Inkonst, an esteemed cultural institution in Malmö. At the event, two video jockeys (VJs) selected and manipulated the video clips in real time, working side by side with electronic musicians/composers who added a soundtrack in real time with both pre-composed material and improvisations. About a hundred people visited the event, watching the clips on a giant screen. The event could also be followed live on the Internet through the live-streaming service Bambuser (see chapter 4).[5]

The performance by the Malmö City Symphony lasted approximately fifty minutes. A documentary film of it can be viewed via blip.tv, The Pirate Bay, and YouTube (in multiple clips). The film contains images from the giant screen, showing what the event audience saw, but it also shows the VJs and the musicians performing, and the audience watching both the performers and the images on the screen. A short summary (see figure 6.13) follows.

Starting with eerie electronic sound, setting up an almost industrial atmosphere, the initial images of the *Malmö City Symphony* documentary show a ferry moving slowly through Malmö harbor. Except for the ferry moving, stillness pervades. From there, movement begins to take over, first in the form of images taken from a train, then people enjoying themselves in Folkets Park. The feeling of realism increasingly diminishes, as images start to glide into and on top of each other, and the VJs start manipulating and distorting the images, using markers to draw new images on top of the old ones. At the same time, the two musicians continue their improvisations, transforming the sound in sections that sometimes support, sometimes clash with the images on view. Halfway through the performance, the tempo slows down again, and the screen is dominated by images of shadows of people, primarily the shadow of a person holding—and sometimes waving—a flag. Then the tempo is raised one final time, with images from a glass elevator, showing once again Malmö harbor. This leads into a closing sequence that begins with the repeated image of a parkour traceur effortlessly jumping between two buildings. Images of police cars compete more and more with the image of the traceur. Finally, the VJs take us back to the train ride from the beginning of the performance. This time, however, one of the VJs systematically uses a black marker to cover the image shown on the screen. The music grows softer. Suddenly all is dark. The performance is over.

The film can be downloaded and shared with others for free through a Creative Commons license. All individual video clips are available for use under the same license. They can be used to create other versions of *Malmö City Symphony*, or for other purposes (as long as proper credit is given).

Malmö City Symphony is a good example of collaborative media work on a tribal level. It is furthermore an example of collaborative media work where the tribal is also connected to one specific physical location. Obviously tribes do not have to be tied to specific locations; neither OurNewsOurWays nor Arduino are location specific. But it could be the case, as with *Malmö City Symphony*.

On the one hand, this means that there is a limit when it comes to the size of the tribe—or even to the potential size of the tribe. It is not likely that a production like *Malmö City Symphony* would ever create interest on a tribal level for people who do not have a special interest in Malmö. It is primarily relevant for people who either live in the city or who have friends or relatives there.

On the other hand, the specificity of place makes it is easier to identify the population that actually could take an interest. In the particular case of *Malmö City Symphony*, the interested population can be described as primarily citizens of Malmö with (1) an interest in culture and politics (defined broadly), (2) an interest in their urban environments, and (3) an interest in expressing themselves.

This definition delimits the population to a smaller segment of Malmö citizens. The segment is strongly correlated to factors such as age, education, and cultural capital. It is also relatively easy to reach. The population of Malmö is about 250,000, and the segment in Malmö as we have defined it is one that to a large extent can be reached with the help of social media and personal contacts, if done by people and culture organizations well known in the segment.

A special webpage[6] was created for the Malmö City Symphony, but advance information about the project was also made available through other channels. It was promoted by the documentary film club Doc Lounge, and shown at one of the club's events. It was highlighted on the Inkonst webpage; Inkonst has staged cultural events in the city for more than fifteen years and its credibility is extremely high. News about the project was disseminated by the School of Arts and Communication, too. Established in 1998, the school has made its mark on the city through its educational programs and public events. A third important actor in promoting was the new regional media cluster initiative known as "Media Evolution." By creating linkages among new media companies and among business, academic institutions, and municipalities, Media Evolution reaches the majority of people working with new media in Malmö and its surroundings.[7] Another important promotion for the event was project member Richard Topgaard's hour-long film based on a bicycle ride around Malmö, which was shown at Doc Lounge some weeks before the *Malmö City Symphony* performance.

The loose communities that Doc Lounge, Inkonst, the School of Arts and Communication, and Media Evolution tie into are to a certain extent overlapping, but not completely. Doc Lounge is all about documentary film and the club events gather people with interests in that particular genre. The focus of Inkonst is on cultural events, and the organization consequently attracts people who want to participate in them. The School of Arts and Communication of course emphasizes subjects dealing with media, design, and communication. Media Evolution adds commercial and technological aspects. Collectively, these actors reach an interesting constellation of Malmö citizens, a constellation that furthermore fits very well in relation to the Malmö City Symphony project.

The tribal aspect of Malmö City Symphony came into being through the introduction of the project's multiple websites. A public blog served as the project's "shop

Figure 6.13 (at left)
Screenshots and action shots from the live performance of the Malmö City Symphony.

window" and was used primarily to communicate with people outside of the "tribe," with the goal of pulling people *into* the tribe if possible. A semi-public "community network" on NING—free, hosted software with functions similar to those of Facebook—primarily targeted the tribe. Although video clip production was done by different actors in isolation, soon after the Malmö City Symphony webpage was launched it was possible to view a number of different clips dealing with the topic of the city of Malmö. But it was also possible to observe the gathering of a potential tribe, given the webpage not only made the videos available but also made the collaborative work visible as it evolved. The webpage highlighted the production process underway, so to speak.

The gathering—the event at which the first version of *Malmö City Symphony* was produced—attracted a large crowd. This was due partly to the interest in the symphony as such, partly to the fact that it was shown before Doc Lounge's screening of the documentary *RIP—A Remix Manifesto* (2008) directed by Brett Gaylor. What also made the evening very special was the fact that the cultural production happened in real time, live, was based on media texts produced by the people attending, and was all about the city in which they live. People interviewed after the event, both media professionals and amateurs, made these same points. Talks were subsequently held with Swedish Television about the possibility of making a television version of the event with the intent of trying to hold onto the tribal feeling in a nontribal setting. Unfortunately, that project never got off the ground. Another spin-off was a discussion around "Byasymfoni Tjörnarp" (Tjörnarp Village Symphony), an attempt to create a village symphony that leaned more toward conservation and digitization of old analog film material but with the same intent of creating a live event. An application for funding was sent to the EU but the project did not receive funding.

Malmö City Symphony attracted lots of interest, and many people wanted to continue working with it. However, as always in projects such as this, funding is the critical issue. Still, the case offers valuable insights into the gestation processes of tribal structures in collaborative media, with a particular emphasis on place-specific design interventions and on a cross-media approach cutting across online, broadcast, and event media.

III Insights and Conclusions

7   〰〰〰   The Uses of Collaborative Media

As digital media increasingly pervade contemporary society, the practices around them become obvious concerns for contemporary social science. One of the characteristic traits of digital media is that they enable new forms of participation and collaboration by offering broad access to means of media production and distribution—in other words, they can be seen as collaborative media.

This is the focus of our interest and this book. In part I, we introduced a number of concepts with which to understand and shape collaborative media practices. Part II was devoted to a collection of cases spanning a decade of collaborative media research combining intervention and analysis. In part III it is time for synthesis, and chapter 7 summarizes our key insights and reflections on collaborative media practices.

The chapter consists of two major themes. The first concentrates on looking at our own work, examining how collaborative media are used and how they *could* be used. As outlined in chapter 2, we consider collaborative media as a particular cultural form for collaborative, mediated practice. This means, among other things, that the practices we observe and help shape through intervention are situated, specific, and ongoing. It does not mean, however, that synthesis is impossible or meaningless. To the contrary, we find that collaborative media practices can be characterized in terms of a few recurrent themes, which we report in this chapter as a step toward communicating a sense of what collaborative media "are." Moreover, we have argued in part I that collaborative media entail three major practices: design, production, and consumption. Here, we discuss each with a view toward relating our experience to what is known in the field and highlighting our contributions to the emerging understanding of collaborative media practices.

The second theme of this chapter, then, takes a step back to sketch a broader perspective on collaborative media practices in society. The organizing principle for that perspective is concerned with power and action, touching on topics such as professionals versus amateurs, notions of quality and authenticity, and hierarchies in the collaborative media arena. In a sense, we revisit the practices of collaborative media with this question in mind: What is the use of collaborative media?

Characterizing Collaborative Media

Based on available concepts and our own theorizing in part I, as well as on the insights gained through the cases reported in part II, we are ready to summarize the specific character of collaborative media in six points.

1. Collaborative media are forms for practice.

We propose that collaborative media are oriented toward action. They are open for interactions. And these interactions lead to the creation of experiences—experiences that change people's dispositions and worldviews.

The propensity of collaborative media toward action should be apparent in all of the part II cases. Two particularly salient examples are Hacktivism (chapter 5) and Parapolis (chapter 4). Consider the manifesto formulated as part of von Busch's reflections on the interventions performed with regard to fashion institutions, where notions of stimulating action through inspiration and facilitation are prevalent in exhortations such as reawakening a spirit, giving voice to the silent, mobilizing resources, and intensifying power.

Similarly, in the Parapolis case, the initial commission from the city of Malmö appeared to presume a more traditional, turn-taking order of events in which citizens were initially invited to provide quick and inspirational ideas on how to address the traffic situation in central Malmö. The next step was for urban planning professionals to develop a handful of distinct and coherent proposals for change, which were then visualized through Parascopes and revealed in turn to the citizens. Significantly, the designers did not settle for a one-off exhibition solution as implied by the commission, but rather spent extra effort on designing the Parascopes in order that their contents could be changed quite conveniently. The rationale for this became apparent in the project's second phase, when the same designers facilitated a series of interventions using panorama studios together with the configurable Parascopes for workshops and collaborative work with citizens on the actual design exploration of future urban planning scenarios.

2. Collaborative media offer a framework with components to combine and appropriate in different ways.

Traditional mass media are based on the notion of specific messages transmitted to a large number of receivers. Collaborative media do not contain specific, easily delineated messages. Instead, collaborative media offer a framework based on versatile components that can be combined and adapted depending on what people want to do with them.

Again, the configurable and modular nature of collaborative media should be apparent in all of the part II cases. For example, consider how the core architecture of Bambuser (chapter 4) was designed with reappropriation in mind. Sharing functions and an embeddable player for Bambuser video clips were among the first features to be deployed once the video transmission functionality itself had been asserted.

Another, even more obvious example is Arduino, discussed in chapter 6. The Arduino community, which is quite considerable in terms of size as well as in terms of devoted energy and effort, is fundamentally driven by component creation, modification, and reappropriation. Several online forums, including not only the core Arduino site but also online periodicals such as *Make* and *Instructables*, publish frequently with high reach and credibility on new Arduino projects—and more or less all of the published projects represent new or recombined components which can then be further reappropriated by other community members. Key factors here are the mandatory open-source licenses ensuring full access and the community culture dictating that new contributions be described with didactic aims, empowering others to repeat and then extend and improve upon the work. The point here is, of course, that all of this activity is performed by people who could not be characterized as designers of Arduino in the traditional sense.

3. Collaborative media entail close interlinkages between media infrastructures and media texts.

Traditional mass media are based on a clear distinction and separation between the media infrastructure—on the basis of which media productions are made—and the media productions themselves. Collaborative media, in contrast, are characterized by a much closer interlinkage, even to the point that the distinction between infrastructure and text (again, referring to all manners of media content) is beginning to blur.

The two cases of MyNewsMyWay (chapter 5) and OurNewsOurWays (chapter 6) are particularly illustrative here, even though the close interlinkage between infrastructure and text is discernible in all of the cases reported in part II.

The premise of MyNewsMyWay was to design new production tools for interactive narrative in the traditional media domain of news and sports. Due to the close alignment of the project with existing media institutions, the work did to some extent retain the conventional producer/consumer distinction while at the same time aiming at offering the consumer new degrees of control over the viewing experience through interactive features such as adjustable playing time and the possibility to go deeper into related material on the fly.

The explorative design work in MyNewsMyWay showed quite clearly that these aims would require an opening up of the infrastructure from the point of view of the consumer. The more or less implicit commitment to traditional producer/consumer structures led the designers in the direction of a fairly complicated scheme for production-time metadata annotation and consumption-time profile specification, an approach that is rather well known from other areas within interaction design to be cumbersome and untenable in actual use.

The alternative approach illustrated in OurNewsOurWays more or less addressed the same issue, but started from different assumptions. More specifically, the tribal scheme of social navigation coming out of OurNewsOurWays was based on releasing the constraints of existing producer/consumer structures to consider a hypothetical future when huge amounts of audiovisual material would be available online and only a small fraction of that material would be produced by traditional media institutions, and an even smaller fraction would have formally standardized metadata. In that hypothetical future, the design of OurNewsOurWays argues that the infrastructure has to be as open for continuous modification as the texts, and that such infrastructural modification needs to occur predominantly as an implicit byproduct of engaging in text consumption and production. In other words, the infrastructure and the texts need to come together, in order for people to perform necessary modifications of the infrastructure while engaging with the texts.

4. Collaborative media are cross-medial and increasingly material.

A traditional mass medium is a distinct entity. For instance, television as a medium has similarities to radio, but is still intrinsically a different medium. Collaborative media, however, cannot be divided into separate, distinct media. In our conceptualization, collaborative media are specific forms for practice that can be tied to different media, and in relation to that, a crucial aspect is that those practices often cut across different media. Thus, collaborative media are cross-medial in character. They are also increasingly material in the sense that the physical properties of the different media increasingly are coming to the fore, as in the development of the Internet of Things.

Several cases in part II illustrate the cross-medial and increasingly material character of collaborative media. An early example is Avatopia in chapter 4. The core idea was to create a positive spiral of engagement and participation by combining an online forum devoted to collaborative creation with a broadcast medium providing credible reach to larger audiences. Significant effort was spent in the project to create an online forum that would support the production of audiovisual "content" for TV broadcasting, and the community-building process was likewise structured as a spiral to draw on the strengths of the cross-medial infrastructure.

Moving forward in time, the recent Malmö City Symphony case in chapter 6 is a decidedly cross-medial treatment of the city symphony genre, where video clips contributed by the general public meet improvisational music at the live performance event, which also included cross-medial references to the physical nature of media through the live mixing of analog video sources including old-fashioned markers on transparent surfaces (and where the physicality of the live overlay is underscored by the fact that the marker and the hand are visible in the superimposed layer).

Finally, as we pointed out earlier, the turn from human–machine interface design to the connectivity of physical objects is represented by the 2009 inclusion of Internet components in the Arduino framework discussed in chapter 6—perhaps the clearest illustration we can offer of the increasing materiality of collaborative media.

5. Collaborative media make possible three forms of practices: design, production, and consumption.

As we postulated in part I, there are three major kinds of collaborative media practices: design of media infrastructures, production of media texts, and consumption of media texts. All three are linked to each other but have their own, specific logic.

In our presentation of cases in part II, we took care to cover these three distinctive practices for each case. Here, we merely wish to draw attention to the variability that results from the different settings illustrated in the cases, and thus to reinforce our notion that collaborative media practices are culturally specific.

The Substrate case in chapter 5 is a story of ongoing transformation of an existing producer/consumer institution, and it is rather obvious that inertia is a significant factor at play. For instance, it is acknowledged in the project brief that the branch of technical information known as B2C (business to consumer) has changed due to the force and widespread penetration of collaborative media on a consumer level, to the extent that traditional producer/consumer structures are more or less obsolete. In the work within Substrate, new strategic positions for B2C technical writers and information architects are being considered as their former primary occupation of developing manuals and user guides for consumer products is being superseded by more current, more relevant, and more accessible technical information produced by global online communities of nonprofessionals and amateur enthusiasts. Still, the main effort of Sigma Kudos within Substrate is devoted to B2B scenarios, given that customers still ask for producer/consumer structures, and such scenarios thus constitute a viable business case for the near term. This means, among other things, that the design work in Substrate is mainly devoted to infrastructures where producer roles and consumer roles are clearly distinct, and neither has much real possibility to engage in design-in-production or design-in-consumption, respectively.

A useful contrast is the Arduino case of chapter 6, which was conceived from day one as an empowerment effort of framework construction where the whole idea was for people to be able to build new components, reuse and modify components, and in general engage in a fluent dance of design, production, and consumption. This ideal has never been abandoned, and the result is a vibrant collaborative media community with strong distribution of design, production, and consumption across many hands, growing widely beyond the original designers and their immediate "clients" (i.e., the students of Ivrea and Malmö).

Our point is that there is discernible design, production, and consumption going on in both the Substrate and the Arduino case, and to describe them in those terms yields analytical leverage in both cases—but the details of how those practices are carried out and of who does what are wildly different due to the cultural separation between the inert, established, and successful media institution and a grassroots initiative growing out of DIY activist open-source values.

6. Collaborative media prioritize collaboration.

The uses of collaborative media are neither necessarily nor exclusively collaborative, but the properties of collaborative media make collaboration especially meaningful and productive.

This last point may be bordering on a truism, but we still find it necessary to include it here to remind ourselves of the essence of collaborative media. The case of Kliv in chapter 5 provides a useful illustration of why such reminders may be necessary. When the Kliv results were publicized, and particularly when the work gained professional recognition in the form of a couple of high-profile national awards, interest was piqued among other medical care organizations. Several regional health care administrations contacted the researchers and visited the Malmö intensive care unit in order to gain inspiration on how to improve knowledge management in their own medical care units. One hospital in particular went as far as developing their own version of the Kliv system, complete with PDAs, barcodes, and video clips. However, they felt that the quality of the system could be even better if medical specialists were enlisted to script the videos, and actors were used to record the videos with as clear diction and pedagogical performance as possible.

The system was deployed and introduced properly in a medical care unit, where it ended up never being used in daily practice. Eventually, it was put out of its misery and disposed of. What the other hospital failed to recognize was that Kliv was not a technical solution as such, but a sociotechnical approach where collaboration in particular occupied center stage. The collaborative aspect of the actual medical staff creating, reviewing, using, and improving upon the video clips together was the main reason for the successful uptake and persistence of the technical system, as an arena for joint articulation of relevant practical knowledge.

This concludes our synthesis of the salient characteristics of collaborative media practices in the cases reported in part II. As noted in item 5, collaborative media make possible three major forms of practices, tightly interwoven but each with its own internal logic. Two of them—production and consumption—are extensively studied in traditional media and communication studies as well as in scholarly work on "new media," whereas the third—design—historically belongs in the realm of design theory. Next, we address each of them in turn with a view toward identifying transdisciplinary insights that might add to our joint understanding of collaborative media practices. In order to avoid the seductive and fallacious sense of a development-process chronology, we introduce them here in the order of consumption, production, and design.

Consuming Collaborative Media

The practice of consuming collaborative media is a comparatively young one, for obvious reasons, but it is one that is already studied and analyzed to some extent in the field of media and communication studies. Scholars have taken an interest in collaborative media consumption and particularly in how it differs from consumption of traditional mass media.

A foundational observation is that the practice of consuming collaborative media has strong elements of picking out and using the materials one wants to use at times when one wants to use them, and of doing so by combining diverse elements of media texts. Traditional mass media, on the other hand, is largely consumed in more fixed units of text, and, particularly in the case of ether media, also at fixed points in time. The vernacular distinction of lean-forward and lean-backward media, suggesting that collaborative media consumption is more active than mass media consumption, is sometimes used to capture this difference.

This tendency toward more fragmented consumption tends to shape the consumption practice in two distinct and concurrent ways. On the one hand, it is found that people typically divide their attention between many different media activities at the same time, perhaps writing an email while checking Facebook and listening to music provided by the digital streaming service Spotify, and without concentrating exclusively on any of the practices. On the other hand, a single collaborative-media practice can be even more immersive than traditional mass media consumption, as the example of many-hour computer gaming sessions illustrates. Both of these developments deviate from the conventional patterns of mass-media consumption, and at the same time both of them are characteristic for the practice of consuming collaborative media (Turkle 1995; Jenkins 2006; Leurdijk and Leendertse 2009; Couldry, Livingstone, and Markham 2010). We find Ito's (2010) notion of hypersociality as a genre of social participation to be particularly apt in capturing the communicative nature of these fragmentation patterns.

Even though the practice of collaborative media consumption is already quite extensively studied, we find that there are a few valuable insights that we might offer based on our analytical model and specifically on the notions of design-in-consumption and production-in-consumption.

On the most general level, the insight we want to offer—and which our model and our empirical material make possible—is the insight that within the moment of consumption, consuming collaborative media is actually more than just consumption. It can also include production and design practices. This is not just another way of saying that people both consume and produce media today, or that people today are prosumers. It is, rather, stating that consumption of collaborative media may *in itself* contain elements of production or design practices. This is, as we see it, a major difference from the consumption of mass media.

As the cases in part II illustrate, design-in-consumption can be explicit or implicit. An example of the former kind would be the panorama studios of Parapolis (chapter 4) where the aim was to facilitate practices of design within the moment of consumption, and to embed such practices deeply in the overall transformative processes of design, production, and consumption in collaborative, mediated urban planning. The latter kind of design-in-consumption is illustrated perhaps most clearly in OurNewsOurWays (chapter 6), where acts of consumption such as choosing to view a particular clip implicitly constitute design-in-consumption since they form the basis for the infrastructure to elicit social metadata and transform itself accordingly for other tribe members.

Production-in-consumption (producing media text while predominantly consuming media text) is already a common idiom in collaborative media, even though recent controversies on the uses and values of generic comment fields for news sites and blogs show that it is a mixed blessing. Another negative aspect of such generic comment fields is their potential use as spam outlets selling Viagra and tricking other consumers into picking up computer viruses by clicking on apparently innocent links. Reverting to human moderation or other techniques to ensure that comments are not malicious must be deemed cumbersome, to say the least. Our own speculation is that production-in-consumption might work better in settings where the medium is inherently more collaborative—it is instructive to compare the general communicative tone of Facebook, if there exists such a simplification, with the general communicative tone of comment fields in newspaper online editions. In our own cases, the most significant example of production-in-consumption is found in the use of the Bambuser back channel (chapter 4), which was designed de facto by early users who immediately responded to the liveness of the first mobile video broadcasts by employing Twitter to create a cross-medial bidirectional live-communication situation, thus engaging in implicit design-in-consumption to create means for production-in-consumption. The owners of the Bambuser infrastructure quickly took this cue by adding a chat room to the core infrastructure.

Producing Collaborative Media

Traditional production of mass media content consisted of professional media producers making distinct media texts (newspaper articles, TV and radio programs, etc.), which in a subsequent step were distributed to a large group of mass media consumers. This is the encoding moment as described by Hall (1980, cf. chapter 2).

The production of collaborative media text looks quite different. First, as already discussed, both professionals and amateurs take part in the production process. This, of course, is a major change and one that has been heavily debated.

Another difference is as crucial, however, and it concerns the character of the texts produced. Just as the media infrastructure is constantly evolving, so is the media output. Obviously, a media production has to be initiated by someone, but once that has been done, other people can appropriate and rework it. This means the producer has the option to either produce original material knowing that someone else may rework it, or use other producers' material as points of origin for the work. The end result of such reworking—or, rather, the intermediate result—can be a new version of an earlier text, it can be a work where two or more earlier works are combined into something new (a mashup), or it can be work made from scratch but based on what others have done (a remake).[1] Most of our part II cases illustrate this form of ongoing collaborative production, but the most salient example is arguably Arduino (chapter 6), where the whole global Arduino community (which is quite sizable) runs on the core ideas of reappropriation and ongoing collaborative production.

So far, we have concentrated on production of collaborative media within popular culture and fiction. As the cases show, however, there are many relevant uses of collaborative media to explore in nonfictional areas such as news, worklife empowerment, and societal change. When considering news production, we expect collaborative media practices to catalyze a shift toward a more curating practice on behalf of media professionals (we will address this further). Another significant shift, which concerns the standpoint of producers more than the practices of production, is to leave the notion of objectivity behind and focus on taking part. This shift can be seen as a response to the sometimes highly rated and appreciated journalistic work produced and published on blogs and other online forums by nonprofessionals; work that is described in journalism literature with the help of words such as "media activism," "alternative journalism," and "moral journalism" (Harcup 2011; Lievrouw 2011; Wiesslitz and Ashuri 2011).

The focus on taking part is not limited to traditional news production, however, but rather follows from the nature of collaborative media. What we find particularly significant, and what our own explorations in part II demonstrate unanimously, is how *taking part is not merely an option, but rather a foundational assumption* on behalf of the people formerly known as producers.

Consider, for example, the panorama studios in Parapolis (chapter 4), or the new possibilities for technical writers and information architects to work as editors, curators, and event producers in the field of technical information (Substrate, chapter 5). In these and other examples, just like in the case of news journalism, producers go beyond disinterested and objective reporting to take a stand and engage in agonistic discursive processes of transformation.

Designing Collaborative Media

The practice of designing is traditionally tied to the notion of the sole designer designing an artifact for a large group of people, an artifact that is functional or aesthetically pleasing—or ideally both. To a smaller or greater extent a designer may take potential users' wishes or needs into consideration, but the distinction between designer and consumer is clear-cut and absolute. In dealing with collaborative media, it would be possible to keep this distinction if the "collaborative" part of collaborative media were restricted to the moments of production and consumption. However, we find that this is not the case. Also, the moment of design is a collaborative one, and thus the practice of design must look different compared to other design situations.

What does it mean to design collaborative media, then? First, as we have stated, the design of collaborative media is, or at least can be, a collaborative affair. It obviously involves professional designers, and they are normally the ones initiating processes during the moment of design. However, as we have discussed, it can also involve amateurs. Cast in more conventional design terms, designing collaborative media is not primarily design for users, but design with users. The Kliv case in chapter 5 is particularly illustrative of what design with users might mean in the context of collaborative media. We saw in that project how a significant part of the professional designers' work consisted of structuring, seeding, and facilitating processes in which medical staff members in the intensive care unit were able to contribute directly to the shape and function of the collaborative media infrastructure, as well as the production and consumption practices taking place.

Second, the design of collaborative media concerns designing objects or services for many different kinds of media. It concerns newer forms of media that are highly suited for collaboration, such as the Internet and mobile phones, it concerns traditional media not as suited for collaboration, such as television, and it concerns objects that are part of the broadening of the whole notion of what media "is" or can be (the Internet of Things). Illustrative cases in the same order would be Bambuser (chapter 4) where the emerging infrastructure of the mobile Internet was deployed to afford a new sense of collaborative broadcasting; Avatopia (chapter 4) where the work revolved around a then-new approach to integrating broadcast TV and an interactive online forum in a cross-medial spiral; and Arduino (chapter 6) where the 2009 move toward Internet connectivity made the whole meaning of the Arduino technology and community change from a workbench for human–machine interface prototyping to an infrastructure for mediated communication based on physical things and objects.

Third, the design of collaborative media consists of the creation of frameworks with components that both producers and consumers can use in different ways. It is a design that makes many different actions possible rather than a particular designated one. The case of Arduino (chapter 6) illustrates this sense of open frameworks particularly well, as it embodies the values and mechanisms of open source sharing and collaboration from its inception. Of particular interest in the Arduino case is how this open-framework nature is due mostly to the sociocultural processes and values with which the Arduino project relates itself, rather than the specific technical choices made in designing the framework components. In other words, multiplicator effects in terms of dissemination and uptake of a purportedly open framework may be contingent primarily on how well the framework is aligned with existing cultures of collaboration and sharing. Technical elegance in terms of creating flexible components and scalable architectures becomes more of a hygiene factor in this perspective, akin to the notion of usability in information systems development: it has to be addressed to avoid frustration among existing users, but it is not in itself a positive factor influencing uptake among potential users.

Finally, the design of collaborative media constitutes an ongoing process. Tools and services are never finished; they are continuously evolving, being constantly worked upon, not only in the design moment but also in the moments of production and consumption (as design-in-production and design-in-consumption, respectively). Consider, for example, the cases of Parapolis (chapter 4) and Hacktivism (chapter 5) as illustrations of the ongoing nature of collaborative media design. In Parapolis, we saw how the Parascopes were intentionally designed for scaling, redeployment, and flexibility beyond the initial brief—and how they have subsequently been used in several places around the world as catalysts of participatory urban planning processes. Similarly, the process reported in the Hacktivism case was one that unfolded moment by moment, never exhibiting an overall plan but rather consisting of activities deemed meaningful in the specific context of the situation at hand and the present state of the intervention into the institutions of the fashion industry.

In looking at these characterizations, it is striking how much they have in common with the design tradition known as participatory design.

As discussed briefly in chapter 3, participatory design emerged against the backdrop of the design of work-oriented systems and the democratization of work practices. Even though explicitly focusing on the notion of democratization, in the initial phase the distinction between the designer and the users was fairly clear. It concerned the relationship between the designer and a small and stable group of users who shared certain clear goals in terms of work-life democracy in a design process over extended periods of time.[2] However, the nature of participatory design has changed in recent years.

The final decade of the twentieth century saw a remarkable shift in the scope of information systems, from being tools for productivity and coordination at work to becoming what essentially amounts to media for everyday communication, leisure, and entertainment. With the widespread penetration of the Internet and all it entailed, it became the norm for information systems developers and interaction designers to address wildly heterogeneous use situations ranging from the private and domestic via the semi-public—such as workplaces and schools—to the truly public spheres of cityscapes. Thus the notion of a small, stable, well-known group of intended users became a rare luxury for developers and designers.

This transformation meant that it became increasing difficult to identify "The Designer," the master planner who initiated and facilitated a participatory design process with a predetermined group of stakeholders participating from start to finish.

Instead of shaping a participatory design process in the traditional sense with an identified group of stakeholders, contemporary participatory design might start with the designer creating a framework for a process of collaborative creation—a process that can only be enabled, never fully anticipated or preplanned in detail. The designer becomes one actor in a large participatory process, not *the* actor.

It is clear that collaborative media design, just like participatory design, is dependent on the participation of different actors. In that sense, collaborative media design can be regarded as a special case of participatory design. But there is a difference between participation and collaboration. A conventional participatory design process, although "democratic," is still based on a fairly clear distinction between the designer and the other actors in the process. These actors participate, but they are not designers. They represent the expertise on their own practices (which were historically work related), but in our language they would largely represent producers and consumers. However, when it comes to collaborative media, even though there is a difference between the three moments of design, production, and consumption, the main point is that people can move between these moments in new ways and the moments all comprise design activities. Producers and consumers can also be designers.

One reason for our pointing out this difference may be our insistence on the malleability of collaborative media infrastructures, something that is not always taken for granted in conventional participatory design thinking. As we have shown in parts I and II, collaborative media infrastructures are subject to continuous design and redesign, ranging from intentional and relatively sophisticated manipulations such as the creation of new components in the Arduino framework to the infrastructural side effects of design-in-consumption, as illustrated by the implicit creation of social metadata in OurNewsOurWays.

Furthermore, in collaborative media processes, there may not even be any professional designers involved at all. One of the implications of the new media infrastructure is that the means for initiating and sustaining a media intervention are available to virtually anyone, from NGOs and activist organizations with well-known brands and ample resources to individuals engaging in innovation, societal change, or play in their spare time. And as we have already shown, these interventions are possible to make without the assistance of professional designers. In chapter 1, we introduced the example of machinima, which originated with using 1990s game engines in ways unanticipated by its designers and which culminated in terms of public recognition in 2005 when Alex Chan reappropriated the game *The Movies* to make the widely noticed machinima movie *The French Democracy*. The point here is that there was very little dedicated professional machinima infrastructure design going on throughout the whole development of this subculture. A similar example might be found in chapter 2, where we argue with Potts and colleagues (2008) that teenage mobile-phone customers jump-started the SMS industry.

The example of machinima in particular illustrates another general difference between participatory design and collaborative media. Even though participatory design processes can be based on notions of democracy, the major motivation behind design processes is historically to solve problems or, more generally, to address concerns. In a nutshell, the essence of design is that of "being in service" (Nelson and Stolterman 2002) or "changing existing situations into preferred ones" (Jones 1970/1992). Of course, that could also be the case in relation to collaborative media design processes, but as the machinima example illustrates, collaborative media are fundamentally about communication and expression. They are media, after all, enabling all manner of human communication—including, but not limited to, addressing concerns. Collaborative media practices may well be playful, hedonistic, indulgent, experimental, tribal, community oriented, seeking validation and confirmation, and a number of other things beyond addressing the concerns of a constituency.

Thus far in this chapter, we have taken the perspective of the human actors and their practices as point of departure. This could be interpreted as stating that actors basically can act freely, without any constraints. As pointed out in chapter 2, such a perspective has been heavily criticized, and we agree with that criticism; it is not that simple.

In dealing with this issue, it is not only a question of putting the practices "in a context." In our case studies, we have tried to include all relevant actors, and in that sense we have taken the context into the picture. It is rather a question of moving one step back, posing the question of what the patterns portrayed actually mean.

Infrastructuring

We have viewed the practices related to collaborative media as consisting of the moments of design, production, and consumption. We have regarded these moments as having separate, internal logic, but related to each other. How can we understand this relationship? We do so with the help of the concept of *infrastructuring*.

We have already talked about infrastructures in relation to media; those infrastructures that need to be in place in order for production of media texts to be possible. These infrastructures have been invisible within media research; they have always been there but often taken for granted.

This research view on infrastructures corresponds well with views traditionally held on infrastructures in everyday life. In a common-sense view, infrastructures are those structures underneath, on which other things depend.[3] Normally they are invisible. They are noticed only when they break down, and their importance becomes clear. But it should also be noted that infrastructures are not objective, existing entities. Infrastructure is a relational concept. The same entity can function as infrastructure for one person and as an object of focus for another person (Jewett and Kling 1991).

The major points to make about infrastructures in this context thus are, first, that they serve crucial roles in many everyday-life situations—they are powerful—and second, that this powerful role seldom is noticed. It is taken for granted by people belonging to the community in which it functions. It is not natural in the sense that it has to be there, but it has become naturalized (Star and Ruhleder 1996, 113).

However, the crucial role played by infrastructures is not a solitary one. The role becomes crucial in relation to other things—to other infrastructures, to people, and so on. It is not particularly meaningful to study them in isolation; it is better to look at the relationships they belong within. As Star and Ruhleder write: "infrastructure is something that emerges for people in practice, connected to activities and structures" (1996, 112).

In 2002, Star and Bowker wrote an often quoted article with the title "How to Infrastructure." As the title indicates, Star and Bowker here look upon infrastructures from a design point of view. They view them from the perspective of how one best can make sure that infrastructures are sustainable. Infrastructures are to be used by different people for different reasons, hopefully over a long period of time. Therefore, for Star and Bowker, it is crucial to design for flexibility (2002, 159).

Their point about designing for flexibility is a reasonable one. However, their perspective is based on the notion that infrastructure comes first and is then subsequently used. But, as we have argued specifically in relation to media infrastructures, even though initially there has to be some infrastructure in order for other practices to emerge, very soon the practice of designing infrastructure takes place alongside other practices.

In order to develop our understanding further, we return to the field of participatory design. In 2004, Karasti and Syrjänen published a report on two cases of participatory design of communication and coordination services for moderately heterogeneous and distributed communities, in some ways quite closely related to the notion of collaborative media but presented rather in the context of design methodology. In the paper, they credit Star and Bowker for the idea to talk about infrastructure as a verb ("to infrastructure") but at the same time advance the notion on several accounts (and, to our knowledge, pioneer the use of the gerund form "infrastructuring").

The blurring of boundaries between use and design characterizes both communities. Integration, local configuration, customization and redesign represent complex, densely structured courses of articulation work without clearly distinguishable boundaries. Participants' embeddedness in various ensembles and activities provides them with a range of perspectives over use, tailoring, training, modification, maintenance, reuse and design. This allows the developing of systems by closely accounting for the ongoing development of the raison d'être activities with which technology development proceeds. (Karasti and Syrjänen 2004, 27)

This quotation points quite clearly to the important insight that infrastructure design is an ongoing process, interwoven with use. Or, in our terminology, that design not only precedes production and consumption but rather that infrastructures are constantly evolving.

Technology change is intimately intertwined with the changes going on in dog breeding and ecological research, as it is the dogs/ecology that drive technology development. Though change is ongoing, it is not necessarily a simple incremental process, nor a wholesale displacement and transformation. Rather, it is informed by enduring, tentative and open interaction between understandings based on the knowledge in the raison d'être domain of practice, in the experience of using and having developed existing tools, methods and technologies, and in the "leaps of faith inspired by imagination" in envisioning new technologies. (Karasti and Syrjänen 2004, 28)

In this paragraph, Karasti and Syrjänen touch on another crucial issue having to do with agency. As introduced in part I, we find analytical value in considering collaborative media infrastructures as (nonhuman) actors. Some of our colleagues have extensive experience in applying the concept of infrastructuring to design for social innovation and to Living Labs (Björgvinsson 2008; Björgvinsson, Ehn, and Hillgren 2012; Hillgren, Seravalli, and Emilsson 2011). Through conducting projects "in the wild," they have shown how complex and conflictual infrastructuring processes are. There are many stakeholders involved, not just designers and "users," and struggles are ongoing, never settled once and for all: "The design researcher role becomes one of infrastructuring agonistic public spaces mainly by facilitating the careful building of arenas consisting of heterogeneous participants, legitimizing those marginalized, maintaining network constellations, and leaving behind repertoires of how to organize socio-materially when conducting transformative innovations" (Björgvinsson, Ehn, and Hillgren 2012, 143).

In their work, Björgvinsson, Ehn, and Hillgren (2012) speak among other things about socio-material organization. What this says is essentially that infrastructuring works with a material of human and nonhuman actors, thus reinforcing our notion from chapter 2 of collaborative media infrastructures as actors. Further, they underline the meta-design character of the work through their use of concepts such as "facilitating the careful building of arenas consisting of heterogeneous participants."

What the preceding quote also shows is the major focus of Björgvinsson and colleagues on the role of the designer-cum-design researcher in infrastructuring processes. This is a natural focus when writing for an academic audience, of course, and it essentially corresponds to our own position in collaborative media. But what about the role of the "ordinary" designer in infrastructuring?

A general move within design has been to focus less on products and more on the user experience of products (or services). A problem with that move, as argued by design theorist Redström (2006), is that it paradoxically may lead to a situation where the designer "overdesigns" the product according to what he or she thinks the user would want to have; there is no space left for the user to do anything constructive with the product in question.

This could never happen in relation to the design of collaborative media. Here it is not a question of whether enough emphasis is put on the eventual user, or whether a product is overdesigned. People using collaborative media products and services—people who produce media texts with the help of the products and services and people who consume texts—continuously take part also in the design processes. Thus, the problem for the designer in this context is not "overdesign." It is rather the problem of how to distinguish oneself from the amateur designer. What happens to the designer when everybody designs?

This question has been a major concern in the design field during the last decade, in the wake of emerging perspectives such as "design thinking" and "open innovation." To simplify, some keys to making progress on the question involve distinguishing designerly activity from being a designer, and concentrating more on the actual activities and their knowledge needs than on formal, exhaustive definitions. There is no space for us to go deeply into the general question, but when it comes to collaborative media it seems clear to us that the concept of infrastructuring as discussed earlier is helpful. Within collaborative media processes, design practices are part of all the three moments of collaborative media, not just the design moment, and the professional designer has a role to play in all three. At the same time, following Björgvinsson. Ehn, and Hillgren (2012), it is reasonable to expect that a major role will be one of facilitating, of enabling other people's designing, producing, and consuming.

Thus, the concept of infrastructuring is crucial in order to understand design processes and the role of the designer. But the concept as such does not by necessity privilege the design actor. It should rather be regarded as generally helpful in understanding the collaborative media process that links humans to nonhumans.

Figure 7.1 visualizes how we view the relationship between collaborative media and the practices related to it; a relationship involving a number of actors engaged in different moments that together make up the processes of infrastructuring, with the outcomes dependent on specific articulations. It also concludes the first theme of the chapter, where we have concentrated on synthesizing insights from our own collaborative media work. The remainder of the chapter is devoted to a broader perspective on the uses of collaborative media.

What Is the Use of Collaborative Media?

To simplify yet attempt to capture the Zeitgeist, existing perspectives on collaborative media fall into two main categories. The first is what could be called the bright side, and it is characterized by somewhat idealistic assumptions concerning the emancipatory powers of collaborative media in terms of enabling direct democracy and grassroots activism, leveling the playing field for creative expression by bypassing the existing media distribution monopolies, and so on.

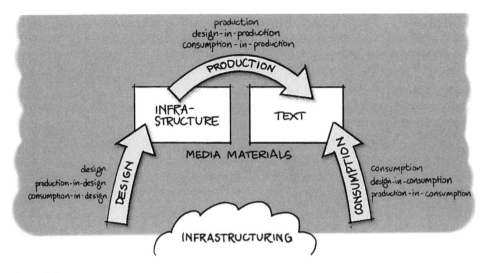

Figure 7.1
The moments and practices of collaborative media, subsumed to infrastructuring.

The second category, the dark side, correspondingly, comprises critical and analytical perspectives emphasizing the dangers, drawbacks, and negative aspects of collaborative media and participatory culture. Typical topics include passivity and interpassivity, long-term detrimental effects on cognition and concentration, social abuse and the growing lack of empathy, quantity taking the place of quality, and how the demands on individual choice grow beyond reasonable limits.

A useful introduction to the overall flavor of the debate is the recent collection by Mark Bauerlein (2011), tellingly entitled *The Digital Divide: Arguments For and Against Facebook, Google, Texting, and the Age of Social Networking*. In it, the most vocal proponents for bright-side and dark-side perspectives are represented with seminal pieces from the last decade of digital media penetration and uptake. It may be argued on the one hand that the bright-side perspectives are naive and overly optimistic, which may be related to the fact that bright-side proponents often include designers, developers, media entrepreneurs, technology providers, and other roles directly involved in creating the tools and platforms that make up the collaborative mediascapes. Dark-side perspectives, on the other hand, are often developed and voiced as analyses and criticism of existing and emerging practices, as is the norm in social science. Consequentially, dark-side proponents and perspectives are generally positioned at a distance from the arenas where the collaborative media are shaped and deployed.

Moreover, there is a tendency in this kind of debate toward taking simplified clear-cut stands for either one position or the other, and toward treating collaborative media as the independent variable in a causal relationship. Briefly, we find this trend makes it hard to make the discussions constructive. In our view, collaborative media are a complex web of situated, ongoing practices. As we have demonstrated throughout this book, it is not very meaningful to conclude that being on Facebook "leads to" symptoms of stress or to small-business success, for example. To us, it is rather a matter of getting on with one's life with the use of many forms of mediated communication, of which Facebook is one.

What we find notable, though, is that Facebook and other collaborative media represent a relative novelty in terms of human mediated communication and that we collectively haven't reached maturity when it comes to engaging in collaborative media practices. From this standpoint, bright-side perspectives as well as dark-side ones come across as rhetorical positions in an ongoing dialogue intended to shape the novel, emerging practices of collaborative media. And that standpoint is exactly what we find to be the most fruitful one, based on our notion of collaborative media as a particular and emerging cultural form.

For us, academic work and the outcomes of such work cannot and should not be separated from the views of the researchers conducting it. Researchers choose some research questions rather than others; work is carried out from one perspective rather than another. These things obviously have a bearing on one's results. And furthermore, there is also the question of taking a moral stand, a question of why we do what we do. As researchers we want to make a difference. We want some things to happen rather than others. We intervene.

Of course, this view of academic work and research is recurrent throughout this book. One concrete example is the Avatopia case in chapter 4. The project emanated from the researchers' appreciation for the energy and passion found among the relatively few young teenagers dedicated to changing society for the better (as opposed to merely complaining about it, or protesting against it, or fighting it through extralegal means). There was no premeditation of exactly what "better" should mean in this context. Still, the researchers' decision to facilitate the project—providing resources in the form of research grants and trusted contacts with crucial actors in "adult society" such as the national public television company, as well as necessary design and meta-design skills—and to coordinate and publicize the joint work was a clear stand in favor of nonviolent grassroots activism.

The ongoing shaping of the cultural form that is collaborative media is marked by extreme bright-side and dark-side positions, reflecting the relative novelty of the topic and the sense in which we as a collective are struggling to come to terms with it. However, by concentrating on more specific themes, we think it possible to advance the dialogue. One such theme that has attracted particular public attention is the openness of collaborative media and how that relates to more institutionalized notions of media structures. We then move on to start unpacking the underlying aspects of power and influence that pervade collaborative media as they do any other cultural form.

The Openness of Collaborative Media

Earlier in this chapter, we outlined the specific characteristics of collaborative media—what makes collaborative media different from other cultural forms. One particularly salient observation is that the cultural form of collaborative media is open, in the same way that texts can be open (see the discussion in chapter 2). In other words, collaborative media can take different shapes and be used in different ways. It is a form with specific characteristics but within the framework of these characteristics things can—and will—change. A telling example of this openness is Bambuser (chapter 4), where live video broadcasts on ongoing revolutions, wars, and other matters of life and death sit comfortably next to the video stream from a grandchild's birthday party.

The development of Bambuser was essentially fueled by the desire to democratize video broadcasting. This ties in with one of the most frequent observations on collaborative media: they challenge traditional media structures by equalizing the access to means of media production and distribution. That observation, in turn, develops in different directions depending on whether your position is one of defending existing structures or one of advocating a leveling of the playing field. Specifically, it plays out in the ongoing discussion of professionals versus amateurs (the Pro-Am issue), and the related topics of the quality and authenticity of media texts.

Professionals versus Amateurs

It is unquestionably the case that the properties of collaborative media have made it possible for more people to take part in the design of the infrastructure and in the production of media texts than was the case for traditional mass media. But will this lead to the disappearance of the distinction between professionals and amateurs? In the future, will there no longer be any media professionals? That could arguably happen, but it will not happen by necessity. The outcome is not settled but rather open to exploration and intervention as illustrated in our own work in collaboration with established media institutions.

Cases such as Avatopia (chapter 4), MyNewsMyWay and Substrate (chapter 5), and OurNewsOurWays and Malmö City Symphony (chapter 6) all represent joint experimentation where researchers and mass media actors jointly investigate new possible roles and positions in a future media landscape marked by emerging collaborative media practices. Specifically, we anticipate a continued demand for the competencies of media professionals, even though the exact tasks will most likely change somewhat. In the field of news media, for instance, we expect a shift of emphasis from writing to editing (to put it simply). When "everybody" produces content in the borderland of citizen journalism and the blogosphere, the scarce resource is rather the skills that have to do with surveying, selecting, compiling, and narrating over time through a trusted and predictable brand—in short, the practice of *curating*. We find it likely that people will start prioritizing their time more realistically in the moment of consumption once the initial enchantment of being able to find your own news wears off and the volume of technically available material becomes obviously overwhelming. If and when that happens, then curating might emerge as the primary monetizable design and production practice in collaborative news media (assuming, of course, that payment mechanisms are sufficiently streamlined as emphasized by Lanchester 2010).

A similar line of argument applies for structurally similar media domains, such as the B2C branch of technical writing as illuminated in the Substrate case. In the argument of Jarvis (2009), it extends more or less to the whole question of Internet content. His epigrammatic prediction is that "algorithm-aided human writing will meet human-aided algorithmic curation; quality will rise."

It should be pointed out, however, that professional journalism is not about curation skills only. In investigative journalism, for instance, the professional role entails a whole package of skills, tools, privileged access to information, and even particular societal rights (such as the guarantee of source anonymity) that stands apart from the infrastructural openness of collaborative media platforms. Similar specific arguments are likely to exist in most domains where professional/amateur distinctions are contested, and need to be considered in relation to the preceding general observations. To further complicate the issue, there is also a reasonable institution-critical position essentially holding that "user-generated content" is a way for corporations to get free labor (Terranova 2004; Andrejevic 2011), in collaborative media as well as open-innovation contexts. It seems clear to us that there are no general answers to be expected, but rather a contested territory of agonistic Pro-Am debate that can fruitfully be approached from several points of view.

Another much-debated issue following from the discussion of professionals versus amateurs is the question of intellectual property. Behind our current notions of intellectual property is the need to assert ownership of nonmaterial products in order to fit them into a monetized economy. A typical position of the music copyright lobby, for example, is that artists and songwriters should be paid for their work. At the same time, heavy criticism has been fielded at the institutions of the music industries for hampering creativity, diverting earnings to middlemen, and overlooking independent quality and talent. It is instructive, for example, to study how much was made in the public debate of Lily Allen's rise to stardom through the use of a MySpace page in the mid-2000s. In a way, she was turned into a symbol of the liberating and disruptive power of collaborative media versus the established institutions (and in that process, it was typically left out that she already had a relatively long career behind her, even including conventional record contracts). At the time of writing, it would appear as if Spotify represents a step forward, perhaps even a synthesis in the Hegelian sense, in the ongoing shaping of an emerging combined music and collaborative media industry. Thanks to enormous amounts of licensing footwork, the Spotify user can access significant proportions of "all available music," thus fulfilling the liberating dream of collaborative media. At the same time, systems are in place behind the scenes of Spotify to ensure that intellectual property owners get paid when a song is played. The general reception of Spotify appears to validate the viability of this synthesis and indirectly also lend support to Lanchester's (2010) point regarding the significance of streamlined payment mechanisms. Thus it can be read as a data point indicating that new positions are being created with respect to the professional versus amateur distinction, at least as far as intellectual property issues are concerned.

Finally, to follow Keen (2007) into our next topic of discussion, one of the traditional purposes of a professional institutional structure is to ensure quality. Journalists are trained and vetted, authors are subject to reviews and editorial judgment before publication, and so on. Keen sees the bright-side rhetoric surrounding collaborative media as a "cult of the amateur," and articulates a concern for the future of cultural production in terms of quality.

Quality

A heated debate is going on concerning the quality of the collaborative media texts. Are we witnessing a steady decline in standards or is it the case that, with new groups of media producers gaining access, we can expect the invention of new genres and new forms of collaborative work that will transform the cultural climate for good? This is also a question awaiting an answer.

Our own work draws attention to the fact that quality is not a simple notion. Let us first have a look at Malmö City Symphony (chapter 6). That project is explicitly set up in relation to one specific film genre. In working within a genre, there are certain rules and conventions to follow. You also must know when boundaries can and cannot be pushed—a general concern when working with genres. In the particular case of Malmö City Symphony, an interesting aspect is that the genre the project is set up in relation to—city symphony films—happens to be one of the most special and highly valued film genres altogether. The demands on people working with this genre, therefore, are particularly intense. Even more, making it collaboratively, and then presenting it live, can be considered a risky endeavor. However, the fact that Malmö City Symphony *is* a collaborative, cross-medial work means that it cannot be judged in traditional terms. It belongs to a cultural form that is not "settled"; there are no commonly accepted hierarchies. It is even difficult to know what it is one should evaluate: is it the performance or the film of the performance, or is it the design of the whole project? Given this, it is probably more reasonable to view the project as one that may feed the ongoing discussions on how to assess quality in cross-media productions, rather than as a project to be evaluated in itself.

Let us move on to the Kliv case in chapter 5. The quality of the video clips did not only have to do with their medical accuracy (although that was certainly a foundational aspect, as indicated by the emergence of a peer review process and several instances of content revision), and not at all with production quality in the conventional sense (the clips were only edited in the camera, and they used its built-in microphone for audio recording, which obviously implies sub-par quality in technical production terms). Instead, the key quality of the video clips was of a sociotechnical nature: the clips represented a shared and ongoing collegial effort to articulate knowledge, improve practice, support one's colleagues, and share individuals' particular expertise. This is the reason, we argue, for the persistent use of the system in the intensive care unit and for our claim that it represented a knowledge management system of high quality.

Contrast the Kliv case with the highly evocative finding in the Parapolis case (chapter 4) concerning the panorama studio process and how it engaged Nydala residents in the joint exploration of urban planning scenarios for their neighborhood. When one of the designers put in a night's effort to take a set of sketches made by residents and turn them into a photorealistic Parascope rendering of Nydala square, the resulting dialogue the next day took on a completely different flavor. Topics pertaining to this more detailed realization were addressed, which is not surprising given the more detailed nature of the new rendering, but there was also a more general exploration of the amount of greenery on the square. This latter point added a new dimension to the participatory planning process and can thus be deemed valuable. A reasonable explanation for its appearance is that the sketching techniques used by residents (including stickies and rough marker drawing) did not offer expressive means to denote greenery, whereas the photorealistic rendering executed by the designer added greenery to the available sketching vocabulary. In other words, what is normally called high production quality was found beneficial in the Parapolis case, unlike the Kliv case.

Thus we can demonstrate by example that the quality of collaborative media texts is a situated and nontrivial concept. This should not come as a surprise given our fundamental view of collaborative media as a cultural form. Moreover, it largely means that quality needs to be problematized in every new collaborative media intervention, rather than being treated as a general and externally defined criterion. This does not mean that everything is relative, however. Turning to the literature on popular culture and fiction, we find a lot of relevance for collaborative media by studying the concepts of authenticity and creativity.

In evaluating pieces of art, *authenticity* has traditionally been regarded as highly important. This concerns both the work created and the intention of the artist creating it. It has to do with the sincerity and the truthfulness involved and it has to do with the artist having a unique voice and the artwork being original. Given the characteristics of collaborative media, it would be difficult to regard authenticity as a central notion if it were to be defined in this way. However, such a definition can be questioned, or at least problematized.

It has been argued that authenticity is less of a quality inherent in either the voice of the artist or in the work of itself, and more of a chosen *style* (Grossberg 1992). A singer using an acoustic guitar is often perceived to be more authentic than a singer using a synthesizer. Obviously, such perceptions are based on conventions regarding what authenticity is all about; a singer/guitarist is not by definition more authentic than is a singer/synthesizer player. From this follows that it is difficult to regard authenticity as a characteristic solely residing in the artist or in the work. It is rather the case that authenticity is tied to the relationship between the artist and the work, and the consumers of the work in historically specific settings (Moore 2002).

This means that collaborative media—even though they consist of components drawn from different places and even though they are not produced by the lone artist having full control—can have a value that could be called authentic. At any particular point in time, there is something that could be called a work that could be consumed—or analyzed in relation to other pieces of work. It is then up to the consumer or the reviewer to perceive it from the perspective of authenticity, if he or she would want to. It has to be remembered that the particular work may look completely different not long after it has been viewed or consumed. But it does not make it by definition less authentic. The video clips of the Kliv case in chapter 5 are a particularly pertinent case in point here. The sociotechnical quality that we alluded to earlier in this chapter could arguably be seen as authenticity, but grounded in a dynamic workplace community of practice rather than in a conventional artistic notion.

Authenticity is closely related to *creativity*, which may be the more constructive notion to apply in relation to the production of cultural works. Creativity is similar to the notion of authenticity in that it is concerned with artistic value and quality, but it is a broader notion. It also has a clearer focus on the production of something new, which obviously is relevant in relation to collaborative media. However, there is also a connotation of uniqueness, which may be problematic in that context.

In analyzing audio mashups, David J. Gunkel (2008) argues that these are evaluated along a dimension where one extreme considers mashups as derivative, inauthentic, and maybe even illegal, whereas the other extreme regards them as innovative and creative. There is no reason to argue generally for the correctness of either position. But, as Gunkel points out, it is crucial to avoid the trap of tying cultural quality to an unreflexive notion of authenticity or originality. In looking at music recordings historically, it has never been easy to identify the primary creator of a particular piece of recording. Is it the musicians? The producer? The songwriter? As Gunkel writes: "The mashup, therefore, does not so much violate authorship as it exploits and demonstrates that the concept of authorship has always been a construct that has its own history, assumptions, and political interests" (501).

The question of authorship is equally complicated in discussing other forms of traditional cultural productions, such as film productions. And audio mashups can be regarded as typical examples of collaborative media productions. Looking at the lineage, it could be argued that there is continuity between traditional cultural productions and collaborative media productions in the sense that the former often have been collaborative as well. The open-endedness of collaborative media productions is different, however, and so is explicitly reusing other people's texts.

Writing songs and making films have always been practices based on the notion of building on other people's works. Works are made within specific genres and new works within a genre are based on previous works within that genre. References to other people's works can then be made more or less explicit in the creation of a new work (Neale 1980).

What is new is the practice of not only referring to but also explicitly using pieces of other people's work. There is a legal side to this, as exemplified by the chapter 1 story of *Downfall* parodies, copyright issues, and YouTube takedown requests. But there is also an aesthetic and creative side. And as discussed before, the possibilities offered by collaborative media tools have enabled nonprofessionals to produce works of their own. They may not always achieve the same technological standard as works produced by professionals. But if they are "good enough" (Engholm 2010) they have the potential to reach large audiences.

Tying back to the notion of quality in general, we might even argue that the home-grown quality of a nonprofessional piece can be particularly appealing to viewers suffering from spectacle fatigue after years of being exposed to professional works of increasingly higher production quality. This position appears to be borne out in several recent examples of advertising campaigns, such as the Levi's jeans backflip videos that went viral in 2008 on the Internet, where large budgets and professional production machinery are employed to emulate the look and feel of "user-generated content." We are also reminded of Theel's (2012) recent study showing that major American news outlets devote forty times more coverage to the Kardashians (a family of reality-TV celebrities) than to ocean acidification. What this study seems to show is that fake authenticity is indeed treated as an institutional panacea for spectacle fatigue. From a collaborative media standpoint, there is comfort in the observation that collaborative practices of a nonprofessional nature appear to be somewhat influential, even though the appropriations of those practices by media institutions sometimes seem more like mockery than anything else.

Power and Action

Earlier we introduced the somewhat exaggerated positions of bright-side and dark-side perspectives, and used them to discuss the openness of collaborative media in relation to the institutionalization of other cultural forms. However, those perspectives are too simplistic to help us unpack the notions of power, influence, and freedom to act. It seems clear already from the preceding discussion that the playing field of collaborative media is not entirely level, in spite of the bright-side evangelism. But how can we understand the power structures and their dynamics more precisely?

According to Michel Foucault, neoliberal societies are characterized by what he terms *governmentality*. By this, Foucault means the ways in which citizens in contemporary societies are subject to control. This control emanates on the one hand from governments and other external actors, but it also comes from inside: individuals subject themselves to being disciplined (Foucault 1991).

This line of reasoning has been applied in relation to information and communication technologies, to new media and to video games, with analyses pointing to how effective these technologies are as tools, aiding in the dual process that Foucault calls "disciplinization." For instance, it has been argued that new media devices make it easier to navigate in urban environments. Cities become visible, maybe even transparent. But, as Brighenti (2011) argues, such perspectives downplay the dark sides of the development, namely the possibilities of surveillance that follow these technologies. Continuous geolocation of mobile devices makes it possible to closely follow any individual, and it makes it possible to fairly accurately predict where he or she will be next. As Lahlou argues: "We are creating a system that will, in a distributed and ubiquitous manner, be aware of all that we do" (2008, 302).

But surveillance and control do not only concern external movements. They also concern the body. Millington takes the Nintendo Wii as an example, a game console with remote controller that enables a player's physical movements to control action on a video screen. It is primarily oriented toward sport-based game play, but the Wii has also been used in relation to health and fitness, with software recording bodily measurements and other data. Thus, the Wii can be used to help people to lose weight and at the same time functions as a tool for controlling people's bodies, Millington (2009) argues.

The surveillance and disciplining described here are made possible by digital media, but also demand that people participate voluntarily; that is the second aspect of governmentality outlined by Foucault. In order for this surveillance and disciplining to work, people have to enable geolocation on their mobile devices, and they have to play on the Wii platform. And people do. It seems as if we are quite prone to giving away in public online settings what would on balance be considered relatively private information, in making the trade-offs between practical benefits and threats to integrity. A related example is, of course, the amount and scope of personal and potentially sensitive information that people give away ownership of and publish for the whole world to see in "social media" such as Facebook photo albums and status updates. More generally, as Lahlou (2008) points out, surveys show that people are concerned about virtual security, but in practice they behave differently. And the worrying part of the development is this: with technology becoming more subtle, it becomes ever easier not only to follow what people are doing but also to predict a person's next move more and more accurately. And when that is done, it is possible to start interfering in a person's choice of action, suggesting things for people to do, thereby not only predicting but also shaping the action.

Foucault's perspective is dark, with basically no openings for resistance, at least if taken to its extremes. We would not want to go that far. The future as projected by Foucault is conceivable, but not inevitable; it is a question of engaging and shaping rather than one of submitting and coping. We have to look at the specific characteristics of collaborative media in order to see what roles are possible—and probable. And we have to look into what action "is," and what it can lead to.

A fruitful approach is to build on the writings of American pragmatist John Dewey and his notion of experience and its relation to action. Often, experience is regarded as something one gathers through life: new knowledge or new skills. To that extent, one's experience is a kind of resource. But that is not the way Dewey viewed experience. For him, experience is forward looking: "experience in its vital form is experimental, an effort to change the given; it is characterized by projection, by reaching forward into the unknown; connexion with a future is its salient trait" (1917, 23). Experience is thus what drives us forward.

How, then, is action related to experience? As Dewey writes, people's actions in everyday life lead to some kinds of experiences all the time. That is life. But for Dewey, in order for something to become *an* experience, it has to be demarcated from other experiences. It has to be a whole, with a beginning and an end. Only then does it become what he calls a *real* experience, something we can talk about as an experience, and something that is forward looking (1934/1980, 36). But this does not happen all the time and it never happens by necessity; there are preconditions. First, experience is not an exclusively private characteristic. Experiences are shared and they develop in interaction. Second, action is driven by both cognition and emotion, and there has to be a meaningful articulation between these two elements. And third, experience also needs an aesthetic quality. This is the quality that transforms action to experience (ibid.). Martha Nussbaum (1995) speaks in this context of the importance of a "literary imagination"; an imagination that makes it possible to see the world from another perspective than one's normal perspective, which in turn leads to the creation of an experience.

We prefer to speak of "meaningful" rather than "real" experiences, but the point is the same. People's actions in everyday life—in social settings—can under certain circumstances be transformative. They can lead to new forms of knowledge and new ways of looking at the world. The power of collaborative media in this context consists of their capabilities for assisting in the creation of such meaningful experiences.

People's collaborative media practices are acted out in relation to other everyday life practices. The field on which they are acted out is not a neutral one in the sense that anyone can do anything or that everything is equally valuable; quite the contrary. The field is shaped by rules on how to act, and some practices seem more natural to carry out for some people than for others. Some practices are furthermore deemed more valuable than others. It is a hierarchical field. And in the terms of Pierre Bourdieu (1984), a person's amount of capital, primarily economic and cultural, shapes one's position in the field.

However, the field is not static. There are continuous movements. In particular, there are movements when new actors enter the field. And collaborative media can be regarded as such actors.

As we have discussed extensively, collaborative media materials, both media infrastructures and media texts, are by definition open for reappropriations and remakes, and they are never completely finished. From the point of view of the person using them, it means that they can be remade time after time in different ways, from different perspectives, making it possible to put the literary imagination to constructive use in new, previously unimagined ways.

One particularly interesting point here is that with the help of collaborative media, it is not only traditional analytical skills that come to the fore but also practical ones. Collaborative media highlight the *making* of things. Such manual skills have traditionally been regarded as less distinguished than analytical ones, but in relation to collaborative media what we can note is a new constellation of practices: mixing the analytical with the practical in ways that may demand other kinds of capital than traditional economic and cultural. This creates new openings, and new possibilities.

Additionally, it is not only a question of *which* practices to carry out. It is also a question of *when* to carry them out. People are able to take part already in the design moments of collaborative media. The importance of this should not be underestimated. If one wants to shape a process, the earlier to take part the better. And even if collaborative media materials can be remade along the way, the first moment of design and initiation is still a particularly significant one. To use Stuart Hall's (1980) terms, it is the determinate moment. Taking part in the determinate moment also means gaining prestige and capital. Thus, one's gain is not only the pleasure of having taken part in the creation of something valuable. The taking part will in itself also create new possibilities—and new positions in the field.

Finally, let us not forget the importance of the "collaborative" in collaborative media processes. Constantinides writes: "The shift in the logic of collective action is creating alternative processes of infrastructure development that are not only popular, but by definition challenge the status quo in important ways" (2012, 608).

In designing media infrastructures collaboratively—in processes including both experts and laypeople—there can be no fixed, predetermined end points. The processes are agonistic, with different stakeholders pushing in different directions. And with new actors continuously joining the game, it becomes increasingly difficult to uphold a position just by virtue of having held it earlier. The status quo is challenged.

In Conclusion

Whenever technology is considered in relation to society, there is the question of power and influence. Does technology shape society, or does society shape technology? Is it engineering progress and innovation that drives societal growth, or rather society that dictates needs and requirements that technology then aims to meet?

On a general level, it is obvious that pitting technological determinism against social shaping creates a false dichotomy (as if they were two separate entities). More important, in our view of collaborative media as a particular cultural form, it is largely pointless to pose the question of power and influence at a general level.

Collaborative media are *forms for practice*; they invite people to act. And collaborative media are *disruptive*. There is thus a potential that transcends the potential of traditional mass media. Can it be fulfilled? That is not only a question for academics. In the end, it is a question for all of us concerned with collaborative media—researchers, designers, "people formerly known as consumers"—to start answering by making future collaborative media and their practices into meaningful experiences.

In order to support this action-oriented take on future developments, we have tried to provide actionable knowledge on collaborative media in the form of concepts and reflections based on our own work as well as the general debate. The intention is for this chapter to complement the case studies in part II by offering a slightly more abstracted level of reasoning. Given our own position in academia, we will now move on to the final chapter where we address in more detail how academic researchers can play their parts in shaping the future of collaborative media.

Although we have argued that knowledge of the cultural form of collaborative media can arise from many directions, academic as well as professional and "amateur," it is still the case that we write in the context of an academic environment and we expect the primary readership of this book will be fellow academics. Thus it seems appropriate to end on the topic of academic research into collaborative media.

What we advocate in part I and illustrate in part II is essentially a design-oriented mode of knowledge production, integrating analysis and intervention in collaborative media research. This sounds rather nice, in the way that most transdisciplinary appeals sound nice in their promises of new constellations and new forms of results if we could only go beyond the established structures of what Kuhn would call "normal science." Still, it is a considerable burden of proof that we find ourselves left with in terms of academic practice. The discipline of media and communication studies, for example, has no experience in intervention and design—the academic criteria for judging "good" interventions as knowledge contributions are not readily available, and it might even be that a design-oriented approach is seen as residing outside the academic scope of the discipline (no matter how worthwhile and meaningful it might be in terms of external relevance).[1] Conversely, the discipline of interaction design is largely alien to analytical approaches grounded in culture and the humanities, having emerged from a perspective of engineering for individual use. The same goes for other academic disciplines that could potentially be touched by the transdisciplinary approach to collaborative media that we advocate.

Hence, we find that the topic of academic quality is a crucial one to address, in order to make sense of the knowledge contributions that we claim to produce from "a design-oriented mode of knowledge production, integrating analysis and intervention in collaborative media research." As we have suggested, the exact standards of academic research are particular to each discipline, but it should be universally agreed that the aim of academic research is to *produce knowledge*. To arrive at a level that enables a transdisciplinary discussion, we might propose following Booth, Colomb, and Williams (2008) that discipline-specific criteria for academic "goodness" in most cases can be abstracted to state that an academic knowledge contribution should be contestable, defensible, and substantive. Briefly, *contestable* means that the contribution proposes a position that at least a significant number of members of the relevant academic community do not already hold. *Defensible* means that members of the community can accept the new position, given the arguments or evidence provided. Finally, a *substantive* contribution is one that is worth the time and effort of the researcher making it and the community members engaging with it.

In this chapter, we address the nature of knowledge contributions resulting from collaborative media design interventions performed in a research context. To conclude, we reflect upon our experiences of doing collaborative media research.

Knowledge Production in Collaborative Media Design Interventions

As introduced in part I, the academic research approach we advocate is a transdisciplinary one of interventions "in the wild" where the analytical and critical stance of social sciences and humanities is combined with a practice-based element. As an example, consider the Kliv case of chapter 5.

The two lead researchers in the Kliv case—Erling Björgvinsson and Per-Anders Hillgren—were PhD students in interaction design, and the project was performed within the framework of an academic research environment. There was obviously an academic agenda at play, involving expectations of academic knowledge contributions. At the same time, Björgvinsson and Hillgren planned and executed an intervention with the distinct aim to help transform the practices of the intensive care unit in the direction of resilient improvement in knowledge management. The dual agenda was in many ways typical for researchers engaging in interventions. We have seen in chapter 5 that the work did in fact lead to persistent change in a beneficial direction. What we need to consider here, then, is the nature and academic quality of the knowledge contributions arising from the work.

The first, and perhaps most obvious contribution was the *design concept* or pattern of the Kliv system itself. The project showed a way in which consumer-grade video cameras could be combined with PDAs and barcode scanners to integrate production and consumption of video in the everyday work practices of nonmedia professionals. The scope of this concept goes beyond the specific technology used, as can be easily illustrated: if the Kliv design concept was applied to a similar design situation today, the designer most likely would suggest a smartphone platform for both recording and viewing. Videos would be stored on a server for wireless access on demand, rather than manually transferred to each handheld unit. The task of determining which video to show at a particular spot could be handled in many ways besides barcode scanning, as the field of available technologies for location-based information has grown considerably since 2001. Some examples would include radio-based tracking (RFID) or near-field sensing (NFC) technologies, phone positioning, or phone-camera optical character recognition (OCR). The point is that even with more contemporary technologies, it would still be very much the same design concept.

Another contribution pertaining to the design concept is enriched understanding of the conditions for its successful deployment, and specifically the conditions under which a sociotechnical system for local management and development of organizational knowledge can grow into a sustainable element of everyday practice.

It should be noted that we are talking about a form of knowledge that resides in the artifact itself, in other words, the system of technology and work procedures that was designed and deployed at the intensive care unit. Now, it is obvious that artifacts themselves are not suited for scholarly communication; when publishing a result like the Kliv system, it is always a question of rendering the knowledge contribution in a form that is suitable for the available communication media (which, in the academic case, consists almost exclusively of paper with lots of text and a few images). This is a recurrent challenge in any academic discipline involving practice-based work, such as design research and engineering; suffice it to say here that conventions do exist per discipline to report artifactual knowledge in ways that are accessible and assayable to the academic community.

At the time, the Kliv design concept was contestable in that its approach to workplace knowledge management was not known previously to the academic interaction-design community. The design concept was defensible due to the way the reporting aligned with the conventions of the academic community being addressed, including a detailed report of the design process and a rich text-and-images rendering of the design concept in use. Furthermore, it was substantive in terms of both internal (academic) and external (practice-oriented) relevance, and in hindsight it is easy to assert that it was perhaps more substantive than many other knowledge contributions reported to the academic interaction-design community around the same time.

Moving on, the work offered *methodological* knowledge contributions. The Kliv design process served as a steppingstone for other researchers seeking to deploy participatory design as a method for action research in the context of workplace learning and collaborative media. This was accomplished by (1) reporting the design process and reflections upon it in adequate detail, and (2) connecting the insights to more general concepts in the academic fields of participatory design, organizational learning, and media theory. The methodological knowledge contributions were deemed contestable, defensible, and substantive by the target academic community in ways similar to those discussed earlier.

Finally, the Kliv case formed part of the basis for *conceptual contributions* to the academic fields of participatory design, organizational learning, and collaborative media. This was accomplished by using Kliv as one case together with other design cases to form the basis for the development of new abstractions. For instance, Hillgren (2006) discusses the implications of viewing participatory design as a series of "fruitful colli-sions" where friction and disagreement among multiple perspectives serve to take the design outcomes beyond the incremental and into the realm of the innovative. Simi-larly, Björgvinsson (2007) initiates a useful discussion on the relation between space and reification in collaborative settings and what it means for collaborative media designers to consider the shaping of space.

To conclude this extended example, it should be noted that the knowledge contri-butions mentioned in this chapter were not made to the field of collaborative media (which arguably didn't exist as such in 2001–2002) but rather to the academic com-munities of interaction design and participatory design. Still, we have argued that the Kliv case warrants inclusion in our treatment of collaborative media, and we find the knowledge contributions identified to be relevant to our nascent field as well. More generally, what Kliv shows from an epistemological point of view is the nature of knowledge contributions that can be expected from a practice-based research interven-tion in a co-production context involving extramural actors as well as academic ones. These insights are every bit as relevant to the transdisciplinary field of collaborative media research.

In the context of participatory design research (which arguably forms part of the academic foundations for the field of collaborative media research), the Kliv case repre-sents a fairly typical situation where the academic researcher embraces the dual agenda of producing academic knowledge and facilitating resilient transformation "in the wild." Some of the other cases, such as Avatopia (chapter 4) and Substrate (chapter 5) are quite similar in this respect, meaning that their knowledge contributions can be identified and assessed in analogous ways. There are, however, other cases in part II of this book where the academic knowledge production process takes on somewhat dif-ferent forms.

The Hacktivism case in chapter 5 was performed when Otto von Busch was a PhD student in an academic environment and therefore academic requirements for the work's knowledge contributions were obviously present. However, unlike the Kliv researchers, von Busch chose to challenge the whole institution of fashion through a series of critical interventions in different places rather than working toward local change in a long-term relation with a particular constituency. Consequentially, his knowledge contributions consist of a "toolbox" of intervention techniques and specific results, along with a more abstracted reflection on the role of the new designer who shapes action rather than fabrics. In what follows, we will elaborate on what collab-orative media researchers can learn from the role model of the new designer that von Busch outlines. For brevity, we will refer to the protagonist as the "researcher," but it should be borne in mind that the researcher-designer-interventionist we describe is an ideal type for the collaborative-media researcher we envision rather than a description of an existing and widespread academic species.

The need for the researcher to serve in an *intensifying* capacity is undeniable. Whether researchers are called facilitators, catalysts, or organizers, it seems clear that they need a keen eye for spotting potentials and initiatives that can be energized by an intervention or by being put into contact with other sparks of energy. You could argue that the researchers in this kind of setting build part of their professionalism on the ability to uphold an eclectic birds-eye view. Most stakeholders in complex structures like fashion or the conventional media are, in practice, fully occupied by keeping their respective pieces of the puzzle in good shape. It is a professional privilege for the researcher to have the opportunity to piece together a bigger picture of the complex structure and to look for new possible pieces that could be added from outside the existing structure.

With the big picture comes the possibility, and responsibility, of the researcher to ask *critical questions*. Every group of stakeholders has its own concerns and heartfelt issues that are not always fully visible to other groups of stakeholders. Practices and stakeholder groups outside the existing structure illustrate other values and concerns that could serve as the grounds for questioning of the existing. If it turns out that such questions are inspiring and energizing, then the researcher is in a position to form new constellations and initiate joint experimentation.

Another aspect of the researcher's responsibility that von Busch captures concerns *tools and craft skills*. If a constellation is formed and there is an urge to engage in joint experimentation, it befalls the researcher to ensure that the action space is opened for the participants. This may entail the provision of tools and techniques for envisioning what is yet to be, as well as the reverse engineering of existing structures to empower experiment participants to act within them.

What we end up with by examining the Hacktivism case is a sketch of a collaborative media researcher, designer, or interventionist (or combination of these roles) whose main responsibilities are to energize and facilitate, create arenas, and provide props for the collaborative design, production, and consumption of media.

The Parapolis case of chapter 4 offers similar knowledge contributions, even though the main initiative in the work resided outside the academic environment. More specifically, Parapolis suggests routes toward agonism and ongoing dialogue as a meaningful alternative to traditional consensus approaches in representative democracy with expert planners making (ideally well-informed and well-grounded) decisions. Moreover, it provides useful insights into how small, highly localized communicative structures of a tribal nature form to engage with collaborative media, and openings for a discussion of how such approaches could scale to loose networks of many tribes.

It seems clear that knowledge contributions of the kind constructed in Hacktivism and Parapolis must be deemed substantive, at least if one accepts our premises as to the emergence and significance of the new cultural form that is collaborative media. That the knowledge contributions are contestable is obvious. The question remains, though, as to whether they can be deemed defensible. Where is the evidence?

On one level, the question can be answered as for any instance of case study research: the proof is in the pudding. The case reports and analyzes what happened, and if the reports are rich enough then the academic community is in a position to independently accept or reject the knowledge contribution. In other words, if the work is criticizable, then it is defensible.

There is, however, another angle that may be worth exploring. First, we need to establish that knowledge construction is an inherently social process, in which knowledge is shaped in ongoing dialogue among members of the concerned academic community. In this discursive perspective on academic research, a publication is a proposition or a claim that is subsequently assessed, appropriated, elaborated, possibly refuted, by peers in ongoing discursive processes. An acceptable contribution in this perspective is one that somehow serves the ongoing processes generatively.

Second, in the context of design research and other practice-based forms of research, proposed design concepts along with reasoning about their merits in comparison with alternative designs do represent knowledge contributions if certain conditions are met. In those cases, the degree to which such contributions are defensible depends on how well they communicate their exploration and comparative analysis of the design space in question to community peers (for a more in-depth discussion of this form of validation in design research, see Krippendorff 2006).

Taking the discursive perspective of research together with the notion of design-space exploration explains how the Hacktivism and Parapolis knowledge contributions can be seen as defensible. The new roles of the researcher in Hacktivism represent previously uncharted possibilities for researcher positioning, just as the specific approaches to agonistic mediation in Parapolis represent previously uncharted possibilities for structuring collaborative transformation processes. In both cases, the proposed directions gain "evidence" through more or less explicit comparison with established approaches. And in both cases, they serve to feed the ongoing discursive process of knowledge construction—in other words, they inspire, challenge, and provoke academic peers to engage with the claims and do further work on them. Thus, in both cases the contributions are said to be accepted by the community given the arguments or evidence provided, where "accepted" under the discursive view of knowledge construction equals being engaged with.

To conclude this section, we take a brief look at yet another form of knowledge contribution represented in part II: the design-led exploration of OurNewsOurWays in chapter 6.

Superficially speaking, the knowledge contribution in OurNewsOurWays consists of a partial design concept for tribal social navigation in a future scenario where TV and online video have essentially melted together into a vast pool of potentially interesting, relevant, and amusing audiovisual material, and where editorial metadata and curatorial efforts only cater for a small fraction of all consumption. The concept is relatively detailed in its core functions, yet remarkably loose in other respects such as exactly how lists of friends and pathfinders are created and maintained. Significantly, the concept has not been evaluated through user tests or other rote methods of empirical assessment from academic interaction design. Still, it is represented as a knowledge contribution, but on what grounds? It is presumably contestable, and if the assumptions embodied in the future TV scenario are accepted provisionally, then it can also be said to be substantive. But we are yet again left with the question of whether the concept is defensible.

The key here would be to relate back to the view of knowledge construction as an ongoing, discursive process. Specifically, the OurNewsOurWays work was carried out in the larger context of a research project where MyNewsMyWay (chapter 5) represented an effort to design new TV viewing modes based on incremental transformation of existing producer/consumer structures. That work led to proposing a scheme of producer-generated metadata and consumer-generated profile information in order to enable the shape-shifting features that constituted the main contributions. However, it is known within other fields of interaction design that such schemes are hard to use and rarely lead to persistent uptake on behalf of users (here: consumers). Taken together with the arguably likely development toward available audiovisual material en masse without producer-generated metadata, the situation in MyNewsMyWay can be understood as posing a question: How can a system be designed that offers audiovisual material worth watching without relying on producer-generated metadata and consumer-generated profile information?

If that is a question in a discursive view of knowledge construction, then the OurNewsOurWays concept in itself is a possible answer to that question (following the argumentation by Cross 2007, on when artifacts do constitute knowledge within design research). To be sure, it is not the only conceivable answer. Design in general deals with envisioning possible futures rather than deducing certain outcomes from premises. What the OurNewsOurWays case does to provide arguments for its chosen answer to the question is (1) to present a number of principled approaches and validate them comparatively in collaboration with the stakeholders of the project to determine which direction to pursue further, (2) to relate the proposed design concept to existing knowledge in the community in the form of empirical studies of existing interactive TV and reasonable predictions based on the reported empirical data, and (3) to ground the proposed concept quite carefully in technically feasible mechanisms. In those three ways, OurNewsOurWays aims to present a claim in an ongoing discourse of knowledge construction, and specifically a defensible claim that did not appear by magic but rather through a reasoned design process with as much grounding and validation as possible.

Doing Collaborative Media Research: Final Reflections

Having spent some effort on the fine details of research epistemology, it is now time to conclude. We would like to do so by reflecting upon what it actually means as academic researchers to do collaborative media research.

As this book hopefully has made clear, collaborative media research is not only about researching collaborative media but also about doing collaborative research. During our more than ten years of collaboration, we have worked closely not only with local and international media companies but quite generally with a broad range of constituencies that in some way or other are engaged in collaborative media practices: local municipalities, cultural organizations, commercial companies, media activists, and so on. We have also worked with informed and interested citizens.

To be fair, it must be noted that doing such work sometimes has come at a cost. The overhead involved in doing co-production research compared to conventional intra-academic work can be considerable, sometimes close to prohibitive. Planning and funding a research project with nonacademic actors is different from doing it by yourself, especially if some of the actors are in situations where their R&D budgets are entirely determined by the bottom lines of the next quarterly reports, the development of volatile markets or political processes, or the availability of charity-like grants. Executing such projects are more often than not exercises in improvisation and bricolage. Furthermore, engaging in an intervention without knowing what the exact research question is and what to expect in terms of results requires experience, and ideally also an academic position where you have nothing to lose.

Is it worth it? Ultimately, it comes to down to thinking through what you want to do as a researcher and why. For us, choosing this path has been easy. We want to take part; we want to change things. With this comes the need for assuming responsibility for what you want to achieve, even when it comes at a cost. And the key point is that we have been able to contribute to, and sometimes even initiate, processes of change by exploring and assessing possible collaborative media futures together with the stakeholders concerned. This we could not have done by ourselves. We are grateful for the opportunities we have been given as academic researchers to take part in these processes.

Spending the last fifteen years working in academic settings toward a transdisciplinary practice of collaborative media research has been pleasurable and constructive. The work has been received with some curiosity and interest, and in recent years we have started to see signs within media and communication studies as well as interaction design of spaces opening up for a design-oriented mode of knowledge production on collaborative media, integrating analysis and intervention. We are, thus, generally hopeful as we draw together a synthesis of cases, concepts, and approaches in this book. However, we would like to make it clear here that our main aim is to inspire academic action rather than to build another silo. To that extent, the choice of the term "transdisciplinary" might actually be an unfortunate one, as it could suggest the emergence of a new discipline. Yet, we find the connotations of transcending existing disciplinary approaches to be appealing, and the perhaps more modest term of "interdisciplinarity" as originally proposed by Jantsch (1972) to us seems less flexible in terms of which disciplines are free to engage in the new field.

To be more precise, we would be happy if actors within our mother disciplines and other academic disciplines would engage with collaborative media in ways akin to what we propose here, working together and joining forces (thus transcending the boundaries of their respective disciplines), but without attempting to create new disciplines. More specifically, what we hope to avoid is all the turf wars and erection of monuments that tend to occur when disciplines or subdisciplines are in formative phases. Resources for the kind of research we propose are fairly scarce, and we would prefer them to be spent on collaboratively producing new and significant knowledge rather than on quarreling over discipline demarcations.

As we hope to have shown, the cultural form of collaborative media is very much in the making. The evolution and experimentation is happening not in the labs but rather in the wild: in society and in people's everyday lives. This is how it should be.

But that does not make academic participation meaningless—quite to the contrary. The cultural form of collaborative media is not predetermined. It evolves continuously, and there are struggles between opposing forces over the power to define what collaborative media should "be," and what roles they should play. The outcomes of these struggles are undecided. And in these struggles, collaborative media researchers can make a difference, particularly by engaging with other actors in collaborative work integrating intervention, analysis, and criticism.

Let the interventionist turn begin.

Notes

1   Introduction

1. See http://en.wikipedia.org/wiki/Social_media (accessed June 19, 2012). Citing Kaplan and Haenlein 2010.

2. An example of this growing recognition is that the *Journal of Visual Culture* devoted a special issue to machinima in 2011, cf. Lowood 2011.

3. Engholm (2010) calls this "the good enough revolution." As long as products reach the minimum level of technical capability necessary to be usable, aspects such as availability and closeness ("this has been created by someone I know") become more important than technical perfection.

4. There are surprisingly few academic works addressing the relationship between interaction design and media and communication studies. For one such example, cf. Koskinen 2006.

2   The Cultural Form of Collaborative Media

1. For instance: *The Handbook of New Media* (Lievrouw and Livingstone 2006); *New Media: An Introduction* (Flew 2008); *New Media: The Key Concepts* (Gane and Beer 2008); *New Media: A Critical Introduction* (Lister et al. 2008); *New Media: Culture and Image* (Fuery 2008).

2. The verb "collaborate" has been used in English since the late nineteenth century. It comes from the Latin "collaborare," which means "working together."

3. An important precursor here is the concept of prosumer (portmanteau of production + consumer), coined by American futurist Alvin Toffler (1980). That concept, however, has more to do with how companies can use the competence of consumers than with the ways people combine production with consumption.

4. "Models perfuse communication studies," as Genosko states in his new book on communication models, a book discussing both the Shannon and Weaver model and Hall's encoding/decoding model (2012, 3). That models perfuse communication studies is not surprising. As he writes: "Models are productive—they do something" (ibid., 7). The actual modeling therefore becomes

highly crucial in one's theoretical work. Or in the words of James Carey (1989), models are not only representations of reality, they also are representations *for* reality.

5. The main social science approaches to media, the media effects approach and the Uses and Gratifications approach, both focus on media use, but they differ widely in their views on how much power people have in making sense of the media. With inspiration coming from film theory (screen theory), much humanities research initially privileged the role played by media texts. This was challenged by reception theory in the 1980s. Today the common perspective is to treat both people and texts seriously (cf. Brooker and Jermyn 2003; Nightingale 2011).

6. It may be argued that to a great extent media and communication studies have moved away from the rather unproductive social science/humanities distinction. Younger scholars do not necessarily think in those terms, and this distinction is not crucial for today's arguably main media and communication studies topics: convergence (Jenkins 2006; Hay and Couldry 2011) and mediatization (Lundby 2009; Hepp 2012). However, and maybe somewhat surprisingly, neither the convergence nor the mediatization discourse, as they have unfolded, is especially helpful in making sense of collaborative media.

7. For a recent treatment of the relationship between media and technology from a media and communications studies perspective, see Morley 2012. On the relationship between media and communication studies and science and technology studies (STS), see Wajcman and Jones 2012.

8. Italics in the original.

9. For example, when two fledgling lovers dine in a restaurant, their interaction is to a certain degree shaped by the seating arrangements: it might be more difficult to engage in intimate conversation if the tables are placed so close together that other guests can overhear what is said. The seating arrangements were made a long time ago, and the person who made them is thus a historical actor.

10. Somewhat surprisingly, actor-network theory (ANT) has not had any particular impact on media and communication studies. For a highly critical treatment of ANT from that perspective, see Couldry 2008. For an ANT perspective on media and communications, see Latour 2011.

3   Researching Collaborative Media

1. http://mediastudies2point0.blogspot.com/ (accessed July 25, 2012).

2. "Ferment in the Field" was the title of a special issue of *Journal of Communication* in 1983, devoted to the transformation of the field of media and communication studies going on at the time.

3. The question of what "practice-based research" means is on one level simple to answer: it is research using practice in order to gain knowledge. However, that would be a rather vacuous truism. Within academia, practice-based research has a long tradition within, for instance, medicine, and is there related to the notion of evidence-based research. When we speak of practice-

based research in this book, we refer to the attempts to gain knowledge by creating products, artifacts, or artistic works.

4. From the journal's webpage, http://www.uk.sagepub.com/journalsProdDesc.nav?prodId=Jour nal200834&crossRegion=eur#tabview=title (accessed July 25, 2012).

5. The anthology edited by Lievrouw and Livingstone came out in 2002, so it could seem a bit unfair to quote it today. However, the article was republished in the 2006 edition of the anthology.

6. Some examples of notable journals in this field include *ACM Transactions on Multimedia Computing, Communications and Applications*; *IEEE Transactions on Multimedia*; *Personal and Ubiquitous Computing*; and *New Review of Hypermedia and Multimedia*.

7. Much work within the field is organized by The Alliance of Digital Humanities Organizations (http://adho.org/, accessed March 16, 2013). The organization publishes the online journal *Digital Humanities Quarterly*. A subfield with connections to digital humanities is software studies (Fuller 2008).

8. These include the journals *Leonardo: Journal of the International Society for the Arts, Sciences and Technology* and *Journal of Artistic Research*, and the biannual conference DAC (Digital Arts and Culture).

9. The most influential publication fora within interaction design include journals such as *ACM Transactions on Computer–Human Interaction, International Journal of Design, ACM Computers in Entertainment*, and *Digital Creativity*, as well as archival conferences such as CHI (Human Factors in Computing Systems) and DIS (Designing Interactive Systems). On a historical note, it could be added that when human–computer interaction was preoccupied with individual use, the subfields of computer-supported cooperative work and computer-mediated communication within informatics were mainly "responsible" for addressing social issues of computer use (albeit focused almost exclusively on work-related use). Even though the subfields still exist, their relative importance has waned, as interaction design grows increasingly aware of social and communicative aspects.

10. This is the argument of Michael Burawoy in his American Sociological Association Presidential address "For Public Sociology" (2005).

11. The term "in the wild" has been used in different contexts. Our usage is related to the one associated with STS researcher Michel Callon (Callon and Rabeharisoa 2003; Callon, Lascoumes, and Barthe 2009); see also the recent plea by Yvonne Rogers (2011) for "wild theory" interaction design research.

12. Media activism, on the other hand—using the media for political purposes—is a lively research subject within media research, not the least new media activism (see Lievrouw 2011).

13. Exception: the rare occasions when the same person actually holds those multiple competencies with sufficient proficiency.

II Interventions

1. A tripartite distinction between the levels of society, institution, and group is commonplace within social analysis. In our particular context, however, the concept of tribe is more apt than the group concept. Discussion follows, and further in chapter 6.

4 Collaborative Media and Society

1. In retrospect, the timing of the Avatopia project was slightly unfortunate. At the time when implementation started, there were no widely available avatar worlds or 3D environments available online. The Avatopia collaborative forum had to be built more or less from scratch at significant cost, and the first version for deployment was finished merely a month before Second Life was introduced to the public in June 2003.

2. One of the original creators was Måns Adler, who at the time of writing was dividing his time between the Bambuser company and the research environment of this book's authors.

3. Sandelin and Torstensson both have a background in the research environment of this book's authors.

5 Collaborative Media and Institutions

1. See http://substrate.se/ (accessed March 18, 2013).

2. An elegant demonstration of such an interface, with some additional interaction features, is Moritz Stefaner's work on Elastic Lists (http://moritz.stefaner.eu/projects/elastic-lists/, accessed March 18, 2013).

3. Refer to http://www.sigma.se/en/Events/Camp-Digital/About-Camp-Digital/ (accessed March 18, 2013).

4. Currently colleagues of this book's authors, Björgvinsson and Hillgren were PhD students in our research environment during the time of the Kliv project.

5. This is similar to the famous story of how Jeff Hawkins, the creator of the Palm Pilot, carried a piece of wood in his shirt pocket for months, taking it out on numerous occasions and pretending to make notes on it, in order to understand the user needs and form requirements for a handheld computer (Jackson 1998).

6. Otto von Busch is a long-term member of our research environment and a former colleague.

6 Collaborative Media and Tribes

1. In academic circles, the concept of "tribe" is primarily associated with Michel Maffesoli and his book *The Time of the Tribes* (1990/1996). A more general-interest take on the subject is Seth Godin's *Tribes* (2008).

2. See http://arduino.cc/en/Main/Boards (accessed March 29, 2012).

3. Refer to http://www.iampoem.net/ (accessed March 21, 2013).

4. Refer to http://arduino.cc/blog/2011/10/10/speed-vest-for-night-cycling/ (accessed March 18, 2013), and http://www.instructables.com/id/Bubblesteen-Bubble-Machine/ (accessed March 18, 2013), respectively.

5. Erik Sandelin and Andreas Kurtsson were VJs and the musicians/composers were Erik Mikael Karlsson and Fredrik Norrgren. See http://citysymphony2009.blogspot.se/ (accessed March 17, 2013).

6. Ibid.

7. Media Evolution website: http://mediaevolution.se/en (accessed March 17, 2013).

7   The Uses of Collaborative Media

1. Even if in this context we touch upon the characteristics of collaborative media texts, our interest in this section concerns the practice of producing such texts rather than the texts themselves. We refer to Bolter and Grusin's *Remediation* (1999) and Manovich's *The Language of New Media* (2002) for important discussions on new media texts.

2. Sources for a more thorough historical introduction to participatory design include Ehn 1989 and Greenbaum and Kyng 1991.

3. "Infra" comes from Latin and means "below."

8   The Practice of Collaborative Media Research

1. This is of course not to say that we are the only ones within the discipline trying to go beyond its traditional boundaries. See, for example, the recent attempt made by Kember and Zylinska to find "a way of 'doing media studies' that is not just a form of 'media analysis' and that is simultaneously critical *and* creative" (2012, xvii). Another example would be Anne Balsamo's *Designing Culture* (2011).

References

Adkins, Lisa, and Celia Lury. 2009. "Introduction: What Is the Empirical?" *European Journal of Social Theory* 12 (1): 5–20.

Adler, Måns. 2012. Personal communication. June 17.

Akrich, Madeline. 1992. "The De-scription of Technical Objects." In *Shaping Technology / Building Society: Studies in Sociotechnical Change*, ed. Wiebe E. Bijker and John Law, 205–224. Cambridge, MA: MIT Press.

Anderson, Chris. 2006. *The Long Tail: Why the Future of Business Is Selling Less of More*. New York: Hyperion.

Andrejevic, Mark. 2009. "Critical Media Studies 2.0: An Interactive Upgrade." *Interactions: Studies in Communication and Culture* 1 (1): 35–51.

Andrejevic, Mark. 2011. "Surveillance and Alienation in the Online Economy." *Surveillance & Society* 8 (3): 278–287.

Arduino: The Documentary. 2010. https://vimeo.com/18539129 (accessed March 30, 2012).

Arias, Ernesto. 1996. "Bottom-Up Neighbourhood Revitalisation: A Language Approach for Participatory Decision Support." *Urban Studies* 33 (10): 1831–1848.

Atzori, Luigi, Antonio Iera, and Giacomo Morabito. 2010. "The Internet of Things." *Computer Networks* 54 (15): 2787–2805.

Balsamo, Anne. 2011. *Designing Culture: The Technological Imagination at Work*. Duke, NC: Duke University Press.

Bambuser. 2012a. "Egypt Celebrating Their 1st Anniversary of the 2011 Uprising." *Bambuser Official Blog*. http://blog.bambuser.com/2012/01/egypt-celebrating-their-1st-anniversary.html (accessed June 7, 2012).

Bambuser. 2012b. "Let Associated Press Contact You about Newsworthy Content." *Bambuser Official Blog*. http://blog.bambuser.com/2012/04/let-associated-press-contact-you-about.html (accessed June 8, 2012).

Banzi, Massimo. 2009. *Getting Started with Arduino*. Sebastopol, CA: O'Reilly.

Bauerlein, Mark, ed. 2011. *The Digital Divide: Arguments For and Against Facebook, Google, Texting, and the Age of Social Networking*. New York: Penguin Group.

BBC. 2004. "Duchamp's Urinal Tops Art Survey." BBC News. http://news.bbc.co.uk/2/hi/entertainment/4059997.stm (accessed August 24, 2011).

Beer, David, and Richard Burrows. 2010. "Consumption, Prosumption and Participatory Web Cultures." *Journal of Consumer Culture* 10 (1): 3–12.

Benkler, Yochai. 2006. *The Wealth of Networks. How Social Production Transforms Markets and Freedom*. New Haven: Yale University Press.

Bernhaupt, Regina, Marianna Obrist, Astrid Weiss, Elke Beck, and Manfred Tscheligi. 2008. "Trends in the Living Room and Beyond: Results from Ethnographic Studies Using Creative and Playful Probing." *ACM Computers in Entertainment* 6 (1): article no. 5. http://dl.acm.org/citation.cfm?doid=1350843.1350848 (accessed March 18, 2013).

Berry, David M., ed. 2012. *Understanding Digital Humanities*. Houndmills, UK: Palgrave Macmillan.

Biggs, Michael, and Henrik Karlsson, eds. 2010. *The Routledge Companion to Research in the Arts*. London: Routledge.

Binder, Thomas, and Eva Brandt. 2008. "The Design:Lab as Platform in Participatory Design Research." *CoDesign* 4 (2): 115–129.

Bird, Elizabeth. 2011. "Are We All Producers Now? Convergence and Media Audience Practices." *Cultural Studies* 25 (4–5): 502–516.

Björgvinsson, Erling. 2007. "Socio-Material Mediations: Learning, Knowing and Self-Produced Media within Healthcare." Dissertation, Blekinge Institute of Technology, Sweden.

Björgvinsson, Erling. 2008. "Open-Ended Participatory Design as Prototypical Practice." *CoDesign* 4 (2): 85–99.

Björgvinsson, Erling, Pelle Ehn, and Per-Anders Hillgren. 2012. "Agonistic Participatory Design: Working with Marginalised Social Movements." *CoDesign* 8 (2–3): 127–144.

Blum, Jeremy. n.d. Tutorial Series for Arduino. http://www.youtube.com/playlist?list=PLA567CE235D39FA84 (accessed April 5, 2012).

Bolter, Jay David, and Richard Grusin. 1999. *Remediation: Understanding New Media*. Cambridge, MA: MIT Press.

Booth, Wayne, Gregory Colomb, and Joseph Williams. 2008. *The Craft of Research*. 3rd ed. Chicago: The University of Chicago Press.

Bourdieu, Pierre. 1984. *Distinction: A Social Critique of the Judgement of Taste*. London: Routledge.

Brighenti, Andrea Mubi. 2012. "New Media and Urban Motilities: A Territoriologic Point of View." *Urban Studies* 49 (2): 399–414.

Brooker, Will, and Deborah Jermyn, eds. 2003. *The Audience Studies Reader*. London: Routledge.

Bruns, Axel. 2008. *Blogs, Wikipedia, Second Life, and Beyond: From Production to Produsage*. New York: Peter Lang.

Brydon-Miller, Mary, Davydd Greenwood, and Patricia Maguire. 2003. "Why Action Research?" *Action Research* 1 (1): 9–28.

Burawoy, Michael. 2005 "2004 American Sociological Association Presidential Address: For Public Sociology." *British Journal of Sociology* 56 (2): 259–294.

Callon, Michel. 1999. "The Role of Lay People in the Production and Dissemination of Scientific Knowledge." *Science, Technology & Society* 4 (1): 81–94.

Callon, Michel, Pierre Lascoumes, and Yannick Barthe. 2009. *Acting in an Uncertain World: An Essay on Technical Democracy*. Cambridge, MA: MIT Press.

Callon, Michel, and Vololona Rabeharisoa. 2003. "Research 'in the Wild' and the Shaping of New Social Identities." *Technology in Society* 25 (2): 193–204.

Carey, James. 1989. "A Cultural Approach to Communication." In *James Carey: Communication as Culture: Essays on Media and Society*. New York: Routledge.

Cesar, Pablo, Konstantinos Chorianopoulos, and Jens F. Jensen. 2008. "Social Television and User Interaction." *ACM Computers in Entertainment* 6 (1): article no. 4. http://dl.acm.org/citation .cfm?doid=1350843.1350847 (accessed March 18, 2013).

Chan, Adrian. 2012. "Principles of Social Interaction Design: An Essay." http://www.gravity7 .com/blog/media/2012/02/principles-of-social-interaction-design-pdf.html (accessed August 8, 2012).

Chesbrough, Henry. 2003. *Open Innovation: The New Imperative for Creating and Profiting from Technology*. Boston, MA: Harvard Business School Press.

Clark, Jessica. 2009. "Public Media 2.0: Dynamic, Engaged Publics." Washington, DC: Center for Social Media, American University. http://www.centerforsocialmedia.org/future-public-media/ documents/white-papers/public-media-20-dynamic-engaged-publics (accessed August 24, 2011).

Clay, Andrew. 2011. "Blocking, Tracking and Monetizing: YouTube Copyright Control and the Downfall Parodies." In *Video Vortex Reader II: Moving Images Beyond YouTube*, ed. Geert Lovink and Rachel Somers Miles, 219–233. Amsterdam: Institute of Network Cultures. http://www .networkcultures.org/publications/inc-readers (accessed June 15, 2011).

Constantinides, Panos. 2012. "The Development and Consequences of New Information Infrastructures: The Case of Mashup Platforms." *Media Culture & Society* 34 (5): 606–622.

Coole, Diana, and Samantha Frost, eds. 2010. *New Materialisms: Ontology, Agency, and Politics*. Durham, NC: Duke University Press.

Couldry, Nick. 2008. "Actor Network Theory and Media: Do They Connect and on What Terms?" In *Connectivity, Networks and Flows: Conceptualizing Contemporary Communications*, ed. Andreas Hepp, Friedrich Krotz, Shaun Moores, and Carsten Winter, 93–110. Cresskill, NJ: Hampton Press.

Couldry, Nick, Sonia Livingstone, and Tim Markham. 2010. *Media Consumption and Public Engagement: Beyond the Presumption of Attention*. Houndmills, UK: Palgrave Macmillan.

Cross, Nigel. 2007. *Designerly Ways of Knowing*. Basel: Birkhäuser.

Cuartielles, David. 2012a. "How Electronics Connect Us to the World. *Medea Talk*, Malmö, March 1. http://youtu.be/knJrXYIVof8 (accessed March 28, 2012).

Cuartielles, David. 2012b. Personal communication, April 10.

De Paoli, Stefano, and Cristiano Storni. 2011. "Produsage in Hybrid Networks: Sociotechnical Skills in the Case of Arduino." *New Review of Hypermedia and Multimedia* 17 (1): 31–52.

Devereaux, Ryan. 2012. "Syrian Government Blocks Live Video Streaming Site Bambuser." The *Guardian*. http://www.guardian.co.uk/world/2012/feb/17/syrian-government-blocks-bambuser (accessed June 8, 2012).

Dewey, John. 1916/1944. *Democracy and Education: An Introduction to the Philosophy of Education*. New York: The Free Press.

Dewey, John. 1917. "The Need for a Recovery of Philosophy." In *Creative Intelligence: Essays in the Pragmatic Attitude*, 3–69. New York: Holt.

Dewey, John. 1934/1980. *Art as Experience*. New York: Perigee Books.

DiSalvo, Carl. 2012. *Adversarial Design*. Cambridge, MA: MIT Press.

Eden, Hal, Eva Hornecker, and Eric Scharff. 2002. "Multilevel Design and Role Play: Experiences in Assessing Support for Neighborhood Participation in Design." In *Proceedings of Designing Interactive Systems (DIS 2002)*, 387–392. New York: ACM Press.

Edwards, David. 2010. *The Lab: Creativity and Culture*. Cambridge, MA: Harvard University Press.

Ehn, Pelle. 1989. *Work-Oriented Design of Computer Artifacts*. Hillsdale, NJ: Lawrence Erlbaum.

Engholm, Ida. 2010. "The Good Enough Revolution. The Role of Aesthetics in User Experiences with Artifacts." *Digital Creativity* 21 (3): 141–154.

Facebook. 2012. "Key Facts: Facebook Newsroom." http://newsroom.fb.com/content/default.aspx?NewsAreaId=22 (accessed July 24, 2012).

Fischer, Gerhard, and Elisa Giaccardi. 2006. "Meta-Design: A Framework for the Future of End User Development." In *End User Development—Empowering People to Flexibly Employ Advanced Information and Communication Technology*, ed. Henry Lieberman, Fabio Paternò, and Volker Wulf, 427–457. Dordrecht: Kluwer Academic Publishers.

Flew, Terry. 2008. *New Media: An Introduction*. 3rd ed. South Melbourne, AU: Oxford University Press.

Foucault, Michel. 1991. "Governmentality." In *The Foucault Effect: Studies in Governmentality*, ed. Graham Burchell, Colin Gordon, and Peter Miller, 87–104. Chicago: University of Chicago Press.

Fuery, Keli. 2008. *New Media: Culture and Image*. Basingstoke, UK: Palgrave Macmillan.

Fuller, Matthew, ed. 2008. *Software Studies*. Cambridge, MA: MIT Press.

Gane, Nicholas, and David Beer. 2008. *New Media: The Key Concepts*. Oxford: Berg.

Gansing, Kristoffer. 2013. "Transversal Media Practices: Media Archaeology, Art and Technological Development." Dissertation, Malmö University.

Gaver, Bill, Tony Dunne, and Elena Pacenti. 1999. "Design: Cultural Probes." *Interactions: Studies in Communication and Culture* 6 (1): 21–29.

Gauntlett, David. 2009. "Media Studies 2.0: A Response." *Interactions: Studies in Communication and Culture* 1 (1): 147–157.

Gauntlett, David. 2011. *Making Is Connecting: The Social Meaning of Creativity, from DIY and Knitting to YouTube and Web 2.0*. Cambridge, UK: Polity Press.

Genosko. Gary. 2012. *Remodelling Communication: From WWII to the WWW*. Toronto: Toronto University Press.

Gertz, Emily. 2011. "Got iGeigie? Radiation Monitoring Meets Grassroots Mapping. *Onearth Magazine*. http://www.onearth.org/blog/citizen-radiation-monitoring-meets-grassroots-mapping (accessed April 5, 2012).

Gibb, Alicia. 2010. "New Media Art, Design and the Arduino Microcontroller: A Malleable Tool." MSc thesis, Pratt Institute. http://aliciagibb.com/thesis (accessed March 29, 2012).

Gibbons, Michael, Camille Limoges, Helga Nowotny, Simon Schwartzman, Peter Scott, and Martin Trow. 1994. *The New Production of Knowledge: The Dynamics of Science and Research in Contemporary Societies*. London: Sage.

Gibson, James J. 1977. "The Theory of Affordances." In *Perceiving, Acting, and Knowing*, ed. Robert Shaw and John Bransford, 67–82. Hillsdale, NJ: Erlbaum.

Gislén, Ylva, Jonas Löwgren, and Ulf Myrestam. 2008. "Avatopia: A Cross-Media Community for Societal Action." *Personal and Ubiquitous Computing* 12: 289–297.

Godin, Seth. 2008. *Tribes: We Need You to Lead Us*. New York: Portfolio.

Greenbaum, Joan, and Morten Kyng, eds. 1991. *Design at Work: Cooperative Design of Computer Systems*. Hillsdale, NJ: Lawrence Erlbaum.

Gregory, Sam. 2011. "Cameras Everywhere: Ubiquitous Video Documentation of Human Rights, New Forms of Video Advocacy, and Considerations of Safety, Security, Dignity and Consent." In *Video Vortex Reader II: Moving Images Beyond Youtube*, ed. Geert Lovink and Rachel Somers Miles, 268–282. Amsterdam: Institute of Network Cultures. http://www.networkcultures.org/publications/inc-readers (accessed August 8, 2012).

Grossberg, Lawrence. 1992. *We Gotta Get Out of This Place: Popular Conservatism and Postmodern Culture*. London: Routledge.

Gunkel, David J. 2008. "Rethinking the Digital Remix: Mashups and the Metaphysics of Sound Recording." *Popular Music and Society* 31 (4): 489–510.

Gruber, Thomas. 2007. "Ontology of Folksonomy: A Mash-Up of Apples and Oranges." *International Journal on Semantic Web and Information Systems* 3 (1): 1–11.

Hall, Stuart. 1980. "Coding and Encoding in the Television Discourse." In *Culture, Media, Language*, ed. Stuart Hall, Dorothy Hobson, Andrew Lowe, and Paul Willis, 128–138. London: Unwin Hyman.

Hall, Stuart. 1986. "On Postmodernism and Articulation." In *Stuart Hall: Critical Dialogues*, ed. David Morley and Kuan-Hsing Chen, 131–150. London: Routledge.

Hannula, Mika, Juha Suoranta, and Tere Vadén. 2005. *Artistic Research: Theories, Methods and Practices*. Gothenburg: ArtMonitor.

Harboe, Gunnar, Noel Massey, Crysta Metcalf, David Wheatley, and Guy Romano. 2008. "The Uses of Social Television." *ACM Computers in Entertainment* 6 (1): article no. 8 http://dl.acm.org/citation.cfm?doid=1350843.1350851 (accessed March 18, 2013).

Harcup, Tony. 2011. "Alternative Journalism as Active Citizenship." *Journalism* 12 (1): 15–31.

Hartmann, Benjamin. 2009. "The Media Experience Environment for PSM: Recognising Opportunities of a Societing Function." In *The Public in Public Service Media (RIPE@2009)*, ed. Gregory Ferrell Lowe, 101–117. Göteborg: Nordicom.

Hay, James, and Nick Couldry. 2011. "Rethinking Convergence/Culture: An Introduction." *Cultural Studies* 25 (4–5): 473–486.

Hayles, N. Katherine. 2012. "How We Think: Transforming Power and Digital Technologies." In *Understanding Digital Humanities*, ed. David M. Berry, 42–66. Houndmills, UK: Palgrave Macmillan.

Hearn, Gregory N., Jo A. Tacchi, Marcus Foth, and June Lennie. 2008. *Action Research and New Media: Concepts, Methods, and Cases*. Cresskill, NJ: Hampton Press.

Heim, Anna. 2011. "The Top Ten Media Apps of 2011." *The Next Web*. http://thenextweb.com/media/2011/12/27/the-top-ten-media-apps-of-2011/ (accessed June 13, 2012).

Hepp, Andreas. 2012. *Cultures of Mediatization*. Cambridge, UK: Polity Press.

Hessels, Laurens K., and Harro van Lente. 2008. "Re-thinking New Knowledge Production: A Literature Review and a Research Agenda." *Research Policy* 37 (4): 740–760.

Hillgren, Per-Anders. 2006. "Ready-Made-Media-Actions: Lokal Produktion och Användning av Audiovisuella Medier inom Hälso-och Sjukvården." Dissertation, Blekinge Institute of Technology, Sweden. (In Swedish.)

Hillgren, Per-Anders, Anna Seravalli, and Anders Emilsson. 2011. "Prototyping and Infrastructuring in Design for Social Innovation." *CoDesign* 7 (3–4): 169–183.

Himanen, Pekka. 2001. *The Hacker Ethic and the Spirit of the Information Age.* New York: Random House.

Howard, Alex. 2011. "Citizen Science, Civic Media and Radiation Data Hint at What's to Come: The Evolution of Safecast is a Glimpse into Networked Accountability." *O'Reilly Radar.* http:// radar.oreilly.com/2011/06/radiation-data-japa-citizen-science.html (accessed April 4, 2012).

Ignatieff, Michael. 1997. "Is Nothing Sacred? The Ethics of Television." In *The Warrior's Honor,* 9–33. New York: Henry Holt and Company.

Ito, Mizuko. 2010. "Mobilizing the Imagination in Everyday Play: The Case of Japanese Media Mixes." In *Mashup Cultures,* ed. Stephan Sonvilla-Weiss, 79–97. Wien: Springer.

Jackson, David. 1998. "Palm-to-Palm Combat." *Time Magazine.* http://www.time.com/time/ magazine/article/0,9171,987979,00.html (accessed August 24, 2011).

Jackson, Lizzie. 2009. "Facilitating Participatory Audiences: Sociable Media and PSM." In *The Public in Public Service Media (RIPE@2009),* ed. Gregory Ferrell Lowe, 175–187. Göteborg: Nordicom.

Jantsch, Erik. 1972. *Technological Planning and Social Futures.* London: Associated Business Programmes.

Jarvis, Jeff. 2009. "Content Farms v. Curating Farmers." *BuzzMachine.* http://buzzmachine .com/2009/12/14/content-farms-v-curating-farmers/ (accessed August 8, 2012).

Jenkins, Henry. 2006. *Convergence Culture: Where Old and New Media Collide.* New York: New York University Press.

Jewett, Tom, and Rob Kling. 1991. "The Dynamics of Computerization in a Social Science Research Team: A Case Study of Infrastructure, Strategies, and Skills." *Social Science Computer Review* 9 (2): 246–275.

Jones, John C. 1970/1992. *Design Methods: Seeds of Human Futures.* New York: Wiley.

Jones, Robert. 2011. "Does Machinima Really Democratize?" *Journal of Visual Culture* 10 (1): 59–65.

Kamvar, Sepandar, and Jonathan Harris. 2011. "We Feel Fine and Searching the Emotional Web." In *Proceedings of Web Search and Data Mining (WSDM 2011),* 117–126. New York: ACM Press.

Kaplan, Andreas, and Michael Haenlein. 2010. "Users of the World, Unite! The Challenges and Opportunities of Social Media." *Business Horizons* 53 (1): 59–68.

Karasti, Helena, and Anna-Liisa Syrjänen. 2004. "Artful Infrastructuring in Two Cases of Community PD." In *Proceedings of the Participatory Design Conference (PDC 2004),* 20–30. New York: ACM Press.

Katzy, Bernhard, and Stefan Klein. 2008. "Editorial Introduction. Special Issue on Living Labs." *Electronic Journal for Virtual Organizations and Networks* 10: 2–6.

Keen, Andrew. 2007. *The Cult of the Amateur*. New York: Doubleday.

Kember, Sarah, and Joanna Zylinska. 2012. *Life after New Media: Mediation as a Vital Process*. Cambridge, MA: MIT Press.

Koskinen, Ilpo. 2006. "Two Solitudes: Design as an Approach to Media Research." *Nordicom Information* 28 (2): 35–47.

Krippendorff, Klaus. 2006. *The Semantic Turn: A New Foundation for Design*. New York: Taylor & Francis.

Kushner, David. 2011. "The Making of Arduino: How Five Friends Engineered a Small Circuit Board That's Taking the DIY World by Storm." IEEE Spectrum. *Geek Life*, October. http://spectrum.ieee.org/geek-life/hands-on/the-making-of-arduino/0 (accessed March 29, 2012).

Lahlou, Saadi. 2008. "Identity, Social Status, Privacy and Face-Keeping in Digital Society." *Social Science Information* 47 (3): 299–330.

Lanchester, John. 2010. "Let Us Pay." *London Review of Books* 32 (24): 5–8.

Latour, Bruno. 2001. "From 'Matters of Facts' to 'States of Affairs': Which Protocol for the New Collective Experiments?" http://www.bruno-latour.fr/poparticles/poparticle/P-95%20MAX%20PLANCK.html (accessed August 1, 2011).

Latour, Bruno. 2005. *Reassembling the Social. An Introduction to Actor-Network-Theory*. Oxford: Oxford University Press.

Latour, Bruno. 2011. "Networks, Societies, Spheres: Reflections of an Actor-Network Theorist." *International Journal of Communication* 5: 796–810.

Law, John, and John Hassard, eds. 1999. *Actor Network Theory and After*. Oxford: Blackwell.

Leadbeater, Charles. 2008. *We-Think: Mass Innovation, Not Mass Production*. London: Profile Books.

Leadbeater, Charles, and Paul Miller. 2004. *The Pro-Am Revolution: How Enthusiasts Are Changing Our Economy and Society*. London: Demos.

Leurdijk, Andra, and Matthijs Leendertse. 2009. "Follow the Audience? An Analysis of PSM New Media Strategies in Light of Media Use and Assumptions about Audiences." In *The Public in Public Service Media (RIPE@2009)*, ed. Gregory Ferrell Lowe, 151–173. Göteborg: Nordicom.

Lewin, Kurt. 1946 "Action Research and Minority Problems." *Journal of Social Issues* 2 (4): 34–46.

Lievrouw, Leah A. 2011. *Alternative and Activist New Media*. Cambridge, UK: Polity Press.

Lievrouw, Leah A., and Sonia Livingstone. 2002/2006. "Introduction to the First Edition. The Social Shaping and Consequences of ICTs." In *Handbook of New Media: Student Edition*, ed. Leah A. Lievrouw and Sonia Livingstone, 15–32. London: Sage.

Lievrouw, Leah A., and Sonia Livingstone, eds. 2006. *Handbook of New Media: Student Edition*. London: Sage.

Light, Marc, and Mark Maybury. 2002. "Personalized Multimedia Information Access." *Communications of the ACM* 45 (5): 54–59.

Linden, Greg, Brent Smith, and Jeremy York. 2003. "Amazon.com Recommendations: Item-to-Item Collaborative Filtering." *IEEE Internet Computing* 7 (1): 76–80.

Lindstedt, Inger, Jonas Löwgren, Bo Reimer, and Richard Topgaard. 2009. "Nonlinear News Production and Consumption: A Collaborative Approach." *ACM Computers in Entertainment* 7 (3): article no. 42. http://dl.acm.org/citation.cfm?doid=1594943.1594954 (accessed March 18, 2013).

Lister, Martin, Jon Dovey, Seth Giddings, and Iain Grant. 2008. *New Media: A Critical Introduction*. London: Routledge.

Livingstone, Sonia. 2003. "The Changing Nature of Audiences: From the Mass Audience to the Interactive Media User." In *A Companion to Media Studies*, ed. Angharad N. Valdivia, 337–359. Oxford: Blackwell.

Lowood, Henry. 2011. "A 'Different Technical Approach'? Introduction to the Special Issue on Machinima." *Journal of Visual Culture* 10 (1): 3–5.

Löwgren, Jonas, and Bo Reimer. 2012. "Designing Collaborative Media: A Challenge for CHI?" In *Proceedings of the Conference on Human Factors in Computing Systems (CHI 2012 Extended Abstracts)*, 31–40. New York: ACM Press.

Lundby, Knut, ed. 2009. *Mediatization: Concept, Changes, Consequences*. New York: Peter Lang.

MacKenzie, Donald, and Judy Wajcman, eds. 1999. *The Social Shaping of Technology*. 2nd ed. Buckingham, UK: Open University Press.

Maffesoli, Michel. 1990/1996. *The Time of the Tribes: The Decline of Individualization in Mass Society*. London: Sage.

Manovich, Lev. 2001. *The Language of New Media*. Cambridge, MA: MIT Press.

Marres, Noortje. 2012. *Material Participation: Technology, the Environment and Everyday Publics*. Basingstoke, UK: Palgrave Macmillan.

Marvin, Carolyn. 1988. *When Old Technologies Were New: Thinking about Electric Communication in the Late Nineteenth Century*. New York: Oxford University Press.

Mateas, Michael. 2001. "A Preliminary Poetics for Interactive Drama and Games." *Digital Creativity* 12 (3): 140–152.

Mau, Bruce. 2004. *Massive Change*. London: Phaidon.

McLuhan, Marshall. 1964. *Understanding Media: The Extensions of Man*. London: Routledge and Kegan Paul.

Melanson, Donald. 2011. "Google Announces Android Open Accessory Standard, Arduino-based ADK." http://www.engadget.com/2011/05/10/google-announces-android-open-accessory-standard -arduino-based/ (accessed April 5, 2012).

Merrin, William. 2009. "Media Studies 2.0: Upgrading and Open-Sourcing the Discipline." *Interactions: Studies in Communication and Culture* 1 (1): 17–34.

Messieh, Nancy. 2011. "Live-Streaming Service Bambuser Goes from Egypt's Revolution to Its Elections." *The Next Web*. http://thenextweb.com/me/2011/11/29/live-streaming-service-bambuser -goes-from-egypts-revolution-to-its-elections/ (accessed August 8, 2012).

Meyrowitz, Joshua. 1994. "Medium Theory." In *Communication Theory Today*, ed. David Crowley and David Mitchell, 50–77. Stanford, CA: Stanford University Press.

Miller, Toby. 2009. "Media Studies 3.0." *Television & New Media* 10 (1): 5–6.

Millington, Brad. 2009. "Wii Has Never Been Modern: 'Active' Video Games and the 'Conduct of Conduct.'" *New Media & Society* 11 (4): 621–640.

Moore, Álan. 2002. "Authenticity as Authentication." *Popular Music* 21 (2): 209–223.

Morley, David. 2012. "Television, Technology, and Culture: A Contextualist Approach." *Communication Review* 15 (2): 79–105.

Mouffe, Chantal. 2000.*The Democratic Paradox*. London: Verso.

Murray, Janet. 1997. *Hamlet on the Holodeck: The Future of Narrative in Cyberspace*. New York: The Free Press.

Murray, Janet. 2003. "Inventing the Medium." In *The New Media Reader*, ed. Noah Wardrip-Fruin and Nick Montfort, 3–11. Cambridge, MA: MIT Press.

Napoli, Philip M., and Minna Aslama, eds. 2010. *Communications Research in Action: Scholar-Activist Collaborations for a Democratic Public Sphere*. Ashland, OH: Fordham University Press.

Neale, Steve. 1980. *Genre*. London: British Film Institute.

Nelson, Harold, and Erik Stolterman. 2002. *The Design Way: Intentional Change in an Unpredictable World*. Englewood Cliffs, NJ: Educational Technology Publications.

Nielsen, Jakob. 2006. "Participation Inequality: Encouraging More Users to Participate." *Jakob Nielsen's Alertbox*. http://www.useit.com/alertbox/participation_inequality.html (accessed August 24, 2011).

Nightingale, Virginia, ed. 2011. *The Handbook of Media Audiences*. Malden, MA: Wiley-Blackwell.

NM2. n.d. "NM2: New Millennium, New Media." http://www.ist-nm2.org (accessed March 15, 2012).

Norman, Donald A. 1988. *The Design of Everyday Things*. New York: Basic Books.

Nowotny, Helga, Peter Scott, and Michael Gibbons. 2001. *Re-thinking Science. Knowledge and the Public in an Age of Uncertainty.* Cambridge, UK: Polity Press.

Nowotny, Helga, Peter Scott, and Michael Gibbons. 2003."Introduction. 'Mode 2' Revisited: The New Production of Knowledge." *Minerva* 41 (3): 179–194.

Nussbaum, Martha. 1995. *Poetic Justice: The Literary Imagination and Public Life.* Boston: Beacon Press.

Oosterling, Henk. 2007. "Interest and Excess of Modern Man's Radical Mediocrity: Rescaling Sloterdijk's Grandiose Aesthetic Strategy." *Cultural Politics* 3 (3): 357–380.

OSHW. n.d. "Definition of Free Cultural Works." http://freedomdefined.org/OSHW (accessed March 29, 2012).

Ozer, Jan. 2012. "Live Streaming Showdown: Ustream, Justin.tv, Livestream, Bambuser." Online video.net. http://www.onlinevideo.net/2012/06/live-streaming-showdown-ustream-justin-tv -livestream-bambuser/ (accessed June 13, 2012).

Packer, Jeremy, and Stephen B. Crofts Wiley, eds. 2011. *Communication Matters: Materialist Approaches to Media, Mobility and Networks.* London: Routledge.

Parikka, Jussi. 2012. "New Materialism as Media Theory: Medianatures and Dirty Matter. Communication and Critical." *Cultural Studies* 9 (1): 95–100.

Peters, Benjamin. 2009. "And Lead Us Not into Thinking the New Is New: A Bibliographic Case for New Media History." *New Media & Society* 11 (1–2): 13–30.

Pingdom. 2011. "Internet 2010 in Numbers." http://royal.pingdom.com/2011/01/12/internet -2010-in-numbers/ (accessed August 2, 2012).

Potts, John. 2008. "Who's Afraid of Technological Determinism? Another Look at Medium Theory." *The Fibreculture Journal*, no. 12. http://twelve.fibreculturejournal.org/fcj-084-who%e2 %80%99s-afraid-of-technological-determinism-another-look-at-medium-theory/ (accessed April 17, 2013).

Potts, Jason, John Hartley, John Banks, Jean Burgess, Rachel Cobcroft, Stuart Cunningham, and Lucy Montgomery. 2008. "Consumer Co-creation and Situated Creativity." *Industry and Innovation* 15 (5): 459–474.

Preece, Jenny, and Ben Shneiderman. 2009. "The Reader-to-Leader Framework: Motivating Technology-Mediated Social Participation." *AIS Transactions on Human-Computer Interaction* 1 (1): 13–32.

Raoof, Ramy. 2011. "Egypt: Timeline of Communication Shutdown during the Revolution." http://www.flickr.com/photos/ramyraoof/5814392791/ (accessed June 8, 2012).

Raymond, Eric. 1999. "The Cathedral and the Bazaar." *Knowledge, Technology & Policy* 12 (3): 23–49.

Reas, Casey, and Ben Fry. 2007. *Processing: A Programming Handbook for Visual Designers and Artists*. Cambridge, MA: MIT Press.

Redström, Johan. 2006. "Towards User Design? On the Shift from Object to User as the Subject of Design." *Design Studies* 27 (2): 123–139.

Ritzer, George, and Nathan Jurgenson. 2010. "Production, Consumption, Prosumption: The Nature of Capitalism in the Age of the Digital 'Prosumer.'" *Journal of Consumer Culture* 10 (1): 13–36.

Rogers, Yvonne. 2011. "Interaction Design Gone Wild: Striving for Wild Theory." *Interactions: Studies in Communication and Culture* 18 (4): 58–62.

Rosen, Jay. 2006. "The People Formerly Known as the Audience." http://archive.pressthink .org/2006/06/27/ppl_frmr.html (accessed March 18, 2013).

Rosenblum, Elsa. 2010. "The Director of *Downfall* Speaks Out on All the Angry YouTube Hitlers." http://nymag.com/daily/entertainment/2010/01/the_director_of_downfall_on_al.html (accessed August 24, 2011).

Sandelin, Erik. 2012. Personal communication, May 31.

Sanders, Elizabeth B.-N., and Pieter Jan Stappers. 2008. "Co-creation and the New Landscapes of Design." *CoDesign* 4 (1): 5–18.

Savage, Mike, and Roger Burrows. 2007. "The Coming Crisis of Empirical Sociology." *Sociology* 41 (5): 885–899.

Schwartz, Randal, and Leo Laporte. 2009. "Arduino." *FLOSS Weekly* 61. http://twit.tv/floss61 (accessed March 28, 2012).

Schön, Donald A. 1983. *The Reflective Practitioner: How Professionals Think in Action*. New York: Basic Books.

Schön, Donald A. 1987. *Educating the Reflective Practitioner: Toward a New Design for Teaching and Learning in the Professions*. San Francisco: Jossey Bass.

Shannon, Claude, and Warren Weaver. 1949. *The Mathematical Theory of Communication*. Urbana: University of Illinois Press.

Shirky, Clay. 2008. *Here Comes Everybody: The Power of Organizing Without Organizations*. New York: The Penguin Press.

Smith, Gene. 2008. *Tagging: People-Powered Metadata for the Social Web*. Berkeley, CA: New Riders.

Snow, C. P. 1959/1998. *The Two Cultures*. Cambridge: Cambridge University Press.

Star, Susan Leigh, and Geoffrey C. Bowker. 2002. "How to Infrastructure." In *Handbook of New Media: Social Shaping and Consequences of ICTs*, ed. Leah A. Lievrouw and Sonia Livingstone, 151–162. London: Sage.

Star, Susan Leigh, and Karen Ruhleder. 1996. "Steps Toward an Ecology of Infrastructure: Design and Access for Large Information Spaces." *Information Systems Research* 7 (1): 111–134.

Svensson, Patrik. 2012. "Envisioning the Digital Humanities." *Digital Humanities Quarterly* 6 (1). http://digitalhumanities.org/dhq/vol/6/1/000112/000112.html (accessed April 17, 2013).

Tapscott, Don, and Anthony D. Williams. 2006. *Wikinomics: How Mass Collaboration Changes Everything*. New York: Portfolio.

Taylor, Paul A. 2009. "Editorial Introduction: Optimism, Pessimism and the Myth of Technological Neutrality." *Interactions: Studies in Communication and Culture* 1 (1): 7–16.

Templeton, Brad. 2009. "Hitler Tries a DMCA Takedown." *Brad Ideas*. http://ideas.4brad.com/hitler-tries-dmca-takedown (accessed August 24, 2011).

Terranova, Tiziana. 2004. *Network Culture: Politics for the Information Age*. London: Pluto Press.

Theel, Shauna. 2012. "Study: Kardashians Get 40 Times More News Coverage than Ocean Acidification." *Media Matters*, June 27. http://mediamatters.org/blog/2012/06/27/study-kardashians-get-40-times-more-news-covera/186703 (accessed August 8, 2012).

Thompson, Clive. 2008. "Build It. Share It. Profit. Can Open Source Hardware Work?" *Wired* 16 (11). http://www.wired.com/techbiz/startups/magazine/16-11/ff_openmanufacturing?currentPage=all (accessed March 30, 2012).

Toffler, Alvin. 1980. *The Third Wave*. New York: Morrow.

Turkle, Sherry. 1995. *Life on the Screen: Identity in the Age of the Internet*. New York: Simon & Schuster.

Underkoffler, John, and Hiroshi Ishii. 1999. "Urp: A Luminous Tangible Workbench for Urban Planning and Design." In *Proceedings of the Conference on Human Factors in Computing Systems (CHI 1999)*, 386–393. New York: ACM Press.

Unsworn Industries. n.d. *Unsworn Visuals Blog*. http://www.unsworn.org/blog/visuals/ (accessed June 6, 2012).

van Dijck, José. 2009. "Users Like You? Theorizing Agency in User-Generated Content." *Media Culture & Society* 31 (1): 41–58.

Varnelis, Kazys, ed. 2008. *Networked Publics*. Cambridge, MA: MIT Press.

von Busch, Otto. 2008. "Fashion-Able: Hacktivism and Engaged Fashion Design." Dissertation. Gothenburg University, Sweden. <http://www.hdk.gu.se/files/document/fashion-able_webanspassahd%20avhandling_OttovonBusch.pdf (accessed August 10, 2011).

von Busch, Otto. 2012. Personal communication, April 5.

von Hippel, Eric. 2006. *Democratizing Innovation*. Cambridge, MA: MIT Press.

Wajcman, Judy, and Paul K. Jones. 2012. "Border Communication: Media Sociology and STS." *Media Culture & Society* 34 (6): 673–690.

Wardrip-Fruin, Noah, and Nick Montfort, eds. 2003a. *The New Media Reader*. Cambridge, MA: MIT Press.

Wardrip-Fruin, Noah, and Nick Montfort. 2003b. "Preface: 'The New Media Reader.' A User's Manual." In *The New Media Reader*, ed. Noah Wardip-Fruin and Nick Montfort, xi–xiii. Cambridge, MA: MIT Press.

White, Miles. 1996. "The Phonograph Turntable and Performance Practice in Hip Hop Music." *EOL Ethnomusicology OnLine* 2. http://www.umbc.edu/eol/2/white/index.html (accessed March 18, 2013).

Wiesslitz, Carmit, and Tamar Ashuri. 2011. "'Moral Journalists': The Emergence of New Intermediaries of News in an Age of Digital Media." *Journalism* 12 (8): 1035–1051.

Williams, Amanda, Alicia Gibb and David Weekly. 2012. "Research with a Hacker Ethos: What DIY Means for Tangible Interaction Research." *Interactions: Studies in Communication and Culture* 19 (2): 14–19.

Williams, Doug, Ian Kegel, Harald Mayer, Peter Stollenmayer, Maureen Thomas, and Marian Ursu. 2004. "NM2: New Media for a New Millennium." In *Proceedings of the IEE European Workshop on the Integration of Knowledge, Semantics and Digital Media Technology*. London: Queen Mary, University of London. http://nim.goldsmiths.ac.uk/papers/EWIMT%202004%20paper%20submitted%20for%20proceedings.pdf (accessed March 21, 2013).

Williams, Raymond. 1974. *Television: Technology and Cultural Form*. London: Fontana/Collins.

Ziman, John. 2000. *Real Science: What It Is, and What It Means*. Cambridge: Cambridge University Press.

Zizek, Slavoj. n.d. "The Interpassive Subject." http://www.egs.edu/faculty/slavoj-zizek/articles/the-interpassive-subject/ (accessed September 1, 2011).

Credits

Writing a book in general represents a collaborative effort; this one is no exception. Here, we credit the people who contributed in various ways to the work reported and to the production of the book.

Cases

The ten cases we presented in part II represent the work of many talented and dedicated people. We list their names in alphabetical order per case, and in deep gratitude for the opportunities we have been given to work with such gifted colleagues.

The core Avatopia design team consisted of Andreas Carlsson, Marie Denward, Ylva Gislén, Marcus Gårdman, Jonas Löwgren, Ulf Myrestam, Andreas Nilsson, Johannes Nyström, and Johanna Wallin.

Bambuser was originally conceived by Måns Adler and Jonas Vig.

Parapolis was the work of Per-Anders Hillgren, Per Linde, Erik Sandelin, and Magnus Torstensson.

The MyNewsMyWay research team included Henrik Larsson, Inger Lindstedt, Tobias Nilsson, Bo Reimer, and Richard Topgaard.

Substrate is mainly the work of Tomas Eriksson, Jonas Löwgren, Niklas Malmros, and Mårten Wikström.

The Kliv project was run by Erling Björgvinsson and Per-Anders Hillgren.

Hacktivism was the work of Otto von Busch.

OurNewsOurWays was the work of Amanda Bergknut and Jonas Löwgren. James Haliburton provided valuable help in production of the video scenario.

Arduino was originated by Massimo Banzi, David Cuartielles, Tom Igoe, Gianluca Martino, and David Mellis.

Malmö City Symphony was created by Erling Björgvinsson and Richard Topgaard. The live performance featured Erik Mikael Karlsson, Andreas Kurtsson, Fredrik Norrgren, and Erik Sandelin.

With regard to all of the work we present in part II, we are immensely grateful to the "consumers"—the individuals who chose to join forces with us and explore the potential of collaborative media: the teenage activists, video broadcasters, citizen urban planners, future TV viewers, technical information users, health care workers, amateur fashionistas, Arduino hackers, and participants in the city symphony project without whose contributions this book would have been an utterly pointless effort.

Illustrations

The authors hold the publication rights to many of the illustrations used in the book. Exceptions are as follows.

4.4. Image courtesy of Måns Adler, used with permission.

4.5. Image by Unsworn Industries, used with permission.

4.6. Panorama by Annika Carlsson, collage by Unsworn Industries, used with permission.

4.7. Image by Unsworn Industries, used with permission.

4.8. CC-BY-SA Unsworn Industries (http://www.flickr.com/photos/unsworn/) and individual panorama creators.

5.8. Image by Otto von Busch, used with permission.

5.9–5.10. Images by Bent Synnevag, used with permission.

6.6. Image by David Cuartielles, used with permission.

6.8. CC-BY Javier Pais (http://www.flickr.com/photos/javierpais/).

6.9. CC-BY-SA Bekathwia (http://www.flickr.com/photos/bekathwia/).

6.10. Image by Baris Serim, used with permission.

6.11. CC-BY-NC-SA webghost (http://thingiverse.com/webghost/).

6.12. CC-BY-NC SafeCast (http://safecast.org).

6.13. CC-BY Malmö City Symphony (http://citysymphony2009.blogspot.se/).

In-depth Interviews and Contributions

We are indebted to our colleagues for giving generously of their time to discuss their work and our interpretations of it with us: Måns Adler (the Bambuser case), Otto von Busch (Hacktivism), David Cuartielles (Arduino), Erik Sandelin (Parapolis), and Richard Topgaard (Malmö City Symphony).

Acknowledgments

Valuable comments and contributions to our thinking have been offered by Magnus Andersson, Pelle Ehn, Anders Emilson, Mads Høbye, and Per Linde. Any errors found in the book are our own responsibility, of course.

To end on a personal note, Jonas would like to thank Christina, Sara, and Ellen for helping maintain a sense of proportion—and for sharing a thing or two about collaborative media practices. Bo would like to thank Maria, Åse, and Tor for their very particular ways of making it all worthwhile.

Index